SECONDARY EDUCATION IN A CHANGING WORLD

Series editors: Barry M. Franklin and Gary McCulloch

Published by Palgrave Macmillan:

The Comprehensive Public High School: Historical Perspectives
By Craig Campbell and Geoffrey Sherington
(2006)

Cyril Norwood and the Ideal of Secondary Education
By Gary McCulloch
(2007)

The Death of the Comprehensive High School?: Historical, Contemporary, and Comparative Perspectives
Edited by Barry M. Franklin and Gary McCulloch
(2007)

The Emergence of Holocaust Education in American Schools
By Thomas D. Fallace
(2008)

The Standardization of American Schooling: Linking Secondary and Higher Education, 1870–1910
By Marc A. VanOverbeke
(2008)

Education and Social Integration: Comprehensive Schooling in Europe
By Susanne Wiborg
(2009)

Reforming New Zealand Secondary Education: The Picot Report and the Road to Radical Reform
By Roger Openshaw
(2009)

Inciting Change in Secondary English Language Programs: The Case of Cherry High School
By Marilee Coles-Ritchie
(2009)

Curriculum, Community, and Urban School Reform
By Barry M. Franklin
(2010)

*Girls' Secondary Education in the Western World:
From the 18th to the 20th Century*
Edited by James C. Albisetti, Joyce Goodman, and Rebecca Rogers
(2010)

*Race-Class Relations and Integration in Secondary Education:
The Case of Miller High*
By Caroline Eick
(2010)

*Teaching Harry Potter: The Power of Imagination in
Multicultural Classrooms*
By Catherine L. Belcher and Becky Herr Stephenson
(2011)

The Invention of the Secondary Curriculum
By John White
(2011)

Secondary STEM Educational Reform
Edited by Carla C. Johnson
(2011)

New Labour and Secondary Education, 1994–2010
By Clyde Chitty
(2013)

*Secondary Education and the Raising of the School-leaving Age:
Coming of Age?*
By Tom Woodin, Gary McCulloch, and Steven Cowan
(2013)

*English Teachers in a Postwar Democracy: Emerging Choice in London
Schools, 1945–1965*
By Peter Medway, John Hardcastle, Georgina Brewis, and David Crook
(2014)

English Teachers in a Postwar Democracy

Emerging Choice in London Schools, 1945–1965

Peter Medway, John Hardcastle,
Georgina Brewis, and David Crook

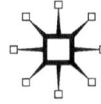

ENGLISH TEACHERS IN A POSTWAR DEMOCRACY
Copyright © Peter Medway, John Hardcastle, Georgina Brewis, and David Crook, 2014.
Softcover reprint of the hardcover 1st edition 2014 978-1-137-00513-7

All rights reserved.

First published in 2014 by
PALGRAVE MACMILLAN®
in the United States—a division of St. Martin's Press LLC,
175 Fifth Avenue, New York, NY 10010.

Where this book is distributed in the UK, Europe and the rest of the world, this is by Palgrave Macmillan, a division of Macmillan Publishers Limited, registered in England, company number 785998, of Houndmills, Basingstoke, Hampshire RG21 6XS.

Palgrave Macmillan is the global academic imprint of the above companies and has companies and representatives throughout the world.

Palgrave® and Macmillan® are registered trademarks in the United States, the United Kingdom, Europe and other countries.

ISBN 978-1-349-43463-3   ISBN 978-1-137-00514-4 (eBook)
DOI 10.1057/9781137005144

Library of Congress Cataloging-in-Publication Data

Medway, Peter.
   English teachers in a postwar democracy : emerging choice in London schools, 1945–1965 / by Peter Medway, John Hardcastle, Georgina Brewis and David Crook.
      pages cm — (Secondary education in a changing world)
   Includes bibliographical references and index.

   1. Language arts (Secondary)—England—London—History—20th century—Case studies. 2. Language arts (Secondary)—England—London—Social aspects—20th century—Case studies. 3. Language arts teachers—England—London—History—20th century—Case studies. I. Hardcastle, John. II. Brewis, Georgina. III. Crook, David. IV. Title.
LB1631.M3995 2014
428.0071′20941—dc23   2014000515

A catalogue record of the book is available from the British Library.

Design by Newgen Knowledge Works (P) Ltd., Chennai, India.

First edition: July 2014
10 9 8 7 6 5 4 3 2 1

Contents

List of Figures   vii
Series Editors' Foreword   ix
Acknowledgments   xiii
Abbreviations and Acronyms   xv
Glossary of Terms   xvii
A Note on the Index   xix

1. Introduction   1
2. The Period, the Education System, and the Teaching of English   17
3. Hackney Downs   47
4. Walworth   79
5. Minchenden   113
6. The Three Schools—What We Have Learned   143
7. Conclusion   169

Notes   191
Index   221

Figures

3.1	Hackney Downs School	48
3.2	The staff, 1946	49
3.3	James Medcalf responds engagingly to an essay by David Ogilvie	62
3.4	Hackney Downs Staff, Summer 1960	69
4.1	Walworth School, 1882 building and craft block in 1950s	80
4.2	Arthur Harvey, senior English master, 1949–1955 with sixth form group	84
4.3	Harold Rosen directing school play, 1956–1958	90
4.4	Simon Clements supervises his third-year class while they film a bombsite scene	97

Series Editors' Foreword

Among the educational issues affecting policy makers, public officials, and citizens in modern, democratic, and industrial societies, none has been more contentious than the role of secondary schooling. In establishing the Secondary Education in a Changing World series with Palgrave Macmillan, our intent is to provide a venue for scholars in different national settings to explore critical and controversial issues surrounding secondary education. We envision our series as a place for the airing and resolution of these controversial issues.

More than a century has elapsed since Emile Durkheim argued the importance of studying secondary education as a unity, rather than in relation to the wide range of subjects and the division of pedagogical labor of which it was composed. Only thus, he insisted, would it be possible to have the ends and aims of secondary education constantly in view. The failure to do so accounted for a great deal of difficulty with which secondary education was faced. First it meant that secondary education was "intellectually disoriented," between "a past which is dying and a future which is still undecided," and as a result "lacks the vigor and vitality which it once possessed."[1] Second, the institutions of secondary education were not understood adequately in relation to their past, which was "the soil which nourished them and gave them their present meaning, and apart from which they cannot be examined without a great deal of Impoverishment and distortion."[2]. And third, it was difficult for secondary school teachers, who were responsible for putting policy reforms into practice, to understand the nature and the problems and issues that prompted them.

In the early decades of the twenty-first century, Durkheim's strictures still have resonance. The intellectual disorientation of secondary education is more evident than ever as it is caught up in successive waves of policy changes. The connections between the present and the past have become increasingly hard to trace and untangle. Moreover, the distance between policy makers on the one hand and the practitioners on the other has rarely seemed as immense as it is today. The key mission of the current series of books is, in the spirit of Durkheim, to address these underlying dilemmas of secondary education and to play a part in resolving them.

English Teachers in a Postwar Democracy: Emerging Choice in London Schools, 1945–1965, by Peter Medway, John Hardcastle, Georgina Brewis, and David Crook, investigates the development of the teaching of English in three key secondary schools over a formative 20-year period. Their research helps us to build on Durkheim's ideas, although in this case it actually concentrates on a single school subject, albeit one of the principal subjects of the curriculum, and the nature of the pedagogy that has been associated with it. At the same time, it certainly addresses the ends and aims of secondary education in vivid and telling fashion. It shows in-depth and detail the innovations involved in English teaching at Hackney Downs, Walworth School, and Minchenden Grammar School, and the ways in which these engaged with broader social ideals. As such, it is a significant contribution to our understanding of secondary education in general, no less than to curriculum history and the teaching of English in particular.

This book also brings to our attention the results of an extensive research project that has made full use of both a wide range of documentary sources and a large number of interviews with former pupils and teachers. It is thus able to explore the lived experience of secondary education, as opposed to the public rhetoric and official plans for the school curriculum. It generates three finely realized case studies, conceived not as typical examples of secondary schools but in terms of the nature, limits, and potential of innovation in thinking and practice in secondary school English. It also highlights the key role played by individual teachers such as Harold Rosen. The work may be rooted in London, and based in England, as well as being framed around two decades of developments in the recent past. Yet it speaks to our contemporary condition, and just as it is relevant to curriculum and pedagogy in broad terms, it provides substantial evidence that will be of significant value for teachers, policy makers, and curriculum planners around the world. It will also establish an important site of study for future research in this area.

As the sixteenth volume in our series, *English Teachers in a Postwar Democracy* takes forward the intricate exploration of secondary education over time that has been such a feature of many of these works. It offers the foundation for additional volumes that might explore a number of emerging trends in educational provision for secondary youth as well as suggesting new areas of inquiry for the series as we extend the focus more deliberately beyond the United States and United Kingdom.

BARRY M. FRANKLIN
GARY MCCULLOCH
Series Co-Editors

Acknowledgments

We wish to thank the following: the Institute of Education, University of London, and King's College, London, for the "seedcorn" funding that made possible our initial studies, on the basis of which we were able to submit a successful application to the Leverhulme Trust; the Leverhulme Trust for the award that funded this project, reference F/07 141/B; Simon Gibbons for permission to quote his interview with John Dixon, and for his help in drawing on the LATE archive; the former teachers and pupils who agreed to be interviewed, wrote to us in connection with our inquiry, or donated or loaned materials; Helen Worger, our transcriber for the entire duration of our inquiry; and for their comments and support the London English Research Group and our Advisory Group for their guidance and help: Richard Andrews, Tony Burgess, Simon Clements, Simon Gibbons, Gabrielle Cliff Hodges, Gary McCulloch, Ivor Goodson, and Peter Newsam.

Individuals who we thank for helping us in other ways are: Cathy Burke, Jon Cook, Peter Cunningham, Bill Green, Patricia Jones, Ben Knights, and Martyn Nystrand.

From Hackney Downs School, we thank Glyndwr ("Willie") Watkins, President of the association for former pupils and staff, and Geoffrey Alderman, the author of a recent history of the school. From Walworth Academy, we thank its principals, Devon Hanson and Yvonne Powell, and administrators, Lorraine Lemmer and Theresa Swaby-Williams.

From the British Library, we thank Emily Hewitt, Rob Perks, and Mary Stewart and from the Archives of the Institute of Education, University of London, we thank Sarah Aitchison. Also from the Institute of Education Archives, we acknowledge permission to reproduce photographic image reference ABB/A/27/32–1 as Figure 4.2.

Copyright on the interviews, both audio files and transcripts, is owned by the British Library and the Institute of Education.

Abbreviations and Acronyms

A level Advanced level (of GCE)
CSE Certificate of Secondary Education
GCE General Certificate of Education
GLC Greater London Council
HMI His/Her Majesty's Inspector[s] of Schools
ILEA Inner London Education Authority
LATE London Association for the Teaching of English
LCC London County Council
LEA Local Education Authority
LMA London Metropolitan Archives
MCC Middlesex County Council
NATE National Association for the Teaching of English
O level Ordinary level (of GCE)
PGCE Postgraduate Certificate of Education
S Level Scholarship level (of GCE)
TNA The National Archives
UCL University College, London

Glossary of Terms

Central school: up to 1944, a selective elementary school, vocationally oriented with entry at age 12 and upwards, normally to 16. Called central because there was one for each local group of schools, to which the ablest pupils could progress (apart from those who went to grammar school.)

Comprehensive school: state secondary school admitting all children in a catchment area.

Elementary education/school: up to 1944, nonselective education/school for pupils from entry to school leaving. Abolished in 1944.

First form, second form, etc.: the first etc. year of secondary school; *first-formers*, pupils in the first-form.

First year (year one), second year etc.: children entered secondary school at age 11 in the first year, continued to the fourth year (when they were allowed to leave) and the fifth (if they stayed on), and then the *sixth form*, which actually comprised years six and seven. (The English system is now closer to the grade system in some other countries: Year 1 is for pupils aged 5, so that pupils entering secondary school at 11 are in Year 7.)

Forms, classes: pupils in London schools in our period were grouped into classes or forms. The latter term derived from the wooden forms on which children sat in Victorian schools, but in our period a form was the group of children who were taught together; in more modern terminology they were called a class.

Grammar school: selective school, academically oriented with entry at age 11 or later, offering a course of five or more years, fee-charging before 1944 and free thereafter.

Primary education/school: up to age 11, 12, or 13 (varied locally).

Secondary education/school: before 1944, selective education in grammar schools; after 1944, postprimary education of all types.

Secondary modern school: after 1944, nonselective, less academic secondary school for children who did not enter grammar schools or technical schools.

Three-form-entry, etc: a three-form-entry school has an annual intake into the first year of the number of pupils that will constitute three forms (classes). An eight-form entry in Walworth School in 1964 was 240 pupils, 8 × 30.

Tests and Examinations

11 plus: test taken in primary school at age 10–11 used as the basis for allocation to type of secondary school. Typically an IQ test, though there might also be tests in arithmetic and composition.

School Certificate: public examination taken at 16 up to 1951.

General Certificate of Education (GCE), Ordinary, Advanced, and Scholarship levels: public examinations taken at 16, 18, and 19 from 1951.

Certificate of Secondary Education (CSE): alternative examination taken at 16 from 1965.

Publications from the Project

John Hardcastle and Peter Medway, "In His Own Words: Harold Rosen on His Formative Years, with Speculations on Working-Class Language," *Changing English* 16(1) (2008): 5–14.

John Hardcastle, "Four Photographs in an English Course Book: A Study in the Visual Archaeology of Urban Schooling," *Changing English* 15(1) (2008): 3–24.

John Hardcastle, "Something More Than Straws and Sticks and Bits of Coloured Paper: English at Hackney Downs (Formerly the Grocers' Company's School), 1876–1881." *Changing English* 18(1) (2011): 17–29.

Peter Medway and Patrick Kingwell, "A Curriculum in Its Place: English Teaching in One School 1946–1963," *History of Education* 39(6) (2010): 749–765.

Peter Medway, "Teachers Learning in a London School: Autonomy and Development in the 1950s," *L1-Educational Studies in Language and Literature* 12 (2012): 1–32.

John Hardcastle and Peter Medway, "English for the Post-War Age," *Teaching English* (2013): 29–40.

A Note on the Index

Our study has involved great attention to detail and to untangling often convoluted stories and relationships. The book cannot help reflecting this complexity and richness. We the authors suggest making active use of the index as a supplementary reading strategy to identify and pursue themes and topics that promise to be interesting.

Chapter 1

Introduction

"Sometimes I see my task, as poet and story-teller, to rescue the centuries' treasure before it is too late. It is as though the past is a great ship that has gone ashore, and archivist and writer must gather as much of the rich squandered cargo as they can."[1]

As our choice of opening quotation from the Orkney poet George Mackay Brown suggests, the spirit of the studies we have been undertaking has in part been one of "rescue archaeology" within the field of a school subject, except that our inquiry has gone beyond the sort of artifacts, like documents, that sometimes survive shipwrecks, and started—though it didn't end—not with relics like documents but with what was preserved in memory. Indeed it started with a simple realization by Hardcastle and Medway that the opportunity had been missed to record the memories of key figures from an earlier generation while they were still able to be interviewed. We accordingly visited a major contributor to the development of the teaching of English, Harold Rosen. We recorded two interviews with him, in 2004 and 2005, from which, in the course of conversations over subsequent years, the larger intention evolved to do something toward filling out, refining, and correcting existing accounts of the postwar history of English up to the mid-1960s, the period in which Harold and others had brought about some decisive changes. Gradually a substantial funded research project emerged, which we think has indeed preserved a portion of the past's "rich squandered cargo" and, beyond that, we hope, has afforded a basis for fresh thinking about the development of a school subject within the context of its times.

This book is an account of that project and a contribution to two specialist studies, curriculum history and the teaching of English, though we hope it will also appeal to those with a wider historical interest in the earlier post–World War II decades. The period we cover, 1945–1965, is one of fascinating change in Britain, from austerity combined with optimistic attempts at reconstruction under a Labour government to rising affluence and a new consumer economy under the Conservatives (with Labour taking over again right at the end) and, accompanying that, the beginnings of far-reaching movement in cultural life. The extent to which and the way in which those social changes bore on what English teachers did in their classrooms in English secondary schools was a question we have pondered continually but that proved to yield no single answer across our cases, though this is not to say that our studies do not illuminate what was happening in society more generally—they certainly do. But that is to anticipate.

Contribution to Curriculum History

The particular contribution that the book hopes to offer to curriculum history derives from the special nature of English. Among the central academic subjects in postwar secondary schools in England, English had features that marked it as different from geography and chemistry. Despite its apparent status as central, its arrival in the curriculum had been relatively recent and its place was for many years insecure. In the universities, English was accepted by the 1830s in London but in Oxford and Cambridge only in 1893 and 1917, and in some major independent (nonstate) schools English was still not included within our own lifetimes, literature being deemed not a real study but a matter of subjective taste appropriate only for leisure pursuit, while competence in reading and writing was assumed to have been taken care of at an earlier stage of schooling. A government report of 1921 on the teaching of English (the Newbolt Report)[2] had to argue vigorously for its admission in schools at a time when the sciences, history, and modern languages were well established. English was unusual as a major subject, secondly, in not essentially comprising a body of facts and concepts to be learned; those specifiable items that it taught—spellings, for instance, or grammatical rules, or the meaning of "fiery cressets" in a Shakespeare play—did not constitute the principal substance of what English was seen by at least some of its practitioners to be essentially about. Much of what English did teach or foster, moreover, was neither new to the learners nor exclusively obtainable from the teaching, since in one sense English was what all native speakers were doing all the time already. Indeed, not only was pupils' English being continuously practiced and extended outside school; it was also learned *within* school, in other subjects, wherever reading, writing, and speaking were engaged in, a point that would be made much of in the "language across the curriculum" initiatives of the 1970s.

These considerations make clear that, to be comprehensive, a theory of the development of curriculum has to take adequate account of the exceptional case of English as well as the more "normal" academic subjects. Work on which we have drawn includes the theory of curriculum history (e.g., Barker 1996, Franklin 1999), teacher life histories (Goodson 2003), studies of individual London schools (e.g., Limond 2002), and historical accounts of the teaching profession (McCulloch et al. 2000).[3]

A curriculum history movement that began in the late twentieth century has provided insights into the development of subjects, subject associations, and school textbooks.[4] This study is specifically indebted to earlier, now rather dated, histories of English teaching (reviewed in chapter two) that offered general accounts drawing mainly on published sources, but it takes them forward by locating evidence about individual schools, classrooms, and teachers within and against those accounts of the general sweep of the subject. This was very necessary because the literature of the 1970s and 1980s presented a story of English that was partial and oversimplified. What we have added has been in some ways a response to Harold Silver's 1992 call for a "social history of the classroom."[5] Since Silver wrote these words there have been some important studies that have risen to the challenge, but perhaps nothing comparable in aims and methods to what was undertaken in this research into English. Our work adds another dimension in that respect to earlier studies of English, but we have also been concerned to rectify notions that we have found to be misleading. These include the apparent orthodoxy that what supplanted traditional English teaching was a 1960s "New English" that subordinated intellectual development to creativity, expressivity, and reading for enjoyment, and, and that the preceding period was largely stagnant and was dominated by textbooks containing abstract grammatical exercises and literature lessons focusing on the appreciation of long-dead great authors.

We have also been impressed by historians of education who have worked with broader methodologies, such as materiality and oral history,[6] and by scholarship exploring connections between content, theory, and history[7] and demonstrating the potential for ethnography and school studies to illuminate understandings of curricula.[8] What we add, that we hope takes account of this work, is a case study approach that enables us to examine English teaching as it was thought about, practiced, and experienced in three London schools. The research employs mixed methods, bringing a strong dimension of "voice" from oral testimony but also drawing widely on unpublished documentary sources retrieved from the schools and provided by informants, all of which add concrete particularity and often vividness to the story. But also, because we remain alert to possible connections between the history of the English classroom and broader developments in postwar British society, we make reference to the writings of social historians and cultural commentators, particularly in chapter two. On this question, although we have arrived at no simple formulation, the detailed and experiential character of our data, offering many glimpses of individual experiences of what Philip Jackson long ago called "life in classrooms"[9]—and staff rooms—will certainly be of interest to social historians.

In short, we offer to curriculum history an account of what can be learned by examining very local phenomena in as much detail as the available evidence allows, given the passage of two-thirds of a century, while keeping in mind what was happening in education in general and society and culture in general.

Contribution to Understanding English Teaching

As a topic, English teaching in the first two decades after the Second World War has not been well served by historians. The main subject histories of English on which we have drawn will be reviewed in chapter two and further assessed in chapter six.[10] The period has been passed over without close attention under the assumption that it was largely a period of unthinking continuation of prewar practices, in a context of few comprehensive schools until the 1960s and with hopes disappointed for a new sort of education in the post-1944 secondary modern schools, while grammar school education was reduced to a grind for examination passes at 16 and 18, dominated by rote learning. While there is some truth in that picture, one contribution of this book will be to show that, in places at least, English was a livelier business than the histories suggest, sometimes far livelier. A major motivation in our studies was to begin to write a more adequate and nuanced account (*only* begin, because in terms of the new data it brings this is a local and particular inquiry). We will show that, at least on the evidence of three good schools (deemed to be good at the time, that is), the picture is more complicated than the literature implies. Coexisting in schools there were different generations of teachers and different notions of English deriving from trends that changed over time in the teaching of English in higher education and in teacher training; teachers learned and changed in the course of their careers, for a variety of reasons including changes in the discipline of English and a new sense of political and cultural possibility. The children and young people in the schools also changed over the 20 years, so that teaching that "worked" in 1948 didn't in 1963, inclining teachers to look for new solutions.

It is a serious limitation of existing histories of English that they rely almost exclusively, as Ball et al. acknowledge,[11] on "the public rhetorics and discourses" comprising books and articles about and for English, without evidence about the English teaching and the pupils' learning that actually went on in schools. Moreover, if existing work uses teachers' oral testimony very sparingly, it draws on that of former pupils not at all, nor on the written evidence of the work they did. The crucial difference in our study has been that its core comprises just three case studies, so that instead of breadth we have gone for depth so as to contribute to a truer and fuller picture of the subject by bringing to the history detailed evidence about the practice and thinking of a relatively small number of teachers. Our evidence from those schools is of two kinds: oral testimony from former teachers and pupils and documentary evidence including pupils' work, school syllabuses, and teachers' mark books and lesson notes. In the light of what we learn from the case studies we are able to place the earlier histories in a new light, at least by raising new questions, bearing in mind always that case studies are local and say nothing conclusive about the general scene, a relationship that Silver (1983) discusses at length, suggesting: "A study of historical detail, of an instance, of a unique event, may point towards wider generalizations, the need for sustained revision."[12]

In the history of English in schools there has long been a need for this particular kind of study. Commenting in his 1990 survey of English in the 1950s and 1960s, based entirely on published sources, Medway observed:

> Little direct evidence is available of what English consisted of in practice in the diversity of settings in which it took place: gaining reliable knowledge of that would require a major research study employing such methods as the collection of school syllabuses, stock lists and surviving pupil work, interviews with former teachers and pupils and a study of textbook sales.[13]

This is such an attempt, pursued through the collection of exactly that sort of material, albeit within the narrow compass of three London schools.

And since we hope to engage readers who bring practical concerns about how English should be taught as well as historical interest, we try to illuminate what seems of permanent educational value in some modes of English teaching that tend to have been dismissed as unthinking persistence in traditional methods, as well as in what was and remains important in the innovations introduced by teachers like Rosen. Although our story is by no means all about "reforms," Harold reminded us of the determination with which these have had to be fought for in the past and confirmed our resolve to record what was achieved and how: "But what I am saying is, we have to record all this...not just mentally. It is about saying there was another way. And some of the best teachers of our generation, generations, fought for that."[14] At the same time, while there *was* a way that was "better" than the sterility of much English teaching in all types of school in the 1940s, 1950s, and 1960s, we have to record what we find admirable in some grammar school practice, although it was experienced by a selective group of the school population.

The Research: Aims, Design, Methods

The research project from which this book derives was entitled "Social Change and English: A Study of Three English Departments 1945–1965." It ran from 2009 to 2012, was funded by the Leverhulme Trust,[15] was directed by John Hardcastle at the Institute of Education, University of London, and was derived from earlier studies by him and by Peter Medway of King's College London. They were joined by David Crook of the Institute and then by Mary Irwin who was succeeded after the first year by Georgina Brewis, with Patrick Kingwell as a volunteer researcher conducting interviews and taking part in project planning, archival research, and presentations.

As we have said, the idea of an ambitious funded project developed only gradually out of an initial realization that we and everyone else had already missed the chance, because of their deaths, to collect systematically the memories of important figures in English teaching, including James Britton, Nancy Martin, and Alex McLeod, people whom Hardcastle and Medway knew and had worked with. We made amends in two sessions with our former tutor, Harold Rosen, before he became too ill. In particular we learned about his time in the 1950s as head of English at Walworth School (a very early comprehensive), where Medway later (1963–1971) did his teaching practice and had his first job. We wanted to know more about Walworth in the period before we started teaching, and also to investigate Hardcastle's school, Hackney Downs (comprehensive in John's time, previously a grammar school). Both schools, we knew, had been influential in the development and dissemination of new approaches to English. We added a third school, Minchenden Grammar, also well known for its contribution to developments in the teaching of English, and applied for a grant.

The design of our research reflected our wish to do something different from the earlier studies we have mentioned. Whereas their sources had mainly been publications in which teachers and teacher educators set out their thinking about the subject, described how they taught it, and explained how they thought it should be taught, we wanted to obtain evidence of their practice. While what teachers told us in interviews was not necessarily more reliable than what some might have written, face-to-face interaction would enable us on the one hand to ask supplementary questions to clarify what they had told us and on the other to check their narratives against interviews with other teachers and former pupils, and against surviving documents such as lesson notes, mark books, and pupil work.

These priorities dictated that we work intensively on a small number of schools in order to construct relatively deep, richly concrete, and fine-textured histories. Three schools was the most to which we felt we could do sufficient justice. Such narrowly focused studies enable researchers to take account of particularities of situation and context the possible significance of which general histories are likely to occlude. Not only do schools differ but differences occur within *categories* of schools. Thus grammar schools are by no means all alike in intake, ethos, or practice. Likewise, broad categories of location such as "suburb" or "inner-city working-class district" conceal a wide range of often quite striking differences.

The three studies would be case studies in the sense that they would describe cases of English teaching in the period, but emphatically without any implication that they were typical (even assuming that it had been possible to determine what was typical). In fact the schools were selected as being precisely *not* typical but, on the contrary—or so we believed at the outset—exceptional leaders of innovation in English. In the nature of case studies, they would not lend themselves to forming general conclusions about English at the time, or even about innovatory English. They would nevertheless carry implications for the further pursuit of understanding in relation to what happened in English more widely. For instance, if a teaching strategy was implemented in one of our schools, that would show that adopting such a strategy was not unthinkable within the conditions of the time and would raise the question whether it might not have happened elsewhere as well; if some of "our" teachers were found to have taken a certain consideration into account as they went about their work, might not teachers elsewhere have based their practice on similar notions? In which case, where had these notions come from? Again, what we find about, say, Grammar School X might corroborate what has been said elsewhere about grammar schools, or alternatively cause us to question the validity of existing general claims.

We were interested not only in teachers and the educational experiences they provided but also in pupils, for their own, possibly diverging accounts of the same teachers' lessons and for what they made of them. ("Pupils," this may be the place to mention, was the term used in the period rather than today's preferred "students," which then referred only to young people older than the statutory minimum school leaving age who attended institutions of further or higher education, post-16 or post-18. We tend here to follow usage from the time.)

We should add that our concern was not only with what teachers did with their classes; we were interested also in what they thought and believed at the time—though the connection between professed and enacted principles is notoriously problematic and needs to be critically assessed rather than assumed from teachers' words. For instance, if an English teacher with a Marxist background teaching in a nonselective school in a working-class area says he believed that the future lay with the working class, that belief may well have reinforced their commitment to the education of the children they were teaching. Beyond that, it may or may not have influenced *what* or *how* they taught: their practical determination may have been either to give the children a good education in traditional terms or to find ways of teaching that were specifically suited to the backgrounds and perhaps the "historical destination" of working-class pupils. On the other hand, an equal commitment to the children and to the job may have sprung from quite different sources, like simple respect and liking, unaffected by any definite philosophy. And whereas some teaching is undoubtedly an expression of core beliefs, aims, or principles, other teaching is driven by the simple pragmatic criterion of "what works"—lesson time is filled, pupils are occupied, "work" is accomplished. Even for teachers who hold strong beliefs, maintaining a teaching timetable of 30 out of 35 periods a week for 40 weeks a year with five or six different classes inevitably dictates some recourse to the criterion of "what works."

A related consideration is that teaching ideas that emerged in innovatory practice as a result of deep thinking about aims and principles by a few teachers in one school would often subsequently become available to be adopted by other teachers—opportunistically or by "eclectic pillaging,"[16] simply as part of the bag of tricks that would get them through the day, often alongside other practices that owed their origin to quite different and incompatible philosophies but that likewise had been found to "work." This, too, poses issues of interpretation. A practice implemented in one teacher's lesson—for instance, getting pupils to relate experiences in home and locality as a preliminary to written work—can plausibly be interpreted by the researcher as the enactment of a principle the teacher may have believed in about the need to start from experience as the first stage in developing in pupils a more acceptable and versatile written discourse; in another teacher's lesson a practice that may look the same may simply have been a way to get pupils writing without too much trouble. One class may be reading *To Kill a Mocking-Bird* because teenagers have been found not to complain too much about reading it, another because their teacher is committed to making them think seriously about race relations in American society.

Although the difference may not be obvious from either observation or the teachers' explanation—because the acceptable rhetorics of justification are well known to teachers being interviewed or writing articles—it may show in their associated behavior and the context in which they embed the work—framing comments, questions, tasks, and feedback, and the relationship that aspect of the work bears to other elements in their program. Most of that behavior tends to be lost to researchers investigating classrooms from years earlier—but not always, as we have found.

A key element in our research design, finally, because we wanted the idea of a publicly available evidence base to influence future research into school subjects, was an undertaking we entered into to deposit all our data, both documents and recordings, in archives available to researchers. This we have done, in the London Institute of Education Archives and the British Library Sound Archive.[17]

The period immediately before we (or at any rate Medway) started teaching interested us because that was when two of us (Hardcastle and Medway) had been at grammar school ourselves and because we had gathered from older colleagues that in those years far-reaching changes had been effected in English teaching. Those changes had by our time influenced teacher training, the teachers who originated them in the schools having become the tutors who taught us about English teaching on their courses in London University, so that we knew we were in effect the second generation to practice teaching in new ways, to be succeeded by many more. (Medway was taught at the Institute of Education, University of London, by Harold Rosen, James Britton, and Nancy Martin in the early sixties and Hardcastle in the early seventies.) The arrival of that second generation suggested a workable end point, as did the recent (1964) return to power of the Labour Party after a gap of 13 years with a commitment to the general introduction of comprehensive schools;[18] besides, changes in economy, society, and culture had started to accelerate rapidly. The obvious starting point was the end of the war and the new dispensation following the 1944 Education Act, while 20 years seemed a manageable stretch of time to study, given what we estimated to be the quantity of data we would be able to collect about English in three schools.

The period is often referred to as "postwar," which is fine when implicitly or explicitly opposed to "prewar" but makes little sense in relation to the second decade, from the mid-1950s, by which time the memory of the war had come to mean far less—to those who remembered it all, which excludes children in the first two or three years of secondary school—and the world already felt very different from that of the late 1940s.

London was the only real geographical choice because we had both spent a large part of our careers there (all, in Hardcastle's case) and we had extensive first-hand knowledge of London schools. "London" meant not only the inner area comprising the then County of London but also outer London areas that fell within other counties including Middlesex, the location of Minchenden School. This broader meaning made sense, not least because teachers from the Home Counties travelled into the center to attend courses and meetings. Choosing London schools meant, of course, that our research could not hope to provide a representative glimpse of the national picture, since the situation for English teachers in London was exceptional in many ways: in opportunities for professional development, the number and quality of courses offered by the Institute of Education and various colleges, and the possibility of gathering together a large enough body of teachers to form a substantial association; also exceptional were the rich cultural resources offered by the capital including theaters, art galleries and museums, and the National Film Theatre and other cinemas showing contemporary British and foreign films. National political groups and events in which some teachers were involved tended to be found in London, including the gatherings around the *Universities and Left Review* that was one origin for the New Left movement in which Richard Hoggart, Raymond Williams, and Stuart Hall were important figures.

Our choice of schools was dictated by their reputations as having been important in the history of English teaching and the access we could count on to contacts, given that we had worked in two of them and knew the major figure in the third. This gave us two grammar schools and one comprehensive, a selection that appears unbalanced until it is pointed out that in the first few years comprehensive schools hardly existed and that the other main type of school, the secondary modern, was not known, as far as we could ascertain without an extensive study, for innovative work in English, most of its teachers being nonspecialists who taught their own classes two or three subjects and who left little impression in one of the main sources, the archive of the London Association for the Teaching of English.

The schools, then, to summarize, were: Hackney Downs, a boys' grammar school run by the London County Council (LCC); Walworth, an LCC mixed-sex "interim" comprehensive school (explained in chapters two and four), and Minchenden Grammar School (mixed) within the County of Middlesex education authority. This selection had the virtue of including a good mix of types in terms of other criteria as well, in that the schools represented three types of origin—nineteenth century institutions established by an ancient trade association (HD) and an elected school board (W), and a post–World War I school created by local government (M); geographically, two entirely urban areas (HD and W) and one suburban (M); demographically, two largely or entirely working-class (HD and W) pupil populations and one mixed but predominantly middle-class (M); and ethnically, one with a homogeneous long-established British population (W) and two with substantial numbers of Jewish pupils (HD and W).

Because of the aftermath of the war, the period we elected to study has implications for the kind of experience the pupils brought with them. Given that, of the pupils who attended our schools between September 1945 and July 1965, some of the earliest cohort (1945–1946) had already been in the schools for six years (being now in the upper sixth and having entered in 1939), our range of birth dates is from 1928 to 1954. Thus not only had some pupils' entire secondary school careers to that point been in wartime, but also, if we assume that children would have some memory of their lives from the age of five, then it would have been 1949 before the first child entered the schools who could not remember his or her experience of at least a couple of years of war; that cohort could have left school as late as 1956. The fathers of a great many children would have been absent for several years, would not normally have come home until well into 1946 or later and often then to the accompaniment of disturbance and conflict;[19] many of their mothers would have suffered years of stress, long hours, and overwork. Schooling might have been disrupted by bombing and rendered unsatisfactory by shortage of suitable staff, and some pupils had spent long periods as truants enjoying the run of a chaotic city. Others, of course, had been evacuated, an experience that might have been brutal and impoverished or enriching and educationally valuable.[20]

We gained much by employing a mixed methodology involving "a combination of documentary and non-documentary sources," as, for instance, when we have been able, in McCulloch's words, "to relate [documentary] records to interviews of living respondents."[21]

Our selection of individuals to interview had to be opportunistic, based on chains of connection starting with people we knew and on appeals on the project's website, the Friends Reunited website and (for Walworth School) Medway's blog. These means of making contact with potential informants were supplemented for two schools by the continued existence, despite the closure of the schools, of a thriving old pupils' association (Hackney Downs) and a school website (Minchenden), the managers of which were helpful when we asked about people we might talk to. Inevitably, given the nature of the information available to us in the absence of surviving school records, we were unable to compile the sorts of lists from which samples might be drawn that were representative of categories such as measured ability or social class. We could invite to interview only those whose names and contact details we were able to obtain. These tended be individuals who had kept in touch with school associations, school friends, and even teachers. Further, those who agreed to be interviewed or to respond to written questions and those who contacted us unbidden to offer memories or documents tended, in the nature of these inquiries, to be those who had enjoyed their English lessons and done well in them, or alternatively had bitter memories of them (not many of the latter). Our experience in general is that most people have little interest in remembering school. Some former Walworth pupils who Kingwell and Medway interviewed as a group commented that they were regarded by friends who had attended other schools as rather strange in being interested in renewing contact with their old school and former classmates, still more in welcoming the prospect of meeting their teachers. For those others, school was something that was best forgotten.

We followed the example of Wells and Cunningham: "Bearing in mind... that a rigid interview agenda discourages interview respondents from pursuing their own recollections and reflections, we sought to devise a minimal semi-structured schedule" and reduced it to a prompt sheet.[22] We completed 81 interviews and had them transcribed. There were also many email exchanges, some very extended and including lengthy notes and memoirs and with scanned documents attached. Potential informants came forward right to the end of the project, and indeed are still doing so.

Individuals' contributions to our stock of memories have varied greatly, the most obvious reasons being the sharpness of their memories, their ability to communicate them, and how extensively they have reflected on their times in the schools in the intervening years. Statements that have a lot of thought behind them tend to be fuller, though there is a risk that memories may have been extensively if unconsciously reconstructed. In the book, although we have tried to represent every significant perspective that we encountered, we do not give all informants an equal say but have made fuller use of testimony that seems to express what many thought but not all have explained so clearly.

We have been conscious that some of those who helped us will be in our audience for the book, as they have been participants in some of our presentations in London; this situation of course has raised ethical considerations, though perhaps not radically different from those that arise in any reporting of research involving human subjects; we have been careful about using only testimony that we have permission to use. The feedback and additional information that has come our way as a result of our written and oral presentations have been a source of strength in our research.[23]

Documentary sources were very varied. Some teachers had saved collections of pupils' work; some pupils had kept their exercise books and folders. Relatives of teachers who had died sent us material or allowed us to inspect copies of books used in teaching, some with significant pencil markings. Documents taken from the schools when they closed had sometimes been saved. Ex-pupils lent us certificates, examination papers, school and class magazines, programs for events including drama productions and exhibitions of work, and photographs. Syllabuses were loaned or donated by teachers, some of whom had also kept mark books and lesson notes. The documentary collections we have been able to hand over to the Institute of Education Archives are rich and substantial. In addition, we looked at documents in the National Archives relating to the schools, particularly inspection reports.[24]

By its nature the research threw up problems relating to finding and interpreting information. The data were often incomplete and fragmentary: what significance should be attached to a pedagogic practice reported from a single school, such as the making of a film by one class in their English lessons? Anecdotes were related to us of something that happened in a single lesson, remembered without context and for which we had no documentary support; pieces of work survived without any indication of how they arose or were received; teachers' notes referred to tasks or readings we are unable to understand; what weight should be attached to a single recollection of something a teacher mentioned in a department meeting? Could an inspector's report on a new comprehensive school be taken as a true attempt to be objective, or did it reflect the writer's concern that the school, the establishment of which he or she had strongly supported as a hopeful democratic experiment, should not be subject to adverse criticism early in its development? It was a strength of our methodology that we were sometimes able to resolve such doubts by reference to a second source. But there was often no finality. Our impression of a particular teacher's style of work could fluctuate as we passed from source to source.

When we began the more extensive and systematic stage of our research, with several interviews about Walworth School already in the bag, we had some hypotheses and questions in mind (which we spelled out in our grant application). We were fairly sure, though we didn't know for certain, that radical innovation in English arose first with significant effect not in the 1960s but in the 1950s or earlier, as Harold Rosen told us was the case in Walworth. We associated that innovation with "a democratic spirit of postwar optimism," to which we tended to attach the Labour Party's 1940s slogan about building a "new Jerusalem." A wider question was, was change in English teaching a product of, or associated with, change in society? It was our interest in the innovations that were adopted widely and with significant effects later that led us to choose schools that we believed had had a hand in originating them. To an extent they also governed our questioning of informants and interrogation of documents.

One sort of outcome of our research, possibly the less important sort, has been an evaluation of those hypotheses and an attempted answer to that question. We did not, however, confine ourselves to inquiries directly relating to them because we felt that our research was probing a period in English about which we knew little, and about which indeed little was known, so that hypotheses formulated in advance would hardly be an adequate guide to inquiry. Our "hypotheses" were, in any case, unlike those that guide research in, say, physics. Our situation had more in common with that of scientists entering an unexplored forest, when pursuing preformed notions could lead to missing the most important potential discoveries. Consequently, a second sort of "finding" has proved equally or more important, that which resulted from "letting the data speak to us"— the equivalent to the scientist's "I took note of everything that occurred, whether or not it seemed relevant, and *happened to notice* that [X]." An example would be our realization, on looking at early Walworth documents (about the school, not English), that the democratic spirit informing English in the school was mirrored in other subjects and reflected the ideology that lay behind many aspects of the new comprehensive school's regime.

Finally, in relation to our purpose, the two initial researchers, Hardcastle and Medway, had both been English teachers for many years and had most recently worked in teacher education, training university graduates as secondary school English teachers. Our interest in the topic, therefore, is not purely historical but also relates to the state of the subject in schools today, which we think could benefit from some attention to what was done in the past. The British experience in the period we are studying might be relevant to other countries, too. While it is not the intention in this book to spell out lessons for today, which in any case, given our competences, would apply to England only, we hope they will not be difficult to draw, despite the extent of the changes since 1965 and the differences, where applicable, between national systems and traditions.

A note may be of interest about what it has been like doing this research. While Brewis, Crook, and Irwin had all used oral history methods in earlier research, Hardcastle and Medway came to it fresh, though with experience of research interviewing in other contexts. One strong impression is of how many resources, human and documentary, are still out there despite the passage of time; not only are there far more documents than we had suspected but teachers whose unfamiliar names appeared on old school lists turned out to be alive, traceable, and ready to talk. Ready and eager, in fact, was the attitude we generally encountered on approaching former teachers and pupils with a view to a possible interview. A former science teacher from one school got in touch from Australia offering to meet us while he was visiting London; it turned out he had also taught English for a period, in place of a regular teacher in hospital, and had brought his teaching notes; he was able to give us valuable memories about his English colleagues in the later 1950s and put us on to another science teacher, living in France, who shared by email his memories of the English department and the school.

The interviews varied in kind. In some instances they represented years of reflection looking back over a career in teaching. Such reflections often included stories and anecdotes that had been rehearsed many times—with events reconfigured in the retelling. In other instances they involved recalling episodes that took on new meanings as the speakers related them and it was common for people to say in the middle of an interview, "I hadn't thought about that before—it just occurred to me now." We met sometimes in our offices, sometimes in public places where we could find a quiet spot but often in our interviewees' homes, at their invitation. Typically they were surprised and delighted that someone was interested in their experiences of school so long ago, and showed this by inviting us to stay to lunch.

We were aware that historical interviews have recently been drawn to public attention because of a surge in documentary television programs on topics at the remoter end of living memory and also in best-selling history books, some relating to our period and making prolific use of interviews, such as the ambitious series by David Kynaston.[25] People appeared to welcome the chance to be participants in this movement. We have had meetings with willing groups of ex-pupils and ex-teachers; a project seminar for both teachers and academic colleagues had no trouble filling a space for 60 places; and we organized two Walworth events,[26] each attracting 60–100 former teachers and pupils, many of whom had helped us and who were obviously delighted to be there. People who met at these events, often old classmates or sports team associates, have arranged further meetings, sometimes as large groups. Some are pursuing our inquiries for themselves and for these groupings, for instance, tracking down the pupils involved in making a film. Our conference presentations typically met with a welcome that seemed to arise from a shared recognition that something like our fine-grained, case-study-based, mixed-evidence research had been needed.

Readers may be surprised by the shortage of women teachers in our report. The fact is that few were prominent in the data, even from the two mixed schools (no women taught English at Hackney Downs). Teachers who were in the schools for many years and so are more likely to have appeared in testimony and documents tended not to be women, perhaps because so many in those days still left teaching on marriage. The head of department at Minchenden right up to 1959 was female but we know relatively little about her. The heads of department in Walworth were all male, as were nearly all the English teachers until into the 1960s.

The findings from the schools are reported in the three central chapters, three, four and five, and our conclusions from the case studies in chapter six. Chapter two briefly sets out the background of the period in terms of society, culture, and the education system, and then explains what is known from, and claimed by, histories and published sources about the state of and changes in English teaching in England between the mid-1940s and the mid-1960s. The discussion of our findings in chapter six will partly be framed by this review and will relate to the earlier historical accounts. Finally, chapter seven will offer concluding reflections on what happened in English in our period in the light of what happened later, and will comment on our research more broadly, its limitations and contributions.

Chapter 2

The Period, the Education System, and the Teaching of English

This chapter is about the context within which English in our case study schools took place, nationally and in London. In it we briefly mention key political, economic, and social developments within the period, the state of the education system nationally and in London, and, at more length, the situation in English teaching. This is not a comprehensive survey and the sources we draw on are a selection from published accounts, contemporary commentary, and archival records.

Britain 1945–1965

The Britain of 1965, the end date of our study, was immeasurably different from the country that emerged from the war in 1945. Radical political change under a Labour government in the early years was followed from 1951 by 13 years of political stability—stability at least in duration—under the Conservatives, until 1964 when Labour resumed office; but social change had accelerated. London at the end of the war had "bombsites overgrown with weeds, dunes of brick dust, rubble piled alongside hastily cleared streets."[1] But a decade of austerity was succeeded by one of growing affluence (though by no means for everyone) and by 1965 Carnaby Street was popularizing new fashions while pop music was played on pirate radio stations that challenged the BBC and the "Establishment" (a term coined by a journalist in a time of declining social deference "to describe a quiet undeliberated conspiracy against the common good").[2] Developments in cinema, television, fashion, advertising, and popular music were accompanied by a new youth culture based in part on teenage spending power. There were challenges to long-established assumptions about nation, empire, gender, and the social order.

Education had not received the same priority of resourcing as other areas of the postwar welfare state, but by 1965 education spending had come to be regarded as an investment. There were ambitions to promote child-centered learning in the primary school, to develop a universal system of secondary comprehensive schooling, and to extend higher education to all young people capable of benefiting from it.

The children in the schools had changed too. For several years after 1945 children entering secondary school at 11 had the war as the dominant memory from their primary school years; those entering from around 1952 mostly remembered little of it beyond the odd incident, while those arriving from 1957 or so were baby boomers and very different children.

The different meanings implied by "reconstruction" reflected an ambiguity in postwar sentiment; it might mean restoration of what was there before or replacement by something new. That divide was characteristic of the "spirit of the times." Some people wanted simply to get back to prewar peacetime normality while other others wanted the opposite—"the construction of a postwar New Jerusalem, planned, humane, and mildly socialistic,"[3] or, for women, not having to give up their wartime jobs that had been a welcome escape from the isolation of the home. The 20 years following the war were a time of both stagnancy and dynamic change. Workers returning to now-nationalized industries found the experience of work essentially unchanged, on the stage chaps in blazers still entered through French windows with tennis rackets over their shoulders, but in council offices planners and architects took up new and exhilarating possibilities for being modern and even Modernist, and grammar school leavers could get good jobs in the previously restricted but now enlarged domain of professional work.

So was it an optimistic or a pessimistic era? There was plenty to be pessimistic about, as numerous novels convey including Kingsley Amis' *Lucky Jim* and David Lodge's *Out of the Shelter*, and a pupil interviewee told us how his home in 1960 had no running water and others still had gas lights. More widely, social optimism was increasingly tempered by a difficult economic and political reality. The 1945 Labour government sought to implement the social reforms proposed in the wartime Beveridge Report (1942) but postwar debt, the costs of the 1950 Korean War, and Cold War nuclear anxieties cast a shadow, and the national confidence following wartime victory was undermined by the loss of empire (starting with India in 1947) and later the Suez debacle (1956).

Mass-Observation diaries, on the other hand, reveal a relatively optimistic mood to do with "a less deferential society in which people came to see themselves less in terms of where they were placed within functional hierarchies, more as autonomous individuals aspiring to relate to one another in egalitarian ways."[4] There was also more money. In the later 1950s the country, at least in parts, became what contemporaries called the "affluent society" and the annual spending-power of (working) teenagers was several hundred million pounds.[5] The situation was characterized by "newly erupted social groups...born of the 'new prosperity' and the cross-fertilisation of English classes."[6] "[M]ore normal two-way communication [between the classes] might at last be opening up. In many of the working-class children who left the new schools was to be noted a new sort of social assurance, a new disposition to speak their minds—in accents and idiom of a new universality."[7]

In formulating our research we had it in mind to relate the history of English teaching to social change. Social change, however, proves a tricky and uneven affair, and what happened in English may have had as much to do with social phenomena that were static as with those being transformed. This study cannot, in the event, be a simple story of English and social change.

Education System and Policy

The Education Acts of 1918 and 1944 owed much to a vision of postwar educational reconstruction as part of building a better society. The raising of the school-leaving age to 14 in 1918 heralded a campaign for "secondary education for all," meaning a wider curriculum than the elementary schools offered, with proper provision for languages, science, and vocational subjects. In 1938, the Spens Report proposed three types of secondary school: grammar schools for the academically able, modern schools for the majority, and technical schools for those demonstrating aptitudes for vocational skills.[8] There was a confident belief that psychometric testing, in the form of the "11 plus" (the test, taken at age 10–11, to measure IQ and sometimes also arithmetic and literacy), could allocate children to the right kind of school. Finally the Education Act of 1944 abolished the charging of fees by local authority grammar schools, leaving admission to be determined by the 11 plus alone. The school-leaving age would be raised to 15 in 1947 and to 16 as soon as possible thereafter (in fact this did not happen until 1973).

One result was rationalization of a confusing terminology. Before 1944 children in the state (as opposed to the private) system had begun their education in a free (no fees) elementary school from the age of five or earlier. At 11 some pupils assessed as more able had transferred into fee-charging *grammar* or *secondary* schools (some with their fees covered by scholarships) while the rest had continued in elementary schools—*senior* elementaries or simply "senior schools."[9] Thus "secondary" education, though available only to older children, had referred essentially not to an age stage but to academic status. After 1944 the nomenclature became more logical; education before 11 was *primary* and that after 11 was *secondary*, and secondary came to include not only the former secondary or grammar schools, now called simply grammar schools, but also the former senior schools, which became modern, or, in the more usual expression, secondary modern schools.

The 1944 Act had nothing to say about curriculum. A Minister of Education explicitly stated

> Once we start any central direction of the contents of text books, we embark on a slippery slope which leads to totalitarianism. It has always been a very important principle of the education system in this country that the Central Department does not attempt to influence the curriculum of the schools in any detail.[10]

The 1944 Act did not forbid the establishment of nonselective common or *comprehensive* schools and when Clement Attlee's Labour Party won a landslide victory in the 1945 general election those who favored the comprehensive system expected the new government, in line with Labour policy, to introduce it. In fact, however, the new minister supported the differentiated Spens system, with the hopeful aspiration that equal value would be accorded to all three types in the interests of undermining the class system—"parity of esteem" was the phrase.[11]

Since technical schools were not established in any numbers, selection in most places meant allocation to grammar or secondary modern school, with the majority of children (75–80%) directed into the latter, which predictably failed to secure equal status.

Many new entrants to the teaching profession and some teachers returning from the war wanted to participate in building a new society. Others, however, shared in what Cox has called the "great longing in England for a return to tranquillity"[12] and in parts of society, including some associated with the teaching of English, there was strong opposition to the 1944 reforms. Denys Thompson, a prominent voice in English, in 1945 attacked the "'levelling-down on which the Ministry seems bent'" and declared that the grammar schools were now "'pearlharboured' by the Act.'"[13] If the ending of fees for grammar schools was deplored by Thompson (and also

T. S. Eliot) on the grounds that a society without strong elites would be unable to uphold cultural standards, how much more offensive to values like his were comprehensive schools.

The establishment of comprehensive schools in, at best, the absence of cooperation from government was a painfully protracted process. By 1958, only 46 comprehensives were operating, and of these few were full comprehensives that included the fifth or quarter of children who would have passed the 11 plus test. This was despite growing dissatisfaction with the 11 plus, as evidence from academic studies questioned the rationale for and validity of psychometric testing.[14] Too many children with latent abilities, it was claimed, were being misallocated to secondary modern schools, while a disproportionate number of those winning grammar-school places happened also to be middle class.[15] There was social dissatisfaction, too, as middle-class parents who could previously have paid for grammar school places saw their less academically able children consigned to the unregarded secondary moderns.

The early 1960s witnessed a "break out" by comprehensive-minded local education authorities (LEAs). The Secretary of State for Education, Tony Crosland, in the new Labour government of 1964 applied pressure on LEAs to "go comprehensive" and privately declared his intention to "destroy every fucking grammar school in England. And Wales. And Northern Ireland."[16] The initiative reflected the fact that "Never before...had public education been...so insistently demanded at all social levels.

> A social survey in 1952 showed that even in the unskilled working class the majority of parents now wanted their children to stay at school till sixteen, while a strong minority wanted them to stay till eighteen. That this represented a real change of attitude could be seen from the figures for children in fact staying on at school, steadily rising, in all classes of secondary school, year by year, through the Fifties.[17]

We should convey something of the character of the school types represented in our study. Since the interim comprehensives were new and few and have not been extensively described, we will briefly address the grammar schools, of which we investigated two. Grammar schools are best described as *academic*. They admitted 11-year-olds judged academically capable and valued "a line of studies which either specifically trains logical thought, the ordering of available facts, the sharpness of rational analysis or are especially open to this approach. The line moves from Latin and the structure of the English language, to physics, chemistry and mathematics."[18]

Associated with this emphasis was a particular social profile. This had changed in the early twentieth century and even more after 1944. After the Education Act of 1902 solidly middle-class Victorian or older institutions were often taken over by LEAs who awarded scholarships exempting a number of poor bright children from paying fees. (The LEAs also established new grammar schools, then and later.) Thus Hackney Downs Grammar School, founded in the 1870s for the middle classes and taken over by the London County Council in 1907, by the 1930s had accepted a large proportion of working-class boys who had secured free scholarship places.[19] Prewar fee-paying grammar schools were already socially diverse, and if they all represented an "elite" education the degree to which they did so varied greatly. Between a grammar school in South-west Hertfordshire and one in Middlesbrough in the later prewar period the proportion of working-class pupils was as different as 16 and 46 percent.[20]

With the complete abolition of fees in 1944 and the introduction of selection solely by the 11 plus test, entry to grammar schools for children from families with middle-class incomes was no longer assured. "[T]he simple right of cash and purse was abruptly replaced by an annual pitched battle of childish wits and nerves." Nevertheless,

> [It] was found [in surveys conducted in 1956] that... in maintained grammar schools, intended for intelligent children of all classes, the middle or professional class was over-represented... This had been the position in the pre-war days of fee-paying; it was still the position when careful allocation was made according to the results of "intelligence" tests. There seemed, therefore, a case for considering whether the "intelligence" test was an objective measure, or whether it merely reflected... the middle-class norm.[21]

In the early 1960s, two sociologists of education, Brian Jackson and Dennis Marsden, drew on interviews with parents and pupils to describe what it was like going to one grammar school in a northern industrial city.[22] The pupils in the school were selected by the 11 plus from a large number of primary schools, a few from each. In most cases they had been the "best" pupils, the most able scholars, team leaders, school monitors, prefects, and so on.[23] In the new school, which was often at a distance from their homes, they were divided into classes and "streamed" according to ability. Most of these 11-year-olds had no friends from their previous school in their class, and found the new school bewildering with its new subjects, new vocabulary (not "playtime" but "break," not "class" but "form") and a "whole body of customs, small rights and wrongs."[24] On top of this, they were immersed in a highly competitive atmosphere. (Colin Lacey observed a first-year history lesson in Hightown: "So many responded to each question that I could not record them. As the tension mounted boys who did not know the answers looked round apprehensively at those who did [...] they stretched their arms and bodies to the upmost as they eagerly called 'Sir,' 'Sir,' 'Sir.'"[25])

Some of the working-class pupils recalled a feeling of "'not *belonging* anywhere'... They found themselves surrounded by more middle-class children than they had ever met before... some already knew some French and Latin, their fathers had told them what 'Physics' was about, a few even knew the teachers."[26] Teachers and middle-class pupils often spoke differently from working-class children, some of whom quickly "learned to speak as others and the teachers spoke" while those who were not good "'mimics'" kept silent whenever possible. [27] But learning to speak in new ways could force a separation from their neighborhood, where they could be perceived as snobbish. Working-class children had to navigate an alien system and manage the daily transition between two environments. Harry Hopkins sets this experience within a wider social context:

> It was the schools in these years that had to absorb the first wave of social change. Two-thirds of the parents of post-war grammar school children had themselves not gone beyond elementary school... [T]eachers reported that it was easy to pick out the middle-class boys by their sense of purpose. For some working-class children and their families, on the other hand, the notion of steady self-directed application, of ambition to "get on in life," was alien. Teachers complained that the parents "hadn't a clue"; parents complained that the teachers were "toffee-nosed."[28]

Schools underestimated the hours spent on homework and working-class pupils found it difficult studying at home: "Our Alfred would be doing his homework in the front room and his father wasn't a bit understanding [...] Eeh, we'd have some rows in this place."[29]

Grammar schools were generally not the place to look for innovation in teaching methods. Very bright children would do well almost whatever the teaching and their teachers had little incentive to find better ways to promote learning. With the lower streams where there *was* such a need (because of factors other than measured IQ, by which all grammar school children were considered to be in the top quarter of the population) it tended to be too easily concluded that these mainly working-class pupils were simply not "grammar school material." The easiness of most grammar school teaching and the sterility of examination work could induce a boredom in teachers that could motivate moves to comprehensive schools.

The teaching profession in state secondary schools was divided between teachers with and without university degrees, the difference being reflected in their pay. Graduates (in British usage, those with university degrees) could be appointed as teachers without further training or could take an additional one-year course in a university department of education to gain a Diploma or Postgraduate Certificate of Education (PGCE). Most graduate teachers found posts in independent or grammar schools. The alternative route was on leaving school at 18 to be accepted in a teacher training college (later, college of education) for a course in both specialist subjects and education, the usual path for primary and secondary modern school teachers. Graduates teaching in grammar schools mainly belonged to a different union from nongraduates. The most significant development of the period, however, was the removal of a ban that debarred married women from teaching.

Over the years covered by our study, a number of graduates were attracted to the comprehensive school ethos or else found themselves in a comprehensive as a result of reorganization. An effect was that teachers with a university education for the first time found themselves in significant numbers working with entire local school-age populations rather with than the minority who had passed the 11 plus.

The London County Council (LCC) was in charge of education in the County of London with its 28 Metropolitan Boroughs. (The LCC had taken over in 1903 from the School Board for London, which itself had assumed responsibility following the Education Act of 1870 and had built the elementary schools most of which were still in use as primary, secondary moderns or comprehensive schools in our period. The County of London had been created in 1889, the boroughs in 1899.) This remained the situation until 1965 when the metropolitan boroughs were amalgamated into 12 "London boroughs," education in which passed to an Inner London Education Authority (ILEA), and joined with 20 other new London boroughs in outer London to create the administrative unit of Greater London.

"London" in this study refers to a wider region, including in our period both the inner County of London and surrounding counties, in one of which, Middlesex, Minchenden School in our study was located. The counties and boroughs that ran education locally in England and Wales were termed "local education authorities" or LEAs. Since the LEAs involved themselves in curriculum hardly more than did the government, they will not feature here except where the LCC's interest in the ethos of new comprehensive schools had implications for the teaching of English in Walworth School. (A Middlesex proposal for a comprehensive system was rejected in 1949 by the minister.[30])

The Second World War impacted disproportionately on education in the capital. six-hundred thousand London schoolchildren, including some complete schools, were evacuated to the countryside at the beginning of the war with some returning before long only be re-evacuated later. Many school buildings were destroyed or badly damaged by bombing.

The LCC's Education Officer, Graham Savage, had spent the war years leading the council's planning of the postwar school system. The vision of comprehensive schools across the city, outlined eventually in the 1947 London School Plan, which was at odds with the tripartite scheme backed by the government, had emerged from a fact-finding tour to North America undertaken by Savage in 1925 when he had been impressed by nonselective high schools. The School Plan proposing reorganization into 11–18 comprehensives expressed the mission as follows:

> Education is a thing of the spirit and, whatever types of school or curriculum may be established, it must everywhere have as its fundamental and overriding aim the many-sided development of human personality. Secondary education must, for every individual, be a liberal education, ministering to three types of interest – cultural interests for the enrichment of personal leisure, vocational interests in preparation for the successful gaining of a livelihood, and community interests leading to responsible participation in the duties of citizenship.[31]

We might note the the absence of intellectual priorities. What, for instance, was to be the place of science education? Such an absence seems striking today, of course, but was not unusual in the immediate postwar period when building a decent society was the priority for many.

New school building on the scale thought necessary (2,500 pupils for a viable comprehensive) being out of the question for the time being for financial reasons, in the interim "certain schools in London were experimentally combined into 'quasi-comprehensive schools' working in more than one building... they are not, however, comprehensive schools in the fullest sense of the term"[32] because the 11 plus test continued and those who passed it could still go to grammar schools, now free of charge. These quasi-comprehensive schools, of which five were set up in 1946 (including Walworth in our study), were termed "interim" or "experimental" comprehensives.

There was considerable opposition to the LCC's eventual earmarking of some grammar schools for closure in the 1950s. A grammar school teacher wrote, "To have built the London Grammar Schools with such high hopes and prospects and just when they were fulfilling those hopes and expectations to cut them down and kill them is a tragedy with no parallel in our history of education."[33] In this context James Britton's reminder is relevant, though his conclusion is quite different:

> In the thirties... the grammar school was seen as the spearhead of social reform in education. It was the bright hope of the public sector, year by year eating away at the areas of privilege of the public schools, the private sector. It stood as it were alone in this democratic role... As in 1930 I looked

for my first job in a state grammar school, so today I would look for it in a comprehensive school and for essentially the same reasons.[34]

It was 1954 before London's first purpose-built comprehensive, Kidbrooke was opened, though it lacked the complete ability range because of the minister's refusal to sanction the closure of a grammar school. Hackney Downs, the LCC grammar school in our study, retained that status throughout the 20-year period of our study and "went comprehensive" only later.

English

Turning to the subject of this book, in the rest of the chapter we must say something of what is known about the teaching of English in England between 1945 and 1965. There are historical accounts to start from: two book-length histories by Mathieson and Shayer and a substantial book section (Peel) that deal with English in general and two books that look at English from specific perspectives (Doyle and Reid).[35] There are also historical theses (PhD and Masters), a variety of chapters and articles, and a new history of the London English teachers' association that is central to our study (Gibbons).[36]

Numerous texts commented within our period or relatively soon afterwards on the recent history of the subject, in the course of or as a preliminary to doing something else, such as reporting a contemporary survey or urging a teaching approach. An example is the major book by Barnes, Barnes, and Clarke.[37] There are also autobiographies and memoirs that describe careers in English teaching and throw light on the state of the subject in general (that by Douglas Barnes is particularly helpful).[38]

Medway (1990)[39] surveyed everything that had been published for and about English in the two years 1958 and 1968—textbooks, articles, and "method" books. It was, and apparently remains (for England),[40] the only such systematically comprehensive survey, albeit limited to two years and, where an age group was specified, to texts relating to the junior secondary period (ages 11 to 13 or 14). He also reviewed historical accounts of English in the postwar period,[41] focusing particularly on those that described coexisting "models," "schools," or "paradigms" of English, those of Hodgson (1975), Hamley (1979), and Ball (1982, 1983, 1985).[42] The tendencies they identify at the start of our period are largely located within long-standing traditions: two majority traditions deriving from the grammar school and the elementary/secondary modern school, together with a minority "progressive" tradition.

Before 1945, and often after, English teaching in the grammar schools was much influenced by the way the subject was taught at Oxford and Cambridge, and, as in the universities, was expected to compensate in part for the reduced domination of Greek and Latin as the core of humane education. Oxford-style literary appreciation and philology-derived scholarly exegesis lay behind the normal version in schools—and in public examinations—while a style of critical attention learned from Cambridge was less widely practiced, though attracting growing numbers of adherents.

The elementary schools in contrast taught a functional English for basic literate competences, tempered with a minimal element of literature that was partly intended, it seems, to inculcate a modicum of respect for the culture of one's betters together with Christian virtues. The grammar and elementary school versions maintained their separate courses well beyond 1945.

The place of English in the secondary curriculum was not securely established at the end of the First World War. An official inquiry complained in 1921[43] that English was often accorded low importance and urged that it be taken seriously; literature had the power "to repair a social fabric grievously damaged by the ravages of the First World War,"[44] while the teaching of grammar was central to a "mission of national renewal." The committee's assumption that working-class pupils (the majority) were linguistically and culturally ill-equipped for education was so deeply embedded that it constituted common sense for most English teachers into the 1950s, if not beyond.

Criticism of the prevailing state of English teaching continued in the wartime Norwood Report on curriculum and examinations. Its proposals included reforms that were reflected in the work of postwar teachers we have been studying: the "simple notion of 'reading' could [usefully] replace…the more pretentious and often harmful idea of 'literature,'"[45] and there was too much focus on essay writing and not enough on oral work that could help pupils "get the 'feel' of correct English on their tongue."[46]

English teachers nationally had no effective organization until the end of our period (an English Association existed but by 1945 it was remote from the interests of most schools).[47] London was better served. In 1947, at the instigation of Percival Gurrey and Nancy Martin, teachers at the University of London Institute of Education, and James Britton, then a publisher, a London Association for the Teaching of English (LATE) was set up. Simon Gibbons, who has written a history of LATE to 1967,[48] shows that motivating factors in its formation were the need for a discussion forum for English teachers (almost all of them were grammar school teachers in the early years) and dissatisfaction with the School Certificate examination in English literature for 16-year-olds. LATE not only ran a program of evening and weekend meetings and conferences but also maintained study groups that met over months or years to consider specific issues, and also sometimes to read literature as a pursuit in its own right, independently of pedagogic considerations. Two of our schools were influential in LATE in the second half of our period. A *National* Association for the Teaching of English (NATE) followed only in 1963.

The English department of the Institute of Education exerted its influence in London and beyond through the one-year PGCE course that prepared English graduates for teaching, including many in our three schools, and also through advanced courses, through its members' participation in LATE as well as through the writings, talks, and other activities of Gurrey, Martin, and Britton (who joined the Institute in 1954 but was a significant presence much earlier). The department was more productive of fresh thinking in English than any other higher education institution. (It is worth noting that, as was not always the case in other countries, university and college staff who trained teachers had generally been school teachers themselves.)

The way English in schools developed was influenced by ideas from beyond the schools and notably from the academic disciplines of literary studies, psychology, linguistics, philosophy and, eventually, sociology and cultural studies.

A school of thought that had a particularly direct influence on teaching in schools was the version of literary studies that was developed in Cambridge University between the wars. *The Meaning of Meaning: A Study of the Influence of Language upon Thought and the Science of Symbolism*,[49] by C. K. Ogden and I. A. Richards (1923), was one point of origin. It was primarily a philosophical work that explored the relationship between words and things, symbolization and reference. Ogden and Richards focused on the role of signs in experience, from a concern to describe mental experience in terms of process rather than content. Richards carried his interest in signs and mental processes forward into his work on the poetic imagination and literary response. For this, he drew on Coleridge (and German philosophy) in maintaining that the mind actively contributed to the formation of knowledge. Richards' concentration on the mental processes involved in responding to literary texts aimed to deliver a scientific account of the poet's experience. His account of the way poetic imagination works and the active mental processes involved in responding to poetry lay behind experiments he conducted in which students read unattributed literary texts. The experiments revealed that the valuations undergraduates made under these conditions were often at variance with the works' conventional places in the canon. Where before it had been assumed that the literary canon was "available" to readers of refined taste and intelligence, after Richards' demonstrations, their authority was called into question, and as a consequence, as Raymond Williams suggests, "literary criticism was offered as – and very locally believed to be – the central activity in all human judgement."[50]

Richards' experiments in close reading were introduced into teaching as a quasi-scientific procedure that was radically different from existing approaches to literary appreciation. Though the "science" that lay behind it was later judged to be flawed, "practical criticism" continued be used in education.

F. R. Leavis, who attended Richards' experiments, was concerned to make literary criticism—judgment—the central activity in English studies, rather than traditional literary biography and scholarly exegesis. He was not concerned as Richards was with the analysis of mental processes or a theory of signs. Texts that were conventionally considered "great works" were submitted by Leavis to a process of critical first-hand revaluation; in fiction he whittled down the canon to, initially, four novelists, the so-called Great Tradition,[51] which gave him a moral platform from which to criticize and resist what he perceived to be the unremitting degradation of language and culture in industrialized society. Poetry mattered to Leavis because the poet "is, as it were, at the most conscious point of the race in his time... 'the point at which the growth of the mind shows itself.'"[52]

Leavis' journal, *Scrutiny* (appearing from 1932 to 1953), though primarily a vehicle for literary criticism, also represented a campaign to renew standards in education and thereby "to meet the pressures of contemporary life."[53] Attempting to carry this work into the grammar schools, Leavis and his student Denys Thompson wrote a book primarily for teachers, *Culture and Environment: The Training of Critical Awareness* (1933).[54] Writers who kept alive the moral values of an imagined preindustrial "organic community" were a bulwark against the decline brought on by industrialization.

Culture and Environment encouraged a broadening out in schools from literature into the analysis of contemporary cultural forms such as newspapers, advertising, and film.[55] Thompson also produced a course book for schools, *Reading and Discrimination*, which aimed to provide "a start in the training of judgements at first hand" by presenting opportunities for practical criticism.[56] "Here it is our concern," wrote Thompson, "to acquire the equipment, the tools for analysis, for detecting through the texture of the writing the quality of the mind that produced it."[57] Practical criticism featured regularly in English classrooms after the

Second World War, to the point in some schools of becoming simply another routine.

In 1949 Thompson, with the help of Boris Ford, relaunched the journal *English in Schools* (created in 1939) as *The Use of English*. Many of its regular contributors were Cambridge graduates associated with Leavis and *Scrutiny* but articles were also written "by practising teachers for practising teachers, thus the word 'use.'"[58] One way the journal sought to be useful was by printing passages for practical criticism along with—a true innovation—extended discussions of pupils' responses.

In 1950 Thompson acknowledged that an English syllabus that concentrated on the study of literature applied chiefly to schools with an "academic bias," while secondary modern schools—the majority—"need something different." Calling for fresh thinking about aims and principles as well as experiment, Thompson offered the journal as a forum for exchange and debate. In the event it fell to teachers coming from a different direction to supply that "something different." Another of Thompson's contributions to the development of English teaching was the creation of local Use of English Groups, about which it was judged in 1966 that "Although these groups have...been foolishly vilified as constituting a 'hidden network of Leavisites,' their activities have been of a non-doctrinaire kind"[59] (a comment that incidentally throws light on the reputation of Leavisite English in some quarters.)

Disciplines outside literary studies also influenced English in schools. One was psychology, which offered fresh hope after the Great War when belief in human rationality had worn thin. The publishing activities of C. K. Ogden, Richards' collaborator, suggest the intellectual urgency surrounding new psychological studies that intersected with work in philosophy, anthropology, and language studies. The ground-breaking series he edited, *The International Library of Psychology, Philosophy and Scientific Method,* included studies in child psychology that linked development to language and symbolization and fostered new thinking in education about the role of language in learning. Among these works were *The Language and Thought of the Child* by Jean Piaget, *The Growth of the Mind* by K. Koffka, and *The Mental Development of the Child* by Karl Bühler.

The Ogden and Richards scrutiny of meaning was continued by William Empson's study of ambiguity in literature[60] but was challenged from a different direction by new work in anthropology. Bronislaw Malinowski questioned the psychological bias in their theory of meaning, stressing instead its *cultural-contextual* dimensions. Malinowski's ideas about *language in use in context* then contributed to the work of J. R. Firth in establishing the London school of linguistics, initially at University College, London (UCL). (The specialized study of the "mother-tongue" at UCL, both language and literature, had emerged first in nineteenth-century English philology.)[61] Randolph Quirk, a key figure in British linguistics after the Second World War, turned in the 1950s toward a grammar of English based on *spoken* usage (*The Survey of English Usage*, 1958). In the late 1950s, Michael Halliday built on Firth's ideas about language in context to develop a fully social linguistics and set up a program in Linguistics in Education to devise approaches for use in schools and colleges.

Effects of postwar advances in linguistics were to hasten a move away from Latin-based grammar and to stimulate an interest in the language of ordinary pupils, though Ian Pringle stresses how far from mainstream linguistics were Firth, Halliday, and the others who James Britton found relevant to the understanding of children's language.[62]

Central to English were ideas about culture. A pamphlet by Leavis, *Mass Civilization and Minority Culture,* had claimed in 1930 that "In any period it is upon a very small minority that the discerning appreciation of art and literature depends: it is...only a few who are capable of unprompted, first-hand judgement."[63] This emphasis on the role of an elite minority sat awkwardly with the democratic impulses emerging from the Second World War, but the views of Leavis were the more insistently voiced by T. S. Eliot in the context of the new education regime. Arguing with Leavis that elites were essential to the conservation and transmission of culture, Eliot asked "whether, by education alone, we can ensure the transmission in a society in which some educationists appear indifferent to class distinctions, and from which some other educationists appear to want to remove class distinctions altogether."[64] He feared in particular the social leveling consequent on the removal of wealth as the criterion of educational access. His claims about the benefits of maintaining a cultural elite appealed to those grammar school teachers who found in *Scrutiny* a restatement of the claim of English to provide a central humane discipline.

But democratic cultural forces ran deep and over our period the adherents of Leavis and Eliot seemed to be gradually losing the battle. These forces, that long predated the American influences so deplored in the 1950s, were apparent in middlebrow educative novels and plays on new themes by H. G. Wells, Arnold Bennett, and George Bernard Shaw; and in a cinema whose products were accessible to all. The intellectual elite was also changing. Francis Mulhern has observed that *Scrutiny's* core readers no longer spoke "as if by right of inheritance," drawn as they were "largely from the petty bourgeoisie, coming up through grammar rather than public schools and—more and more likely—the 'civic' universities rather than Oxford and Cambridge."[65] Prominent among them were grammar school English teachers. The audience envisaged for the

BBC's highbrow Third Program, launched on radio in 1945, "was a hardworking, Labour-voting schoolmaster in (say) Derby, who was interested in international theatre, new music, philosophy, politics and painting."[66] And people of all classes were claimed to be among the ten percent of the population estimated in 1956 to read intellectually serious Penguin and Pelican paperbacks.[67]

The conviction that culture could be simply identified with what Matthew Arnold, Leavis, and Eliot meant began to be challenged by George Orwell with the rival claim of working-class life and values. He found in seaside postcards and boys' weeklies[68] and also in his experience of working-class life[69] moral qualities and a sense of real life that were lacking in the works of university-educated intellectuals. This insight was developed with far-reaching consequences by Richard Hoggart in *The Uses of Literacy* (1957).[70] His analysis was Arnoldian and Leavisite in its claim that literacy was giving access to the wrong culture (a degraded popular press and American "shiny barbarism") but at the same time, drawing on his childhood in working-class Leeds, it affirmed the reality and value of a working-class culture that manifested itself in cooperation, self-organization and family values—culture as a whole way of life. Hoggart's work led to a new discipline of cultural studies, while another working-class provincial writer, Raymond Williams, published *Culture and Society* (1958),[71] the title an allusion to Arnold's *Culture and Anarchy*. This historical study, positioned mid-way between Leavisite literary studies and sociology, presented culture not as set against social and economic relations but as arising from them and indeed contributing to their production. Culture, far from being simply the "best," was "ordinary,"[72] people's common inheritance, a whole way of life.

Sociological studies of class also had a profound effect on socially conscious teachers. They included, first, studies of slum clearance and working-class communities[73] and, second, a sociology of education whose first focus was class in relation to 11 plus selection, achievement, and destination.[74] *Education and the Working Class*, discussed earlier, was a sociological study of a grammar school, based on interviews.[75]

Conceptualizations of English teaching in schools also drew on syntheses based on ideas from more than one discipline, among which literary studies were not always dominant. We have described how Cambridge ideas were brought to the attention of English teachers by the work of Denys Thompson and *The Use of English*. A separate line of thinking about English in schools was developed in a university department not of English but of education, in London not Cambridge, and drew on additional quite different sources. In the Department of the Teaching of English as a Mother Tongue at the University of London Institute of Education, the principal theorists, Percival Gurrey and James Britton, were educationists first, not "Eng Lit" people who had gone over to an "applied" field. This is not to minimize the importance they attached to literature or the work of Leavis and his colleagues, but rather than literary criticism their thinking was focused on learning as it occurred in the processes of writing and responding to literature. To this end they felt the need to take account equally of other disciplines such as those referred to above: psychology, especially child development, linguistics, philosophy, cultural studies, and sociology.

Percival Gurrey taught in grammar schools and in 1926 joined the London Day Training College (which became the University of London Institute of Education in 1932). He left in 1948 to work in the Gold Coast[76] but his contributions to the teaching of English in England continued for many years. In a departure from conventional thinking about English, he and Britton urged a focus on the place of language in a child's learning and development: "Among teachers the conception is still rife that it is the business of the teacher of English to teach grammar, précis, paraphrasing, essay writing, without concerning himself with the mental development of his pupils."[77]

Gurrey's prewar *The Appreciation of Poetry* refers[78] to Richards, Leavis, Eliot, and *Scrutiny* writers, especially William Empson and L. C. Knights; but his primary concern was not literary criticism but the processes involved in responding to literature. Following Coleridge and Richards he held that "[t]he appreciation of poetry is not primarily a critical activity, it is creative"[79] and that (quoting Empson) "[t]he process of getting to understand a poem is precisely that of constructing his poem in one's mind."[80] (The quotation is firmly underlined in Britton's copy of Gurrey's book.) The development by children of their own first-hand responses was an active process of construction. He cited Percy Nunn, Principal of the LDTC: "To lead pupils to 'appreciate' is not merely to lead them to admire or to take pleasure in a beautiful thing, but to make them become in a sense its re-creators."[81] This was a crucial insight behind the reforms to English in our period.

Gurrey found that current composition tasks and exercises "do not go deep enough to have much effect in developing the linguistic powers of the child, for they have little relation to the child's real life."[82] English had to be concerned with pupils' "linguistic expression of experience."[83] Britton later pointed out that "imaginative writing and creative response are essentially parts of one process... That... to see them as distinct or separable activities is damaging to both."[84]

Gurrey's view of the role of language in development called for a new synthesizing theory spanning psychology, philosophy, and both literary and language studies. He was well-placed to bridge new developments in Cambridge (literary criticism and the philosophy of language) and London, where a new linguistics was emerging from the work of his friend, J. R. Firth.[85]

Britton, Gurrey's former student, continued the search for a synthesis. Where Richards found marked differences between the mental capacities of poets and ordinary people, Britton placed at the center those human symbolizing processes common to everyone. This more universal account of human productivity informed the democratic view of education maintained by Institute thinkers and many in LATE, and was starkly opposed to the Leavis-Eliot stress on an elite and on high cultural production.

Britton taught in grammar schools and after the war worked in publishing. Although moving to the Institute only in 1954, he had participated throughout in developments in London, contributing with Gurrey to the founding of LATE in 1947 and providing from the start some of its most stimulating thinking. Britton was for many years the most influential British figure in English teaching. His importance was evident at the time of the Dartmouth seminar of 1966 (see below and chapter six) and increased with his later publications.[86] He led the Writing Research that produced *The Development of Writing Abilities, 11–18*,[87] played a major role in the Schools Council's work on English, and in the 1970s was a member of the Bullock Committee which produced *A Language for Life* in 1975, the most influential chapter of which, following an initiative developed in LATE, was on "language across the curriculum."

Britton differed sharply from the view of George Sampson and the Newbolt Committee in the 1920s that children's natural speech, in Sampson's terms, needed to be "cleansed" or "purified." He argued that personal and academic development depended on children's free and habitual handling of information, ideas, and concepts, and particularly their own experience, in the language that came readily to them. Hence English teachers, and teachers across the curriculum, should allow and encourage the use of "expressive" language, spoken and written.

The two strands of English, Leavisite and Institute-centered, engaged in active debate at the transatlantic Dartmouth seminar in 1966, where they were thrown into relief by contrast with North American practice comprising an academic approach to literature and writing "instruction" based on grammar and structures like the five-paragraph essay (though there were also very different American voices). In the Dartmouth context at least the distinction between LATE/NATE positions on the one hand and those of Cambridge-oriented educators on the other was clear. (An American and a British report of the seminar were published, the former in effect sinking without trace while the British book by John Dixon, *Growth through English*,[88] which argued his own version of the NATE position as much as synthesizing the proceedings, was taken up as the manifesto of that side of the internal UK argument, and in Australia as well.)

Although there was no theorist in the Britton sense on the Cambridge/*The Use of English* side, a widely welcomed book written from that perspective was *English for Maturity* by a student of Leavis who, most unusually, had gone to teach in a secondary modern school.[89] David Holbrook's book persuaded many that teaching the majority, and not only a grammar school elite, was an exciting way of realizing the cultural mission implied in a literary education. He also produced a series of innovative prose and poetry anthologies for schools, offering, for instance, excerpts from Lawrence's *Sons and Lovers* and *Lady Chatterley's Lover*.[90] Although like Denys Thompson's his vision was informed by preindustrial romanticism, he had discovered that ordinary children could write, while his literary critical background enabled him to demonstrate the quality of that writing to striking effect. He was critical of grammar schools for being over-academic while secondary moderns had failed to realize their purpose, the pursuit of O level examination success by some confirming their failure.

That the positions of Holbrook and his sympathizers on the one hand and Britton and his on the other had much in common is brought out by Frances Stevens' account of values implicit in the Cambridge view, namely honesty and straightforwardness about one's experience.[91] Confirming this, Holbrook claims that in the current content of English "common life and common decency are everywhere absent. The joys and difficulties you and I encounter everyday are absent. The kind of people, good and bad, you and I would meet if we went out into the street for ten minutes are absent, too."[92] This is a criticism no less keenly felt by Britton and his colleagues.

Official sources offered few ideas for teachers. An exception was the 1954 Department of Education and Science publication, *Language: Some Suggestions for Teachers of English*, written by Her Majesty's Inspectors of Schools under the lead of Percy Wilson. In its awareness of current thinking about the role of language in ordering experience the following could have come from Gurrey or Britton:

> It is language that enables an individual, not only to seize the immediate experience, to fix it and to distinguish it finally from the welter of experiences to give it greater vividness, but also to transcend the immediate world. By creating more occasions for reflection, and by making it possible and easy to recall experience, language enables man to dwell upon the past and to incorporate it into his present way of life. So, too, it enables him to contemplate the future and to formulate purposes and ideals. In this sense,

language is woven into our experience, and is not merely a parallel activity. In so far as language is interpenetrated with experience, transcending the present and the individual, it is the basic element within a tradition, and so within a culture.[93]

Equally remarkably (not least when we think of schools inspectors today) the authors appreciated philosophical ideas on the role of language in cognition, observing that "We no longer live in 'a merely physical universe, man lives in a symbolic universe...a symbolic net, the tangled web of human experience.'"[94]

In the rest of this chapter we review both the situation of English teachers and what they are known to have been doing in their classrooms and professional activities. The account is most conveniently taken in two parts, dealing with roughly the first and second halves of our period.

English to the Mid-1950s

Starting with the first decade or so, we consider the conditions of English teachers' work and then their practice. The former covers examinations, resources, associations and institutions, and inspection.

Grammar school teaching was dominated by the public examinations taken at 16 and 18. Syllabuses and examination papers were prepared by a number of examination boards, run at arms length by certain universities, among which schools could choose. The School Certificate, taken at 16, and the Higher School Certificate at 18 were replaced in 1951 by the Ordinary (O) and Advanced (A) levels of the General Certificate of Education (GCE). GCE offered separate Language and Literature examinations at O level, Literature only at A level. The textbooks on which teachers tended to rely were often written by grammar school teachers expressly to prepare for those examinations. Growing dissatisfaction was expressed by teachers with many aspects but particularly the separation of Language and Literature, the choice of Literature texts, the content of the Language paper and the appropriateness of the questions.

For several years after the war, provision of books in schools was restricted by shortages both of funds and of suitable titles, particularly cheap and hard-wearing editions of the modern and contemporary works that some teachers would have liked to teach. Publishers' catalogues were dominated by the classics, especially Shakespeare.

Though schools were short of money to buy them, Heinemann's New Windmill series, launched in 1948, met a clear demand for "reading matter of the highest quality, at a low price...with the appearance of good modern novels" (the publisher's words.) The first titles included C. Day-Lewis' *The Otterbury Incident,* Jack London's *The Call of the Wild,* and H. G. Wells' *The War of the Worlds.* American titles followed, including novels by Steinbeck and Hemingway. Postwar fiction written for adult audiences, such as George Orwell's *Animal Farm* and William Golding's *The Lord of the Flies,* found its way into 1950s classrooms. Pupils' literary experience was gradually transformed, at least in years one to four (ages 11–15) before examination syllabuses determined the reading.

Among new textbook offerings, Ronald Ridout's *English Today*[95] presented a modern appearance, though in fact it was mainly traditional fare in a new guise. The bestselling series offered a term-by-term course and dominated many pupils' classroom experience. Cedric Austin's *Read to Write* series[96] offered a more integrated and stimulating course, and Nancy Martin's books of passages for comprehension work, *Understanding and Enjoyment,*[97] stood out as successful.

BBC schools radio broadcasts were welcome, though their usefulness depended on the timings of the programs fitting those of the classes. *Senior English,* with readings and dramatizations,[98] was joined in the mid-1950s by *Poets and Poetry,* presented by Robert Gittings and Cecil Day-Lewis. Poems by pupils as well as the work of well-known poets[99] were read.

Schools were inspected nationally by His/Her Majesty's Inspectors of Schools (HMI), some five hundred in number, and locally by LEAs. They visited the schools in an area individually and formed into teams for national inspections, during which some concentrated on the subject in which they were expert. It is difficult to know how effective the inspectors were. HMI normally published little beyond reports of individual school inspections, which occurred at intervals that could be of many years. They apparently ran one annual national summer course on English, for less than one hundred teachers, but it seems they had little influence on how English was taught in the schools.

HMI did, however, wield some power through their seats on official bodies. In the last years of our period George Allen, HMI, chaired the English Advisory Group of the Secondary Schools Examinations Council, was then influential in the new Schools Council, helped to set up NATE, and arranged for two former Walworth teachers, by now in teacher training jobs, to be given national courses to run.[100] John Dixon believes that Allen wrote Schools Council Working Paper 3, setting out the program for English, "probably in consultation with Jimmy [Britton]."[101] Another HMI, Percy Wilson, was chair of the Schools Council English Committee.

HMI who were English specialists met centrally as a panel whose views seem to have been relayed to the minister. Their position, certainly in their own view, was in advance of that of most of the profession they spent their time inspecting and the 1954 DES document[102] discussed earlier which they wrote, was still recommended reading on the Institute PGCE course in 1963–1964.[103] The panel anticipated an end to the separate examining of Language and Literature,[104] shared LATE's dissatisfaction with existing O level examinations ("hair-splitting questions on grammar and the niggling attitude of examiners"),[105] expressed a need for books "that did not perpetuate the present gulf between 'real' books and 'school' books," and in writing argued for pupils to "be led to express in a vital way the truth of their own experience."[106] They are not in general pleased with the state of English in either secondary modern or grammar schools. Though their opinion was divided, they wanted the teaching of grammar to be reduced if not abolished, though they worried that the reduction in grammar in some grammar schools was leaving a vacuum. "'Practical Criticism.' Can it be overdone?" was a topic for a meeting in 1950.[107] They disliked the diversion of what they saw as the proper concerns of English into "'social English' which used advertisements and similar material as a basis of study."[108]

Some comments by Percy Wilson in internal memos seem particularly enlightened. "[S]ome progress [in the teaching of writing] is happening and this is due...to a realisation...that...you need to have something to say, you need to have an interest in it and you need to visualise your audience or your reader...The worst thing that could happen is that we should go back to grammatical grind and formal essay writing. They never did much good and they are more responsible than anything else for the subject having been, for so long, dead, and even decomposing."[109] Having something to say, having a sense of your audience, and discussion before writing were key themes in the more imaginative teaching in our period.

English as it existed in the schools at the start of our period was derived, as we have shown, from two quite distinct traditions: in the account by Barnes, Barnes, and Clarke, the elementary school tradition concentrated on orthographic conventions and the secondary (grammar school) tradition "saw writing in terms of the 'essay.' Elegant, disengaged from context and from any purpose but amusement, the essay was the goal of the kind of writing we are calling *belles lettres*."[110] Across both grammar and secondary modern schools the general practice was to devote separate lessons to the elements of English: grammar, composition, comprehension, précis, and literature. A textbook might deal with one or more of these. The amount of time devoted to English in schools varied greatly and many classes were taught by nonspecialists. HMI in 1951 found English in both modern and grammar schools to be competent but dull.[111]

Other sources supplement inspectors' impressions. Medway[112] characterized English in the 1950s as a tired and conventional subject in which pupils worked from books that had, even the new ones, "drab covers, cheap paper, cramped print and bad artwork."[113] Poetry collections included little that was recent and much that was trivial, though good modern alternatives were available like James Britton's *Oxford Books of Verse for Juniors* (1957),[114] that excluded "'the pixie-and-toadstool nonsense.'"

Grammar was a major component in all types of school and writing took place in the context of instruction in conventions. In the subject matter for exercises and composition, no significance was attributed to real everyday experiences, which were not deemed worthy of treatment in an essay unless simply for practice in some skill. Subjects worthy of attention in their own right included conventionally recognized occasions like birthdays and speech days and exotic topics outside normal experience (Africa, adventures). The real wider world was absent (not least its conflicts: Korea, South Africa), as were the cities most pupils lived in, the environment generally referenced being rural or small town.

Critiques of this state of affairs are not lacking. A writer complains that grammar school English is too heavily influenced by its Latin ancestry, with undue attention given to the rules of grammar, structure and form, parsing and analysis:

> The fear of making the learning of their own language too easy is leading us, I believe, to make it, for many adolescents, unnecessarily difficult. They find English parcelled out into quite a number of separate subdivisions…The books chosen for them to study are not always well suited to their age, and the study of them is often, under the influence of examiners, prematurely critical and analytical. Between English as a school subject and all other forms and uses of their own language, there appears thus to be a gap: "Literature" on one side of it, their own books and magazines on the other; on one side of it analysis, and the niceties of the pluperfect, on the other the living tongue in which they express themselves.[115]

Another teacher observes in 1947 that few teachers read for pleasure the literature that they teach, such as essays from *The Spectator* and *Silas Marner*. Instead they read *modern* literature. What many adolescents and adults read in their own time they often know to be rubbish but they will read any rubbish rather than Shakespeare. They "would like to try something better if they knew what to look for—but emphatically not the dead authors they associate with English literature as taught in school." If schools taught modern literature like Hemingway or Graham Greene, pupils would realize there were alternatives that were both good and enjoyable.[116] This line of thinking, as we shall see, became widespread in certain circles in the later part of our period.

English from the Mid-1950s to the Mid-1960s

Change in English teachers' professional situation was brought about by the growth of true English departments in schools, impending reforms in public examinations, the establishment of the Schools Council for Curriculum and Examinations, and the increased influence of LATE and, eventually, its national equivalent, NATE.

At the start of the period there was little concept of an English *department* in grammar schools, and in secondary moderns teachers tended not to have single-subject affiliations. Grammar school teachers operated essentially as individuals, with Senior English Teachers assigning classes to staff and ordering and allocating books. Harold Rosen described how "a quick chat over coffee would solve what few problems needed solution."[117] Within the limitations of examination syllabuses and book stocks, teachers chose their own classroom material and activities. By the mid-1960s, however, an LATE conference on "The Work of the English Department" thought a change had started a decade earlier, when teachers' responsibilities began to be considered "not as individual tasks but as co-operative endeavors."[118]

The existing public examinations remained in place though LATE was eventually successful in introducing an alternative syllabus in London. There were experiments by other examination boards, including trial tests of spoken English. A powerful body of opinion had meanwhile been urging the need for a second public examination at 16 more suited to the needs of the ability group (in comprehensives and secondary moderns) below the one for which O level was intended. The new Schools Council was charged with setting up the Certificate of Secondary Education (CSE) to be run by regional boards under the control of teachers, not universities. The first CSE examinations were taken after the end of our period of study in 1965.

The Schools Council came into existence in 1964, too late to have an effect within our period. Of its first six planned programs one was to be about English.[119] Working Paper 3, *A Programme for Research and Development in English Teaching*, set out its rationale and intended coverage,[120] which included major research projects on writing and spoken language.

LATE had gone from strength to strength, not least through a new interest in the education of the majority that was brought by members from the new comprehensive schools and grammar school teachers facing comprehensivization. Douglas Barnes has recalled that

> We designed alternative examination syllabuses and persuaded an examination board to adopt them; we edited and published books of materials for

classroom use; we collected material on such topics as students' writing and the criteria of assessing students' scripts and found a publisher for them; we set up working parties to consider aspects of our teaching; and we organized conferences on new topics in teaching.[121]

In 1963 a National Association for the Teaching of English was finally set up, its members (some of them also in LATE) influencing the committees and publications of the Schools Council; London members in this category included James Britton, Douglas Barnes, and John Dixon.

Parts of two reports addressed the teaching of secondary English. The Newsom Report, *Half Our Future*,[122] urged that the education of the majority be given more serious consideration, and the Plowden Report on primary education[123] proclaimed a position labeled, with approval or hostility, as "progressive." Plowden spoke to a vigorous strand of LATE interest in primary schools, encouraged by Connie Rosen, a primary school teacher, and her husband Harold. They promoted contacts with primary teachers and with education authorities noted for outstanding primary practice, especially Alec Clegg's West Riding of Yorkshire; Clegg's anthology compiled from his schools, *The Excitement of Writing*,[124] was received with enthusiasm.

The resources in the second half of our period were better and more plentiful. Shayer remarked on a "dramatic change in the form of English school textbooks, after something like sixty years of grammar-based conformity."[125] Medway confirms this impression.[126] A new generation of course books featured the sort of material that some teachers had been designing and duplicating for themselves, drawing sometimes on very different sources from those the examination boards relied on. The bestselling English course of the 1960s, *English through Experience* by A.W. Rowe and Peter Emmens,[127] also embodied changes in methods. Volume one, for the first year, was ordered into thematic chapters around topics such as "fire," "smells," and "flight"; each began with a section soliciting personal writing. Summerfield noted, however, that underneath the modish coating of "creative" sugar there remained the old pills of verbal manipulation, sentence-combining, exercises in usage and the like.[128]

The provision for class reading was much improved. Whereas 11-year-olds in 1950 might have been set to read *Lorna Doone* by R. D. Blackmore or *Silas Marner* by George Eliot, in 1965 their text might have been Ian Serraillier's (1956) *The Silver Sword* about the Second World War in Europe.[129] Novels about contemporary working-class life made their way into schools; *A Kid for Two Farthings* by Wolf Mankowitz,[130] set in the East End rag trade, was one example (see chapter six). There was a flowering of recent children's and adolescent fiction. Overall, teachers' classroom choices of literature were transformed.

New poetry anthologies appeared including James Britton's *Oxford Book of Verse for Juniors*, David Holbrook's *Iron, Honey, Gold*, Michael Baldwin's *Billy the Kid*, Ted Hughes' *Here Today*, culminating in Summerfield's *Voices* shortly after our period (1968), when Penguin Education started publishing books for schools.[131]

BBC radio had new English offerings for schools, including the outstanding *Listening and Writing*, the contributors to which included Ted Hughes and James Britton. As tape recorders became cheaply available schools could record them for use in the most appropriate lessons.

There has to be an important note of caution: all the above is about available resources but we know very little about how they were taken up and used. Moreover, although fine new books were published, plenty of books in the older style also appeared, old books continued to be reissued and existing book stocks could remain in use for 20 years or more with little added. The new developments recorded above must be treated very cautiously as indications of a widespread change in English teaching.

Few writers have a good word for the public examinations at 16, in which Shayer observes "an astonishing degree of continuity and sameness" from 1920 to 1960[132] while George Allen, HMI, speaks of the damage done by literature exams, repeating arguments made in the 1930s: "Do [candidates] in fact read the texts at all, or do they 'get them up' well enough to answer the questions?...Real reading is something different..." Language and literature will indeed continue to command their own disciplines but too often the students have experienced not the reality of language and literature but "meaningless requirements deriving from obsolete theory and boring practice."[133]

The CSE was introduced in 1963 and first examined in 1965. Under "Mode 3" regulations schools could choose to write their own syllabus, something which became popular with LATE/NATE English teachers, not just those in comprehensive and secondary modern schools but also in grammar schools like Minchenden.

Among the published evidence on English after about 1955, contemporary or near-contemporary overviews are perhaps the most useful sources. They agree there has been an acceleration of change. Writers speak of "the present period of intensive curriculum revision and planning"[134] and of "somewhat febrile endeavour."[135] For HMI George Allen, although "As recently as 1960 English as a school subject was in a state of suspended animation which had hardly changed over forty years...somewhere about the year 1960 something began to stir"; he lists new publications and institutions that manifest the change.[136]

Accounts that are closer to schools suggest that some English teachers at least are now pursuing different aims. Frank Whitehead's formulation is "developing in children the ability to use the mother-tongue as effectively as possible, as sensitively and expressively as possible, in a really all-round way; in listening, speaking, reading, writing, and drama";[137] the aims of English in one comprehensive school were "to encourage accurate writing; to widen and deepen the child's experience of reading upon which imaginative response, a vital motive power behind written work, depends; to develop self-confidence through oral lessons; to link the more formal aspects of English, vocabulary and comprehension, grammar, spelling, punctuation to the more informal at appropriate stages."[138]

Various authors offer general characterizations of the state of English, often with implied criticism. Summerfield, from a comprehensive school noted for its English work, finds that the English teacher "prefers the kind of 'knowledge' represented by, say, D. H. Lawrence's *The Rainbow*" and that "The proponents of literary study" [the Leavisites] tend to take from Lawrence and Leavis "a belief in the inalienable centrality of literature as an instrument of moral education." Some of that group, he says, are by now sounding second-hand, tired, fractious, and petulant. A different but widespread style of teacher "is aroused by and responds to the peculiar quality of the individual moment...[This can lead into] teaching from hand to mouth, a chronic non-co-ordination of learning, and a non-policy of ad hoc excitements."[139] A graphic illustration of this tendency was provided by Peter Emmens, coauthor of the *English through Experience* series, in a 1962 BBC documentary: Emmens is shown blowing soap bubbles in front of his secondary modern class, eliciting and providing adjectives ("iridescent") and writing them on the board.[140] It may have been lessons like this that led American observers in 1969 to report that in British schools "'Intellect is out; feeling is in.'"[141]

Hollins comments on the grandiosity of some English claims: "One often meets enthusiasts who believe that English studies can form a good basis for the development of all the necessary qualities a civilized human being will need. It is usual to give literature this all-powerful role."[142]

The impression of accelerated change is strengthened when we look at specific aspects of English. There is said to be less teaching of *grammar* in 1965 than ten years earlier. Doubts had grown about its claimed *cognitive* benefits,[143] and debates about the value of grammar divided the profession.

An account based on experience of a progressive school and of the teachers who went to LATE and NATE meetings tells us that in the teaching of *literature* "Teachers [had become] more hesitant to hand over authoritative readings, ready-made literary opinions; the idea of 'personal response' meant that each reader should shape his or her unique interpretation of a literary work."[144] But while literature remains the heart of English for one set of teachers, Hollins[145] and Dixon[146] suggest a movement toward placing *experience* at the center, with literature serving to induce reflection on experience.

As regards *writing*, "English teachers," so Barnes, Barnes, and Clarke claim, "discovered that most pupils wrote better if they wrote about something that mattered to them, and if their teachers accorded validity to what they wrote by responding to it as a serious message. Writing was seen as a purposive act, not merely the exercise of skills but the shaping of linguistic resources by the desire to communicate."[147] Summerfield ascribes the improvement he finds in school writing in part to the enhanced value now placed on speech, so that "the fluency of informal speech is found in [children's] written work. In writing, children are learning to trust their own native vivacity," resulting in work that contrasts strikingly with the "ill-fitting, derivative style of the traditional examination-type essay, with its off-the-peg prescriptive structures [the *belles-lettres* tradition]...The business of writing [has changed] from a miserable chore to keen pleasure and intelligent personal application." As evidence Summerfield cites new collections of children's writing by Michael Baldwin[148] and Sir Alec Clegg.[149] He also credits the influence of the BBC's *Listening and Writing* broadcasts.

A Schools Council research project on *spoken English* ("oracy") parallel to one led by Britton on writing, sought to meet the imperative that, in Summerfield's words, "The working-class boy, relatively inarticulate in the bourgeois context of the school, [who] can cheerfully hold his own among his peers...must increase his oral range so as to embrace increasingly sophisticated skills, to cope more or less adequately with new kinds of social demands."[150]

Change in the latter part of our period can be considered under a number of broad headings:

Thematic content: Whereas, as Medway discovered,[151] at the start of our period rural themes dominated (even in books used in city schools), there emerged a new appreciation of the city as the locus of what was interesting in the contemporary world, and work was developed around the urban and suburban neighborhood and community; the city where most pupils lived at last became an acceptable topic and resource.

Experience: The shift from rural to urban themes was driven by a recognition of the need for matter that related not only to most children's experience of the city—streets, flats, and parks—but also to their lives more generally: home, grandparents, neighbors, weddings, shopping, visits to the dentist, and all the topics which earlier had either been despised as possible topics for English except for treatment in arch or whimsical "essays." Significance was, it was discovered (with Lawrence's help), after all to be found in our own everyday lives and the things and people around us.

Language: The only way in which many children would be induced freely to explore and reflect honestly on those themes in spoken classroom exchange was if they were not inhibited by the expectation that they express their thoughts in an alien language.

The changing feel of classrooms: It may have been because young people were getting more difficult to teach, not least working-class children trapped in low streams, that there seems to have been more of a bid to engage pupils' willing participation. Whatever its educational justifications, the move toward recognizably real-life topics, the acceptance of language that would formerly have been frowned on and the use of more appealing material is likely to have had at least something to do with avoiding disaffection. A new emphasis was placed on active involvement and collaborative working. The incorporation of classroom talk as a major element (as opposed to speech practice) had consequences for the feel of classrooms—noise, movement, groupings.

The existence in the 1960s of two camps within English—Institute/LATE/NATE versus adherents of Leavis—was and remains a widely shared perception. The situation was in reality more blurred. While Lightfoot is almost certainly right in his impression that the concept that underpinned *The Use of English* "of the classroom as a haven of intellectual and cultural values, with its ultimate objective as the appreciation of literature, was widely held,"[152] another writer finds that the picture of rivalry between the two versions "suggests a division of loyalties within English teachers at large, which is, in fact, not there."[153] Stephen Ball, a sociologist of education, undoubtedly distorts reality in positing a binary opposition between "Cambridge" (literature-based) and "London" (language-based) versions of English.[154] On this view the "London School" put the "role of language" first, the "Cambridge School" literary criticism. Ball's "London School" issued in what he calls "the sociolinguistic paradigm" of English. (Martin Lightfoot observes "how odd it is to find James Britton in the linguists' camp and opposed to the promoters of literature.")[155] The two camps view oversimplifies the complicated relationships and cross-fertilizations among groupings of thinkers and constellations of ideas that went into shaping English both in schools and universities.

Moreover, Hardcastle and Medway know from their own experience as pupils that grammar school English was by no means limited to Leavisite-literary and belles-lettristic versions and recall teachers who primarily valued rationality, argument, and ideas. These teachers emphasized unpretentious writing and "clear thinking" and valued Shaw's plays for their intellectual excitement and rhetorical vigor; nonfiction texts such as Vance Packard's *The Hidden Persuaders* and Rachel Carson's *Silent Spring* might equally earn a place in their lessons.

Grammar school teachers generally regarded sixth-form teaching as the high point of their work, and lower school work as less rewarding. Those who moved successfully into comprehensives with small or no sixth forms needed to learn to find their satisfactions lower down the school, and less in children's performance in argumentation and ideas than their stories, poems, and drama.

It has to be stressed that the above is a survey based on sparse and unsatisfactory evidence—publications and sporadic first-hand contemporary impressions that fail to cover probably the bulk of schools. What is sadly lacking is seriously designed, large-scale research from the time. The picture we have drawn from what we have is largely a rosy one of sustained change for the better. Anecdotal evidence we have gathered informally suggests, however, that in many, perhaps most schools, change was superficial.

Chapter 3

Hackney Downs

Background

The Grocers' Company School, later known as Hackney Downs Grammar School, was established as a middle-class day school for boys in 1876. "Grocers" was an imposing Gothic building wedged between two railway lines feeding into the commercial heart of the City. The scheme to build the school was proposed by Worshipful Company of Grocers, a City Livery Company, following the Endowed Schools Act of 1869.[1] Boys between the ages of seven and eleven "of good character and of sufficient bodily health" were admitted, leaving at age fifteen.[2] Places were gained by passing an examination: there was both an entrance fee and an annual fee. Scholarships were open to competition and depended on the Headmaster's recommendation as well as the results of the entrance exam. The establishment of a middle-class school, a new kind of institution, stemmed partly from the widespread perception that Britain lagged behind its international rivals and competitors, and partly as a response to demands for secondary education from the tradesmen, minor professionals, and skilled workmen that made up a large proportion of the local population.

In 1907 the school was transferred to the London County Council (LCC). The LCC acted as trustees, with agreement that the selective entry boys' grammar school would be known as "Hackney Downs School, formerly the Grocers' Company School." Under the LCC Junior Scholarship scheme, boys from working-class homes, who attended public elementary schools and who could not afford private schooling were able to obtain places at the grammar school and as a result the number of working-class pupils increased (Figure 3.1).

Figure 3.1 Hackney Downs School: an imposing Gothic building wedged between two railway lines feeding into the commercial heart of the City.

By 1952, Hackney Downs was a three-form-entry school with 539 pupils on roll. After a devastating fire in 1963, following much negotiation and extensive rebuilding, the school reopened in 1969 as a six-form-entry comprehensive for 900 boys. During the 1970s, it became a successful comprehensive with a strong reputation for addressing the needs of children from diverse backgrounds. Following a troubled period in the early 1990s, the school closed and today Mossbourne Academy stands on the site of the original school.

The way the school evolved reflected complicated demographic changes in the local area. For much of the nineteenth century, Hackney had been a prosperous residential suburb of North East London with a relatively settled population. However, around the turn of the century, many middle-class families moved out, mainly as a consequence of the capital's expanding transport system: land development followed railway development and new suburban housing estates were built further out from the commercial center, north of Hackney, to attract middle-class house buyers. Working-class families from the traditional East End—Whitechapel, Hoxton, Shoreditch, Mile End, Stepney, and Bow—moved into neighborhoods vacated by the middle classes. Among these working-class families were large numbers of immigrants, many of them Jewish families, refugees from Central and Eastern Europe. Many of these families had originally settled in the East End, close to the docks, where some of the worst housing and the highest levels of poverty in the capital were concentrated.

Although they were not well off, many boys from working-class Jewish families obtained scholarships under the LCC scheme, which meant that the number of first-generation grammar school pupils at the school was disproportionately large.[3] However, middle-class families also continued to send their children to the school, which by this time had become socially mixed. During the interwar years, slum clearance and rehousing became national political priorities and large new estates of social housing were built close by the school. During the war, the bombing of East London created an unprecedented further demand for new housing.

In 1945, the school provided a five-year course at the end of which pupils took the School Certificate examination with a sixth form for those accepted for a further two years' study. After 1951, pupils were entered for the new public examination at GCE O level, with about a quarter staying on into the sixth form. Regarding English, there were separate exams in language and literature with only a percentage of pupils entered for the literature paper. The basic pattern of English teaching had been established before the war. Because younger men were occupied with the war effort, an older generation of teachers continued teaching largely on prewar lines. In 1951, the HMI report on the school observed that no less than eight

Figure 3.2 The staff, 1946: "A group of prewar Masters—loyal, experienced, and faithful guardians of tradition." James Medcalf is sitting first from the left on the front row. Joe Brearley is fourth from the left on the back row.

current members of staff had been present at the previous inspection in 1936: "a group of pre-war Masters – loyal, experienced, and faithful guardians of tradition" (Figure 3.2).[4]

After the Great War, English teaching in England lacked clear aims, coherence, and academic prestige, yet by 1945 it had come to occupy a central position in the secondary school curriculum. For the principal English teachers at Hackney Downs their subject was a liberal, humanizing discipline: however, they had no picture of an English syllabus catering for all abilities and there was no vision of equality of provision or common entitlement. In sum they were not concerned with a picture of *"English for all."*[5]

An Overview of English at Hackney Downs After the War

The version of English that evolved at Hackney Downs assumed that it was the main purpose of the selective grammar school to give an education that would be a basis for continuing studies at a university and a preparation for entry into the professions. The curriculum was meant for a minority of the national population and the syllabus was tailored for those pupils who were considered the most able. Grammar school teachers generally perceived it to be the responsibility of other kinds of institutions—technical and modern schools—to offer children with different capabilities and experiences an education suited to their particular ages and strengths.

In 1945, English teachers at Hackney Downs relied heavily on existing course books and single lessons based on textbook exercises were the order of the day. We know from former pupils' exercise books as well as from teachers' records and correspondence that prewar text books such as *Grammar in a New Setting* (1928) by Guy Pocock, *Thought in English Prose* (1930) by J. C. Dent, and *A Year's Work in English* (1921) by J. W. Marriott were still in use in the 1940s and early 1950s. Grammar was a staple. As the 1951 HMI report noted, "the provision for Grammar and Language is, if anything, generous,"[6] implying that there was possibly too much of it.

To give a flavor of the kind of work that went on, consider this typical grammar lesson from an exercise, "Word Making," that appears in *Grammar in a New Setting* (1928).[7] The instruction is spare: "Exercise. Re-write the following sentences using adjectives of quality instead of abstract nouns: (1) The sheep showed remarkable fatness." The task invited a mechanical response : "The Sheep looked remarkably fat."[8] The justification for such lifeless tasks reflected a long-standing and widely held assumption that sound grammar teaching, which in practice meant a diet of course book exercises, constituted the only foundation for mastering language. Yet HMI hinted that that more might be achieved: "The general standard of written work was respectable, but lacking in the originality and distinction which might have been expected in some of the ablest boys."[9] They went on to suggest: "Greater elasticity in the work in English, especially in the manner of composition, might produce good original work from some of the boys."[10] Thus they implied (further to the suggestion that the amount of grammar teaching was over-generous) that the scope of English might be broadened to include more engaging, more imaginative, more rewarding tasks.

The unduly heavy concentration on grammar teaching reflected prewar priorities. To be fair, Guy Pocock's *Grammar in a New Setting* represented an attempt to make grammar interesting at a time when it was universally acknowledged to be hard. Pocock tried to kindle pupils' interest in the history and principles of language study. "Grammar even in its elements is not a particularly easy subject," he conceded. "All the same, there is no reason whatever why the grammar lesson or the grammar book should be DULL."[11] Thus he aimed to present "all that is necessary for common use and the passing of junior examinations—in a fresh and interesting setting." As he put it, "It is not 'Grammar made easy' that is aimed at, but 'Grammar without boredom.'"[12]

Grammar in a New Setting dealt with formal grammar. There were no additional suggestions for composition, comprehension, or précis. Later, views about the importance of grammar and details of usage would be modified as précis and comprehension came to the fore and the teaching of accurate reading became a priority.[13] With some course books written after the Second World War, such as *Complete English* by J. H. Walsh (1949), there was a conscious attempt to dovetail grammar and composition. Evidence from pupils' surviving exercise books, however, does not suggest that English teachers at Hackney Downs made sustained efforts to combine grammar, composition, and précis with literary studies to forge a coherent, unitary whole and as a consequence English remained fragmented.

We should say a word about practical arrangements. Hackney Downs was originally planned to accommodate five hundred boys, with fifteen classrooms "fitted on the Prussian system," a library and a large semicircular theatre capable of seating eight hundred persons. Rooms were equipped with double desk benches up to the sixth form, when individual chairs were introduced. There were no dedicated English classrooms and no designated spaces for wall displays exhibiting pupils' work. Lessons typically lasted 40 or 45 minutes. Following the reorganization of the timetable before the war, school began at 9 a.m. with a break for lunch at 1.15 p.m.[14] The extended morning session allowed five lessons each day and the variable pattern in the afternoon accommodated after-school societies and clubs. The time allotted for English varied from six periods a week in the first and fifth years to just three in the fourth year. Pupils were issued with a homework timetable and each teacher had his appointed day for setting homework which was done in the same books as classwork.[15] In the first year there were two subjects each night and homework was meant to take about an hour and a half, though it often took longer. The amount of work increased to two hours in the second year and three hours (sometimes more) in the third, fourth, and fifth years. Books were given out at the start of the school year and changed as necessary. There were no free periods or officially timetabled slots for private reading. The library was well stocked, but it appears that teachers only rarely recommended books for pleasure. Pupils used standard blue or green exercise books with supplementary (extra-thick) rough books for cross-subject use. The exercise books had printed lines, but pupils had to draw their own margins in pencil. There were ink wells and ink-monitors, although those pupils who could afford them were allowed to use fountain pens. The use of ballpoint pens was forbidden.

There was minimal consultation with pupils about the content of English work and teachers' academic authority was rarely challenged, which is not to say that pupils were always well behaved. And yet according to the former pupils we interviewed English lessons were often stimulating. There was much lively appreciation of stories, poems, and plays with pupils' work read out in class and, as was established practice at the time, boys took turns reading round the class. Learning a poem by heart was occasionally set for homework and tested in class the following day. One of our informants recalled, "I remember getting by heart almost all the poems in the book of poetry. We had [*Daffodil Poetry Books, I* and *II*], as a set book, I had almost all of them by heart. I must have taken them home, because I wouldn't have had time in school to learn them, and we didn't buy them."[16] Scenes from plays were occasionally acted out at the front of the class, although we have found little evidence of drama intended as a learning activity involving the whole class. Classroom discussion was vibrant, with talk increasing proportionately as pupils progressed through the school. The vibrancy of classroom interaction was frequently attributed by informants to the strong London working-class and Jewish presence in the school.

Grammar was taught as a separate topic and teachers relied on textbook exercises rather than dealing with aspects of grammar related to ongoing English work.[17] In the upper school there was increasing concentration on grammar, especially clause analysis, with the approach of public examinations. In the lower school grammar lessons usually involved pupils copying definitions such as the parts of speech, followed by formal exercises to test their knowledge. Unsurprisingly, some former pupils, such as Terry Gasking, said they found grammar lessons tedious.[18]

Teachers' reliance on course books reduced the need for planning and, as a consequence, there was an overall lack of coherence. Several former pupils recalled that there seemed to be no obvious principle of organization, and therefore it must have been difficult for them to appreciate any continuity or progression. As one former pupil put it, "You didn't know until the teacher began the lesson what was going to happen."[19]

As a rule, grammar school teachers took their bearings from their subject as they had studied it at university or college. Writing about the relatively new English Language O Level exam in 1955, James Britton, observed: "And this is the dilemma – not for the fortunate in fortunate places [public schools and grammar schools], but for the others: the conflict of loyalties – to the subject they teach or to the child who is taught."[20] Grammar school teachers generally looked to the universities for their procedures and standards as well as for their sense of what the subject was for. Their loyalties were principally to their specialism rather than to ideas about pupils' learning needs. This is not to say they were indifferent to pupils' welfare—we have found much evidence to suggest that pupils' well-being was taken very seriously—but teachers focused their energies on teaching their subject. As a result the pupils' own language and culture was overlooked as a potential starting point for work in English.

The teaching of written Standard English figured strongly in the school, but we should not assume that "correct" English was treated simply as a matter of linguistic authority. Teaching about Standard English involved looking at "living language." Consider this example from a pupil's surviving exercise book. The pupil was instructed to make distinctions among Standard and "slang" forms and to estimate whether or not a particular word would "live" in the language.[21] We traced the source, a textbook exercise, "New words and Phrases," in Guy Pocock's *More English Exercises* (1934).[22] From the pupil's exercise book we can see that he described "best-seller" correctly as "slang." However, the teacher duly amended the answer, adding the following words with underlining for emphasis: "*was* slang now *Stand. Eng.*" Thus he conveyed the principle that what constitutes a "correct" Standard form is not fixed for all time but rather it is dependent on changing usage. Such responses, which invited further discussion with the pupil, point toward a view of "correctness" derived from "living language"—albeit "educated" usage—rather than an ideal form abstracted from classical and literary models. New work in linguistics based on language in use encouraged a move away from Latin-based English grammars of the kind employed in prewar textbooks, but such work was not generally available to secondary school teachers at the start of our period.

In 1951, HMI noted that "boys read with spirit and an effort at expression of meaning of what they read."[23] However, they also observed: "in most cases their reading is marred by an uncouthness of utterance which survived longer than was necessary," adding, "a little regular practice in the lower forms might eliminate certain unwelcome diphthongs."[24] The mildly deprecating phrase, "unwelcome diphthongs," of course, refers to the boys' London accents. Yet working-class varieties of spoken English were largely tolerated by the staff. From what former pupils told us it appears that the boys "moderated" their natural way of speaking, adapting it to the way their teachers spoke partly out of respect. It would be both inaccurate and misleading to describe the school population as "cockney": Hackney Downs was not an entirely working-class school, although there was a strong London working-class presence.

We found no evidence of attempts by teachers at Hackney Downs to address the issue of language diversity, and yet linguistic diversity was a striking feature of many pupils' daily lives. Whereas the school remained a traditional grammar school in most respects, many pupils came from households where Yiddish, German, Russian, and Polish were spoken. Indeed, Yiddish words and phrases were often heard in the school corridors between lessons and in the playground. As Barry Supple, a former pupil put it, after the war, the school became increasingly "cosmopolitan."[25]

Pupils' ways of speaking could bring submerged prejudices to the surface. Harvey Monte, who was born in the East End, and who came from a Jewish background, suggested how teachers' perceptions of pupils' language occasionally betrayed their prejudices:

> [...] He used to openly say – now, we can take this two ways, things like–"I know people from where you come can't speak properly." Now, he could have meant kids generally from the East End, but if you are Jewish you tend to say [*breaks off as if to say that the inference is clear*] "He means us," yes. And he took every opportunity of being disparaging: "You kids from the East End," sort of thing. [26]

Such instances of overt prejudice were rare, but social judgments about pupils' speech were relatively commonplace.

Three Senior English Masters

The story of changes to postwar English teaching at Hackney Downs can be told best with reference to three striking personalities: James Ellis Medcalf (1891–1962); Joseph Brearley (1909–1977); and John Kemp (1929–2010). In their different ways all three were exceptional teachers who shaped the character of English at the school. They were not the only English teachers, of course. Immediately after the war, at a time of acute teacher shortages, there were several short-term appointments and some English teaching was done by nonspecialists. For three-form-entry grammar schools with around five hundred pupils on roll an establishment of three specialist English teachers was a typical staffing arrangement. Other English specialists included David Ogilvie, a former pupil who joined the staff in 1957, Bernard Law, who joined in 1958, leaving in 1969, and Roger Adlam, who was appointed in 1956 and who with Law continued at the school into the comprehensive era. But it is Medcalf, Brearley, and Kemp who best exemplify the changes to English that occurred in our period.

These three senior masters were themselves the products of grammar schools. After military service in the Great War, Medcalf was appointed to Hackney Downs as a French teacher (1921). Brearley, who also taught modern foreign languages, had studied under F. R. Leavis at Downing College, Cambridge, joining the staff at Hackney Downs in 1939. He returned after war service overseas to teach at the school for a further two decades. Brearley will be remembered principally as the teacher of the playwright, Harold Pinter, who attended the school from 1944 to 1948. In contrast to Medcalf and Brearley, who went to schools in the North of England, John Kemp was a Londoner. He attended a North London grammar school, read English at King's College, London, and was appointed assistant master at Hackney Downs in 1954. Kemp was promoted to senior English master and went on to become head teacher (1974), after the school had become a comprehensive, retiring in 1989 shortly before the school closed.

Stanley Day (1901–1957) was the senior English master immediately after the war. He was a graduate of London University in French and English and one former pupil described him as, "friendly, conservative, unadventurous and unromantic."[27] Day, and Medcalf who succeeded him, relied on four prewar course books: J. C. Dent, *Thought in English Prose* (1930); Guy N. Pocock, *More English Exercises* (1934) and *Grammar in a New Setting* (1928); and Norman L. Clay, *School Certificate English Practice* (1933). Such heavy reliance reflected the general problem of wartime shortages, but it was also the case that the School Certificate examination syllabus had changed little and there was little incentive for change.[28]

English Under James Medcalf

When Day left at the end of the Autumn term in 1947 to take up a post as senior lecturer at Trent Park Emergency Training College, James ("Jimmy") Medcalf was appointed as senior English master, taking over Day's duties. He is universally remembered as a scholarly, humane teacher who devoted himself to the whole life of the school. He attended Cowley Grammar School, St Helens, Lancashire (1900–1903) and St Helens College, Southsea (1903–1909), and in 1916 he was awarded a First Class Honors degree (External) from University College, London, in French and English. Later, he served in the Labor Corps (1917–1919).[29] After teaching briefly in the Welsh Marches—Malvern, Worcestershire, a town with strong English neo-Romantic associations—and in Streatham (1910–1919), a South London suburb, he was appointed to Hackney Downs as a French specialist. As one of our informants put it, "Really, he [Medcalf] was a French teacher. And then he did English."[30] In 1931, Medcalf took charge of a new, well-stocked library at a time when the head master, Thomas Oscar Balk, was president of the School Libraries Association. Spencer Moody, a colleague, paid this tribute to Medcalf that appeared in the school magazine, *The Review*, on his retirement in 1956:

> In the thirties, too, J. E. M. took up his place as Prince of Librarians in the newly-created library. There he would sit, after lunch and after school, endlessly good humored, surrounded by more or less helpful boys, cataloguing, inscribing, chaffing, perhaps verifying some recondite allusion in a crossword puzzle, and certainly spreading his own love of literature and sound learning. He knew all about the books, and all about the boys. He was devoted to the welfare of both; time and trouble did not seem to count.[31]

Raoul Sobel, a former pupil, recalled the way Medcalf showed a keen concern for individual boys' well-being: "I thought, of all the masters I had, certainly in English, he was the one who was most interested in my academic welfare."[32] He was also well regarded by HMI, as this short extract suggests: "The Senior English Master, who holds a First Class Honours Degree of London in French and English, has been on the Staff since 1920; he is a man of culture, widely read and of many intellectual interests and his influence is a very great asset to the school."[33] Moody recalled Medcalf's presence in the staff room: "[I]n the 30s, James would be in the Common Room, meticulously correcting in red ink and in an incredibly beautiful script, a huge pile of exercise books, occasionally interrupting his work to relight his pipe."[34] Barry Supple, remembers Medcalf as a "traditional type"—a "tranquil," "avuncular figure" who was "never fully resigned to the preponderance of Jewish boys at the head of the classes he taught."[35] To Supple, who came from a Jewish background, Medcalf seemed a typical English academic: "He suited an academic gown more than any other of our masters."[36] Harvey Monte, who came from a similar home, recalled writing a bogus quotation on the blackboard as a joke: "'*Time is no man's enemy but his compatriot.*' It drove him up the pole for nearly a week and I never told him that I was the author."[37]

Yet English lessons with Medcalf were neither dry-as-dust nor uniformly dull. Former pupils singled him out as a teacher who had the ability to make lessons interesting despite the ongoing preparations for public examinations that dominated lessons in the higher forms, where past papers and tests was the staple diet. In 1951, HMI reported that the school syllabus laid special stress on drama and choral speaking. They also noted that English teachers held regular library periods and pupils were expected to keep personal reading lists.[38] Reading for pleasure was widely encouraged, but rarely directed by the teachers. Monte recalls reading *Macbeth, Merchant of Venice, Midsummer Night's Dream, Journey's End,* and *Good Companions* as well as a fairly comprehensive list from a poetry anthology.[39] Some texts (such as *Lorna Doone, Black Beauty,* and *Treasure Island*) were chosen because they were considered suitable for younger readers. However, immediately after the war there was little in the way of literature written for adolescent readers. There was little money to spend on new books and very few pupils bought their own books because they were too expensive.

We have found little in the way of planned innovation under Medcalf. From the evidence available to us, it appears that there were few departmental meetings with little in the way of new materials or theorized practice. A small specialist English establishment meant that although there was plenty of informal discussion there seemed little need for formal departmental meetings. So whereas there was much lively conversation about books, there was little sense of organized collective endeavor.

The "assignment" of classes and the allocation of textbooks was a key administrative mechanism by which the senior English master managed his department. In 1953, Medcalf wrote to John Kemp shortly before he joined the staff as a relatively inexperienced teacher.[40] In the letter, Medcalf set out Kemp's teaching responsibilities, his "assignment," for the coming year. Classes and text books were matched in an overall scheme but it could hardly be described as a syllabus.

> For the first two terms you'll have rather a dull set of forms, I fear; certainly one scarcely worthy of a man with a first. I assure you that we've done

our best, and that we shall do much better when we have a re-shuffle at Midsummer. This is your assignment (to use a horrid jargon word). This gives you seven free periods, which isn't too bad.

The letter reveals how Medcalf managed professional relationships. His style resembled what Harold Rosen once referred to as "paternal autocracy." First, he reassures Kemp that he (Medcalf) appreciates his (Kemp's) outstanding qualifications (a first-class degree in English from Kings' College, London); second, he gives assurances that the "assignment" of classes in no way reflects a perception that Kemp might be better suited to teaching the less able pupils; and third, he implies that academic attainment is of paramount importance among the staff at the school. The tone is personal, confiding, half-amused, especially where he speaks about his energetic second in department, Joe Brearley: "I have rather weakly let my brilliant second in command have all the best forms; but he has lately become second master [deputy headmaster], and won't be so greedy for work when the collar begins to gall."[41] Medcalf is skillfully negotiating a complicated set of hierarchical relationships and his tone is calculated to bridge the distance between himself, the established senior master, and the newly appointed assistant master. Further, it implies that Kemp's assent will be freely given—thus rendering the assertion of managerial authority unnecessary. Medcalf concludes on an urbane, friendly note: "The staff are a very decent crowd: as for the boys, they're like all boys, *ni ange ni bête*; I've stood 'em for 33 years anyhow."

A supplementary sheet accompanying Medcalf's letter gives details of books for use with various classes as well as informal notes about pupils' abilities. It is hard to know what to make today of Medcalf's descriptions of pupils: "a band, mercifully small, of duds who are forlornly preparing for the GCE English Language paper"; "a hearty set of boobs"; "too doltish"; and so on. A generous view might be that they represent a manner of speaking about boys that was common among teachers at the time, and not meant to be taken too seriously. There is ample evidence of Medcalf's kindness, yet his remarks reveal common assumptions about pupils' academic and cultural deficiencies. He writes: "The general standard is lamentably poor: they come from bookless and uncultured homes." Yet our evidence suggests to the contrary that many pupils came from working-class homes where books were highly valued.

After the first year, classes were streamed. According to Geoffrey Alderman (2012) in his recent history of the school, Vernon Barkway Pye (the fifth head master, appointed in 1952) and his staff were "responsive to contemporary thinking on the value of modes of 'streaming.'"[42] Under Pye, streaming was extended through the provision of an "Alpha" form in the third, fourth, and fifth years for pupils who were considered especially able. The "Alpha" stream was meant to provide an accelerated O level course ("an elite within an elite," as one member of staff put it), but the experiment was not a success.[43] However, a positive outcome was that the best teachers were not necessarily reserved for the ablest pupils.

The dramatist, Steven Berkoff entered the school in 1950. He recalls the misery he felt at being placed in the "C" stream:

> For some reason, which even today I cannot fathom, in Hackney I was placed not in an equivalent A group or even a B group but a dreaded and shameful C! I assumed they wanted to test me out or else thought that the standards of Hackney Downs Grammar School were far superior to those at [my former school] Raines. In any case, the damage to my self-esteem was terrible and I remember going home for lunch on the first day, even though it was a half-hour bus journey, because I couldn't bear the humiliation and the low white trash in my class. I was intensely proud and tearfully crossed a dreary damp Hackney Downs which reflected my mood as I made for the bus stop.[44]

Berkoff speaks bitterly about the demoralizing effects of streaming. He also suggests that pupils in the "C" stream followed a different syllabus: "The higher grades did drama and wrote creative essays. I remember begging for a chance to write essays since I had enjoyed doing them so much at Raine's [School], but this was always denied. I felt it a shame—I had written essays since a child at primary school."[45] But it was not always the case that pupils in the lower streams worked from different books. Medcalf's letter indicates that although 3A and 3C were considered of different ability they shared the same textbooks: Marriott's *A Year's Work in English* (1921) and Dent's *Thought in English Prose* (1930). Furthermore, it appears that Joe Brearley, Medcalf's "brilliant second in command," actually taught 4C, a low stream, which supports Alderman's claim that, under Barkway Pye, the best teachers were not necessarily reserved for the ablest pupils.

There is no doubt that pupils from a wide variety of backgrounds often found English under Medcalf stimulating. He had the ability to fire pupils' imaginations and to engage their interests—sometimes at the deepest levels. His lessons were neither unvaried nor dull, but of their time. Monte recalls reading Longfellow's poem, "The Slave's Dream," when he was in the middle school: "I was intensely moved by the image of the Black Prince sold into slavery: suffering and cruelty and hardship in the slave column; that he found relief and almost happiness in death."[46] However, it is also fair to say that we have found no evidence to suggest that Medcalf gave sustained thought to the cognitive needs of pupils in the lower streams.[47] Terry Gasking, who came from a severely disadvantaged background, was in the "C" stream in the mid-1950s. He told us: "I was never going to make anything really in "C" Form, going through and struggling – struggling with everything really."[48]

From surviving exercise books we have reconstructed the pattern of English lessons for the years 1941–1947. Our reconstruction reveals the way that English teachers tried to vary the lessons by making selections from the course books rather than working through them slavishly, exercise-by-exercise. However no clear principle of selection or ordering is discernible beyond the apparent wish to balance the diet of grammar, précis, and composition with literature teaching. Here are some indicative examples from 1946: on January 29, pupils were instructed to write two paragraphs about a parrot who said the wrong thing at a tea party; on February 3, they worked through exercises on word-making; on February 8, they focused on punctuation; and on February 17, they retold the story of a poem, "The Lion Going to War," in prose.[49] These tasks were interspersed with the usual tests, comprehension exercises, clause analysis, précis, and parsing, but there were also one or two opportunities to write in a freer manner.

Let's focus on the experience of an individual pupil, David Ogilvie. Ogilvie was a working-class boy from a Scottish family background who went on from Hackney Downs to read English at Oxford. His father, who had served in a Scottish regiment in the Great War, worked in the post office. In 1939, along with a number of pupils from Hackney elementary schools as well as a large portion of the secondary school—some four hundred boys—Ogilvie was evacuated to King's Lynn, Norfolk. During his time there, he wrote "Sunday" letters to his parents in Hackney.[50] These "Sunday" letters offer rare glimpses of classrooms and we want to touch on one episode to bring out what we will call the "atmosphere" of English lessons. Ogilvie writes, "Mr Medcalf, our English master calls Norman [Norman Rule, a fellow pupil] the 'Oppressive Rule'; and me 'The Bonny Earl of Airlie.' I was doing something or other in the class the other day—moving about I think, when Moo-cow (Mr Medcalf) said, 'When this barbarous Scotsman of ours has finished fluttering his kilt about and causing a draft, we will proceed.'"[51] Ogilvie's anecdote is meant to amuse his parents, but it affords us an insight into the good-humored relationship between teacher and pupils in extremely difficult circumstances. The anecdote also says something about the way that discipline was maintained (by mild sarcasm) as well as the way that the teacher's knowledge of pupils' backgrounds counted for something.

Ogilvie returned from Norfolk to a dreary world of bombsites, rationing, and housing shortages in Hackney. Several of our informants told us that both teachers and pupils welcomed the restart of school. We touched on the atmosphere of Medcalf's lessons. Now we want to focus on the way he responded to pupils' work. Marks out of ten were commonly given in the lower school. Further up the school there would be extended comments at the end of essays and compositions with supplementary points and corrections. Medcalf's classes copied a key to corrections on the inside cover of their exercise books. However, in responding to their work, the teacher went further, and we want to look at one or two instances in detail.

From a surviving exercise book, we see that on February 16, 1947, Ogilvie, wrote a piece entitled "All I ask, the heaven above and the road below me," which included a paragraph about leaving the "smoky, soot begrimed town for the open country": "How I long to wander at my leisure over the hills and down through the green and peaceful valleys where Nature alone governs all things."[52] Medcalf responded by underlining the words, "Nature alone governs all things" and wrote in the margin in neat red ink, "Where is this?" Thus he gently mocks the *artificiality* of Ogilvie's bucolic prose. However, it is hard to imagine—harder to reconstruct—what Ogilvie made of the comment. Nevertheless, what is progressive in Medcalf's approach is the engaging nature and the length of his responses to pupils' work at a time when it was more common for teachers at the school to give marks out of ten with a brief comment at the end (Figure 3.3).

Pupils at Hackney Downs read a lot of nature poetry in the 1940s. The English countryside had been especially significant in the period of national cultural reconstruction following the Great War. Later, at the start of our period, the bias toward nature poetry in English remains striking.[53] In 1945, Ogilvie listed poems from two class anthologies, *Daffodil Poetry, Books, I and II* (1920): the list included: six "Patriotic and War Poems"; three "Supernatural and Spiritual Poems"; eight 'Ballads'; and forty-three "Nature Poems."[54]

The title of Ogilvie's composition, "All I ask, the heaven above and the road below me," was taken from a (then) well-known poem, "The Vagabond," (1896) by Robert Louis Stevenson. The poem and its central theme, the artist outsider, would have been a familiar one to the educated English middle classes. Reading Stevenson in schools was common at the time largely as a result of the widespread use of a series of anthologies produced by the English Association, *Poems of Today*.[55] Later, in April 1947, Ogilvie wrote an appreciation: "Poems of R. L. Stevenson," and Medcalf asked (as if continuing a conversation in red ink), "Do you know your R. L. S.–novels and verse?" Behind the inquiry lie the teacher's own tastes and values into which Ogilvie was being progressively initiated. Where Ogilvie writes about events in *Lorna Doone*: "John [Ridd] sets him on his horse which rides off," Medcalf responds, "A performing horse." The teacher's joke calls attention to Ogilvie's insecure grasp of the way language works, but elsewhere, for example, in connection with *Macbeth*, Medcalf

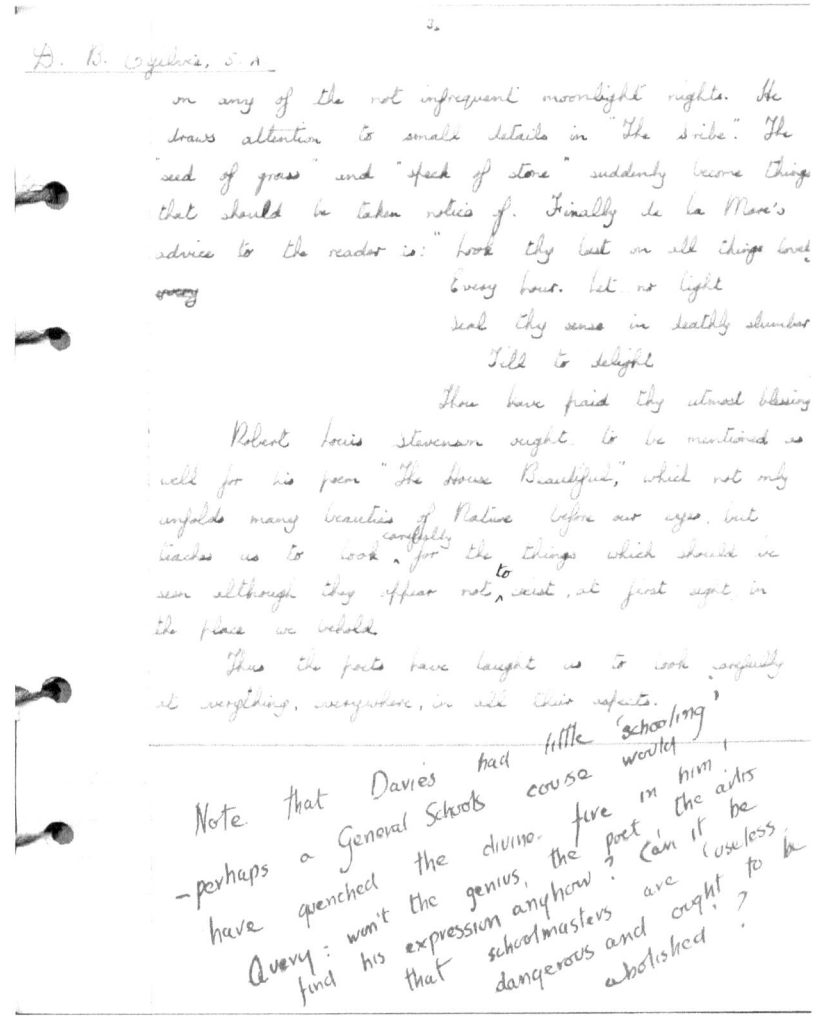

Figure 3.3 James Medcalf responds engagingly to an essay by David Ogilvie, 1947.

questioned Ogilvie's grammar (the use of a feminine ending on "villainess") to make a substantive point about the significance of grammatical forms in the world of the play: "An unnecessary fem. form if it exists. She is determined to be wicked as a saint is to be good: the Devil has his Saints and Martyrs, too, and they strive to attain preeminence like the saints." Although separate formal grammar lessons continued, such comments suggest how Medcalf drew on pupil's grammatical knowledge to deepen their understanding of literary texts.

Ogilvie was an exceptionally able pupil who was singled out and encouraged to apply to Oxford. After National Service in Berlin, where he taught formal grammar to battle-hardened NCOs, he went up to Oxford to read English, eventually returning to Hackney Downs as an English teacher. When we interviewed him shortly before his death in 2011, he recalled his time at Hackney Downs with immense pleasure, especially English lessons with Medcalf: "But then, I mean, we had really quite gifted teachers, like James Medcalf, who taught me, and was also librarian, and he wrote reviews for learned magazines and, you know, publications, and he introduced me to Helen Waddell, who wrote about medieval times and wandering minstrels and all that sort of thing."[56] The continuities between Ogilvie's school and university interests are especially striking. The fact that he enjoyed reading Anglo-Saxon, Middle English, and Medieval French at Oxford—Medcalf's own long-standing interests and passions—says much about his intellectual formation at Hackney Downs.

English Under Joe Brearley

Joseph ("Joe") Brearley was appointed to Hackney Downs in April, 1939. Shortly afterwards, in September, the school was evacuated to King's Lynn, Norfolk. In March the following year, Brearley was seconded to West London Emergency Secondary School, and subsequently, from October 1941 to May 1946, he served overseas. On route to the Far East, he was torpedoed, surviving to spend much of the war in the Middle East. He rejoined the school in 1945.

Born in 1909, Brearley grew up in Batley, a small industrial town in the West Riding of Yorkshire. We have a rich and detailed account of his intellectual development from a collection of his writings, *Fortune's Fool*,[57] which gives us a picture of an English teacher's intellectual interests as well as their influence on his teaching. Whereas Medcalf was a practicing Anglo-Catholic, Brearley came from a Methodist family. And it was from an intense, often turbulent religious background that he went up to St John's College, Cambridge, to read English in 1928. He writes, "I came under the influence of Dr. I. A. Richards and had my own personal studies supervised by Dr. F. R. Leavis [...] Even now I cannot express my great debt to these two men."[58] Later, he reflected, "from Cambridge the whole town of Batley seemed small, provincial and unimportant."[59]

Cambridge continued to shape Brearley's teaching at Hackney Downs. He recalled that I. A. Richards' new book, *Science and Poetry* (1926), made a great impression on him at the time. He writes, "For many years as a teacher I made this [distinction between two kinds of belief] my basic assumption when arguing with Arts sixth form boys in practical criticism lessons," adding, "Since many of our discussions were recorded on tape it is now possible to hear them again and to estimate how far my basic assumption was modified as the years went by."[60] We have not been able to trace the original open-reel tapes, but we have managed to recover some transcripts. Thus we can see that topics for discussion included: "poetry and religion," "intellectual belief and emotional belief," and "the poet and his audience." As far as we can tell the transcripts were used to hold the contributions for further analysis and to give continuity. The tone of the discussions is uncompromisingly cerebral and although Brearley intervenes sparingly we can easily trace his controlling presence.

We have mentioned that examination syllabuses constrained what went on in English lessons and we have shown how English teachers were reliant on course books. Yet some teachers cut back against the grain.[61] David Ogilvie was in Brearley's Arts sixth form along with Harold Pinter and Henry Grinberg. He describes Brearley's unconventional approach like this: "He had very little patience with the official syllabus for A level.[62] I remember him one day trying to sort of do his job, and one of the set books was Wordsworth's *Lyrical Ballads*—language "such as ordinary men do use"—you see [...] putting them against the ornate eighteenth-century stuff, and he sort of made a start on this, and his face changed suddenly and he just threw the book at the wall, and turned the lesson into something much more interesting."[63] Some pupils found Brearley's high-handed disregard for the syllabus disconcerting. Raoul Sobel contrasted Medcalf and Brearley's differing styles. Medcalf's lessons, he told us, were structured: they related to the syllabus in a systematic way: "With Brearley," Sobel complained, "you had no idea what was going to happen. Tennyson was on the syllabus, [he] said, "If anyone wants to read Tennyson they can fetch the book. Tossed it out of the window."[64]

If Medcalf fostered keen literary appreciation, Brearley injected a new critical spirit into English teaching. Barry Supple recalled the way that he introduced practical criticism into lessons: "What he said was, 'Look, these are poems, you don't know anything about the background or the person, what do you think?' which was really very good."[65] Supple writes, "Joe Brearley–a free spirit, entirely unconventional, given to unschoolmasterly singing and play acting, someone who had no inhibitions about encouraging youngsters to express themselves to the point of ill-disciplined anarchy."[66] He continues, "[H]e treated us like fellow men, but was at once undisciplined and formidable."⁶⁷ Henry Grinberg recalls sharing a front-row desk with Pinter in the "Tower," Brearley's private domain, "a wonderfully secluded room on the top floor of the School's massive, sprawling Victorian brick building, just under the belfry, with its own private staircase."⁶⁸ Pinter's lifelong friendship with Brearley is well-documented.⁶⁹ Michael Billington, Pinter's biographer, has described long walks through the run-down streets and parks of North East London.⁷⁰ In the course of these walks they would declaim lines from Webster's *The Duchess of Malfi* or *The White Devil*. As Pinter himself recalled: "That language [Webster] made me dizzy. Joe Brearley fired my imagination."⁷¹ As Billington, remarks: "Brearley seemed to have found his *métier* in Hackney [Downs] and passed on his passion for English poetry and drama to Pinter and other pupils."⁷²

Grinberg makes a further, telling observation about his Jewish contemporaries' families' aspirations. "Their parents [he is speaking about Pinter and others] took it as a point of pride that their sons did not have to work. Despite a postwar Labour Government and our hopes for a Worker's Paradise, the class system was still very much a reality, and the quality of one's accent definitely so."⁷³ There was little distinction between schoolwork and what they did outside and as consequence, Grinberg says, they were "massively absorbed" by their studies: "We were expected to read widely and constantly–and we did so–and when we were not reading, we were expected to be thinking and writing about what we had read."⁷⁴

Drama flourished after the war. In 1940, during the school's evacuation, Brearley was involved in a successful production of *Midsummer Night's Dream*. But it was his 1947 production of *Macbeth* that established school productions in the postwar era, with Pinter in the leading role. The production was in modern dress and Kenneth Hooton, a left-wing history teacher, who was nominally in charge of the school's Literary and Debating Society, wrote a review: "Probably the most striking example of this [production] was his [Brearley's] frankly outrageous treatment of *Macbeth* where he clearly saw that violence, revolution and dictatorship were the salient points and could be brought out to telling effect to the modern stage only by converting the whole thing into present-day costume."⁷⁵ Hooton noted how the production drew freely on "the established techniques of film, radio and variety," which suggests that Brearley was alert to the potentials of popular cultural forms as resources for staging Shakespeare. The following year, Brearley produced *Romeo and Juliet,* with Pinter in the role of Romeo. Subsequently, Albert Calland, a young geography teacher, took over responsibility for school productions. He turned the semi-circular theater to great advantage with a series of challenging plays: Ibsen's *An Enemy of the People* (1955), *Julius Caesar* (1956), Shaw's *Caesar and Cleopatra* (1957), Thornton Wilder's *Our Town* (1958), *Oedipus Rex* (1959), T. S. Eliot's *Murder in the Cathedral* (1960), and Bertolt Brecht's *The Life of Galileo* (1961).

Theater figured large for many, though not all, of the pupils at Hackney Downs. Harvey Monte recalls visits to plays: "We [saw] Lear with Donald Wolfit at the Camden theatre and there were various visits to [West End] London theatres. Plays included *Death of a Salesman, School for Scandal; Antony and Cleopatra* and *The Duchess of Malfi* [...] One trip that I remember vividly was to a theatre in Toynbee Hall, Commercial Street [in heart of the East End] to see *Great Expectations*."[76] Raoul Sobel described to us how these trips were organized: "What happened was the teacher would take down how many people [...] wanted to go – send away for the tickets and then the tickets would come, and then we would each be given a ticket, and then we'd make our own way there." Pupils were not always accompanied by a teacher and they were expected to make their way independently to the theater. Thus they avoided the "crocodile" (two-by-two procession), schools matinee, set book approach that was more usual at the time.[77] Sobel reflected, "I was introduced to the theatre in that way. My parents had never gone with me to the theatre. It was just this new world."[78] After Pinter had left the school, Sobel played a leading role in Brearley's production of Sheridan's *The Critic*, which Brearley recalled as "a triumphant success."[79] But it seems there were inconsistencies in Brearley's treatment of pupils, as Monte recalled: "He gave immense support to Harold Pinter, for obvious reasons, and after Harold went, he turned his attention to Raoul and they did *The Critic*. Raoul had one of the starring parts there, and he [Brearley] really built [him up] and then dropped him afterwards."[80] Sobel went on to become a successful film editor.

As a general rule, pupils from the lower streams did not participate in school productions.[81] Terry Gasking's family was evacuated to Wales after a bomb fell directly on their air-raid shelter in Tottenham, North London. After, his father, who was blind, formed a small touring variety act, touring South Wales. Gasking was in the "C" stream and not good at English, yet he remembers Brearley as an inspiring teacher: "You couldn't switch off with Brearley. He was as mad as a hatter. Moments of inspiration, [...] he'd come out with wonderful things. I'm just sad I was far too shy to do any of the shows that Brearley used to put on. I was never encouraged to anyway, by him, or by mum, really, who didn't want me to go on the stage because dad had been."[82]

We mentioned how Medcalf responded at length to pupils' writings. Brearley also responded with extended comments, particularly in connection with advanced level studies. The following comment was made in response to an outstanding, essay by Geoffrey Alderman entitled, "A

Passage to India by E. M. Forster: Some aspects of the world and universe inhabited by Forster's characters in his novel." At the end of the essay Brearley wrote praising the seriousness of Alderman's approach. He also responded to what appears to be a timed essay (undated) on the same theme. Alderman had written: "What Fielding [the central character] fails to see is the wider, political background to the racial situation in India. He bases his analysis of the situation in observations of individuals alone." Brearley commented: "This is important. (The old [Liberal] idea–change the individual and you'll change society. But to change *India*, is some all-embracing economic plan necessary? Forster seems unaware of this aspect of the problem.)"[83] In his relationships with sixth-formers there was no sense of reserve on Brearley's part, just as there was no sense of deference on the part of the pupils. His sense of "things that matter" and what pupils should know about, extended beyond English to world affairs. Supple recalls that it was from Brearley that he first heard the news of Gandhi's assassination in 1948. He sums up the incident: "a communication in a school corridor which even then I realized reflected a relationship of near equals."[84]

After the war, in school clubs and societies, pupils from mixed social and religious backgrounds learned to practice democratic participation. The Literary and Debating Society under Hooton held highly charged debates on current issues such as the future of Israel and the Suez crisis. However, the mock election in 1951 is probably the best indicator of the school ethos of open debate and discussion. Harvey Monte stood as the Communist candidate:

> They were amazing times. I mean, I remember when we had this mock election in '51, [...] the final speech was made in the amphitheatre [lecture theatre]. Brearley came to this final debate, and it was pretty full, and we opened the thing for questions when we'd finished. And Brearley asked me this question, because Nasser had just come to power in Egypt, and he said, "What is the policy of your government towards Nasser?" And I said, 'In view of the fact it was a nationalist movement we would be bound to support it. And he saw me the following day, and he said, "That answer was brilliant."[85]

English Under John Kemp

John Kemp came from a "respectable" working-class background. His father worked in the post office (as did David Ogilvie's). He attended Trinity Grammar School in North East London (1940–1947) and went on to read English at King's College, London (1947–1950) where he obtained a first class honors degree in English Literature.[86] Following his first degree, Kemp took a PGCE at King's to qualify as a teacher. In 1953, he was awarded an MA in English, which was rather unusual for students from similar backgrounds at the time. From September to December 1953, he taught at our third school, Minchenden. Then, in January 1954, he was appointed to Hackney Downs (Figure 3.4).

In 1951, Kemp undertook a brief period (three weeks) of teaching at White Hart Lane Primary School (formerly Earlsfield School), Tottenham, a working class suburb of North East London, not far from where he grew up.[87] We have a surviving account written by Kemp of teaching at White Hart Lane and from this account we can begin to reconstruct something of the evolution of his ideas about teaching and learning. He writes about discipline, the unforeseen difficulties involved in teaching simple arithmetic (primary teachers were usually generalists), and his first encounters with pupils with special educational needs—"backward children," in the terminology of the day:

> I wondered whether the backwardness of children with quite a fair I.Q. was due partly to their social environment. The school serves one of the sad suburbs, built around the turn of the century, whose only purpose seems to be to fill out the vacant vacuum between one shopping centre and the next; council estate-ish, too limp to be a township, too shapeless to lead anywhere, eminently respectable in the main, but spiritually void. Since many of the children lack a lively intellectual background, the school has its work the more difficult.[88]

As was common at the time, Kemp unhesitatingly attributes working-class children's learning difficulties to their (perceived) culturally impoverished environment. References to the "sad suburbs" and a "spiritual void" suggest that Kemp took a disdainful view of Tottenham. But he was full of praise for what teachers were able to achieve and he writes enthusiastically about the way the school managed to enter the lives of working-class children, especially those in the "A" stream. Further, he admires the "ever-changing series of collections and wall displays," something it would have been rare to find in grammar schools at the time. Finally he describes a successful lesson where he invited children to imagine themselves miners trapped in a pit that was given shortly after the Knockshinnoch pit disaster (1951). Overall, the account reveals both his dislike of shabby, featureless suburbia *and* a socialist belief in transformative power of education for the working classes.[89]

Figure 3.4 Hackney Downs Staff, Summer 1960: from the left, David Ogilvie is ninth on the back row, John Kemp is fifth on the middle row, and Joe Brearley is sixth on the front row.

Kemp carried his university interests forward into his teaching. In his master's thesis (1953) he wrote about "the position and function of the artist and his work in society as seen in the literature of the years 1880–1920."[90] "The sheer ugliness of the new [industrial] cities is obvious," he writes, "but more important is the attitude of mind they bred, the way of living they enforced. A vast, cultureless, and uprooted proletariat was employed by a class whose test of value was industry and utility."[91] Kemp's initial aim was to raise the cultural level of individual children and lift them out of their "dreary" surroundings toward a "better life." Later, when Hackney Downs became a comprehensive, his perspectives and aims would change.

As schoolboy, Kemp told us, he was drawn to the Romantics: "I spent months wandering around Dartmoor when I was a kid, because it was Bronte and Wordsworth, and that very emotional response to literature went on for a year or two at university."[92] As an undergraduate student in his final year he was drawn to F. R. Leavis' literary criticism. In 1953, he received key texts by Leavis including *New Bearings in English Poetry* (1932) and *The Common Pursuit* (1952), as gifts from his mother. He referred specifically to Leavis and Denys Thompson's book, *Culture and Environment* in his thesis. We know that he acquired *The Great Tradition* (1948) and from his personal copy we see that that he got it from Foyles Booksellers, Charing Cross Road in December, 1954, which was the month he left Minchenden for Hackney Downs. From his personal collection of literary journals we also have surviving issues of *Scrutiny,* for 1953 and it clear that Leavis' ideas figured powerfully at a critical moment in the young teacher's intellectual development.

In 1994, after his retirement, Kemp recalled the impact that Leavis made on his thinking in his final year at King's (1950):

> It was simply a matter of what happened in the last year of the degree course – [my] last year of college, when I found Leavis. Coming across Leavis's criticism as it happened, in the third year, suddenly gave a different way of looking at everything. Gave a shape to everything, and for a time it became a bit of a salvation. [...] I got caught hook, line and sinker for about six months. He had a way of looking at things which really pulled my head into shape.[93]

Whereas Medcalf's sensibilities were Georgian in taste and feeling, Brearley and Kemp were attracted by Leavis' penetrating literary and cultural criticism. Kemp engaged with *Culture and Environment* (see chapter two) from the very start. The book, which claimed to offer a training in critical awareness, was designed principally for use in schools. With similar intentions behind it, *The Use of English,* a key postwar journal edited by

Thompson, aimed to give direct practical aid to English teachers by means of regular features one of which was called "stocktaking." The first issue contained advanced notice of a forthcoming article by Raymond Williams: "*Stocktaking I: English and the Background* will examine the books available for relating the study of English to the environment and provide an extensive bibliography."[94] *The Use of English* broadened significantly the scope of English. William's article duly appeared during Kemp's final year at King's. For Williams, an adequate education in "culture and environment" involved "the extension of English into the critical analysis of a variety of cultural forms—newspapers, magazines, and advertisements—including forms that do not depend on the written word—broadcasting, cinema, architecture and town planning." Such ideas lay behind sustained work on advertising which began in earnest after Kemp was promoted to senior English master in 1956.[95]

We have traced a surviving example of such work: a pupil's analysis of a Persil advert from October, 1960, entitled: "When a mother cares – it shows." Tim Dowley (age 13) wrote perceptively about the way words and pictures combine to produce psychological effects: "to make the mother wonder if she is doing enough."[96] Further, we have reconstructed the pattern of the year's work from Kemp's surviving mark books. Although we have not managed to secure work from the academic year 1958–1959, we can see plainly from Kemp's records that a task on advertising was set for a top stream at the same point in the year, which, in view of the fact he continued with similar work in 1960–1961, suggests an established pattern.

We have mentioned the influence of Leavis on Brearley and Kemp. We have also indicated lines of continuity between their experiences at university and their teaching in the grammar school. We suggested that Kemp (more so than Brearley) was attracted to the project that Leavis and Thompson set out in *Culture and Environment*. Now we want to go wider to show how new ideas about English pedagogy of the kind proposed by *The Use of English,* the journal Thompson edited, made their entry to the school under Kemp. We shall concentrate on one particular instance of new work to show how the introduction of what we are calling the "village" sequence of lessons broke the pattern of single lessons based on course book exercises that we spoke about at the start of this chapter.

First, it is worth pausing to say where the "village" sequence came from. It has a long evolutionary history going back to the publication of James Britton's seminal course book, *English on the Anvil* (1934). In it Britton fashioned a template for planning coherent *sequences* of lessons around central ideas or themes. In the first volume, "For Junior Forms," he used a passage from the Robert Louis Stevenson's 1892 story, *The Isle of Voices* to introduce English work that involved the creation of an imaginary island.

Work stemming from *"The Island"* suggested ways of combining whole sequences of lessons within a unified scheme of work. Whereas Pocock's *Grammar in a New Setting* focused on formal grammar with no further suggestions for composition, comprehension, or précis, in contrast, *English on the Anvil* offered a *unified* course in language and composition. Each chapter was divided between a section on grammar and suggestions for composition. The early chapters introduced the notion of an imaginary island which as the course unfolded became a unifying theme—"How I discovered my Island"; "My first Day on the Island"; "How I explored my Island"; and so on. The idea for the project—in essence, a composition syllabus for junior forms—was taken from Harrow Weald County School, the Middlesex grammar school where James Britton was senior English master.

English on the Anvil was recommended by tutors at the Institute of Education. In 1954, Percival Gurrey's book *The Teaching of Written English* offered a sample composition syllabus that suggested that an "island" project for first years should be "started on *Anvil* lines" and "kept going for at least a term."[97] Gurrey, Britton's teacher and collaborator, also proposed a sequence of composition lessons for third-year pupils based on a "village" project which covered an entire academic year, with various activities including descriptions of a fictional village seen through the eyes of its inhabitants, mystery stories written round village life, preparation of a country magazine, and an attempt to look at changes to village life through imagined interactions with the new Citizen's Advice Bureau. The "village" constitutes a specific instance of a shift—a major change—toward thematically organized sequences of lessons. It was a watershed for the way that it implied both a new way of working involving extensive teacher planning as well as a deeper understanding of pupils' development. In sum, the "village" project held out new possibilities for coherence, continuity, and progression in secondary English involving several kinds of language-related activities: oral work, description, mystery stories, a magazine, a pageant, and citizens' advice. However, Gurrey also included the idea of "Town Development,"[98] which signaled a further departure in line with the kind of critical analysis that Williams proposed in his article, *Stocktaking I*.

A careful inspection of John Kemp's mark book for 1959/60 reveals that his first-year classes (age 11) worked on "the village" over several weeks—in other words, for an *extended* period of time. The task headings in the mark book suggest that Kemp adapted the original (Harrow Weald) plan by reducing its scope slightly, but the main features of the original project were retained: a village map, a description of the place, descriptions of village characters, and so on.[99] Crucially, Kemp had the freedom to plan such work for the lower school; higher up the school, such freedom was constrained by exam preparation.

Raymond Williams' article, *The Use of English, Stocktaking I* (1950), had proposed to equip secondary age pupils with the analytical tools they needed to join public debates as active participants in a democratic process.[100] Kemp brought fresh resources to the original "village" project. From his personal library he drew on a classic study of postwar rural planning, *The Anatomy of the Village*, by Thomas Sharp (1946).[101] *The Anatomy of the Village* was one in a series published by Penguin that engaged with postwar debates about the built environment. Kemp developed strong views about the need for rational planning and reconstruction as exemplified by the series to which *The Anatomy of the Village* belonged within an enlarged picture of the aims of English.

We have traced an example of pupil's work relating to the "village" by following up contacts on the internet. Tim Dowley, a former pupil who supplied the example, came from a middle-class background. His father, a solicitor and a fundamentalist Evangelical Christian elected to live in the traditional East End.[102] Dowley recalls that as a child he "stuck out like a sore thumb" in a working-class neighborhood. He was a conscientious student who produced a first-rate map of "Shaybridge Village" (after the manner of the illustrations in *Anatomy of the Village*), when he was in his first year at Hackney Downs (1958).

Dowley, now a successful publisher, told us that he enjoyed Kemp's lessons and that he thought highly of his teaching: "He [Kemp] was always very considered with his viewpoints. He never made a rushed judgment about anything. He was a very admirable person." As an instance of Kemp's concern for pupils' well-being, Dowley recalled the way that he ran the school library: "[...] because every day, after school, he [Kemp] was in the library, until whenever. And it was a sort of...I used to use the word 'sanctuary,' you know, it was a sort of area of safety for the odd bods."[103] Above all, Dowley recalls reading stories—*The Machine Stops*, *The Odor of Chrysanthemums*, *The Secret Sharer*, and so on. It was the richness and excitement of Kemp's literature teaching that stood out for him and which he remembers most vividly.

Kemp's preparation notes are contained in 16 surviving exercise books. The books are frail, brittle with fire-damage, and whereas ten of the sixteen books came from LCC stationery supplies, two books are from Middlesex County Council and it is highly likely that they date from when Kemp taught at Minchenden (1954), which was an MCC school.[104] One of the books, dated (retrospectively) by Kemp himself, contains a list of "possible lesson methods" arranged under various headings: "Grammar," "Composition," "General," and "Reading and Comprehending," "Play,"

"Prose Reader," "Poetry," and "Reading to them [pupils]." The headings derive from the PGCE course that Kemp took at King's and it contains a wealth of suggestions for activities: practical suggestions for getting children to do things such as: "making up their own plays that they act first from the basic idea"; "describing parts in character and mock trials"; and so on. The general aim was to involve pupils as active participants in lessons and to use drama as a resource for learning. However Dowley recalls what happened when Kemp tried to introduce new "active" approaches to Shakespeare:

> [W]e did it [*Macbeth*] for a lesson, or maybe a lesson and a half, and it was chaos. It didn't work. You know, people had no idea what was going on, and people were messing about, and he [Kemp] threw, I think, as far as I know, a mock tantrum, and shocked us, he said, "You will not piss upon my Shakespeare" – or something. [He] shocked us when he said "piss." And then after that we didn't do any more Shakespeare with him until year five.[105]

Grammar school pupils were not unfailingly biddable and new methods were not always welcome.[106] According to Kemp, who was sanguine about such "reversals," many if not most of the methods associated with progressive practice in English were already around in the 1950s: "the various methods of approach weren't very different, I think, from those we had in the sixties and seventies."[107] Talk—debate, discussion, argument—was a central activity throughout our period. David Ogilvie told us that class discussions were always central to the way English was taught at Hackney Downs: "Apart from the weekly grammar lesson there were discussion lessons on some sort of theme, which was really sort of trying to teach pupils, even from year one, how to manage a discussion in civilized terms, and stick to what the discussion was about, in other words relevance. And that [discussion] was usually pretty popular."[108] However Ogilvie also suggested that projects, which gave pupils greater control over the pace and direction of their work, came in around 1963, which is considerably later than the entries in Kemp's mark book for the work we have been describing would seem to indicate. (We have not been able to resolve this issue.) Certainly, projects were described in an article, "Projects for the English Specialist" by Cyril Poster in *The Use Of English,* 1953. The appeal of single subject project work—Poster gives the example of work around the fictional village of Fenham—is that it "counteracts age-old tendencies to subdivisions within the subject into poetry lessons, Punctuation lesson and so on." "Above all," he continues, "it provides both material and incentive for the development of the practice and the standards of criticism."[109]

About grammar teaching in the late fifties, Kemp recalled, "We didn't do much formal grammar work. We didn't do lists of vocabulary." Yet an exercise book from 1953/54 contains 19 pages of painstaking preparation notes on clause analysis and parsing with additional material on methods of teaching spelling. All of this suggests that grammar teaching figured strongly, at least during Kemp's early years of teaching. It is possible that Kemp played down grammar teaching, which was actually a sizeable proportion of the work, in retrospect because his chief interest was in teaching literature.

Literary criticism, the critical analysis of demanding literary texts became *the* central activity under Kemp. He prepared lessons on set books with assiduous care, making systematic, first-hand critical notes on the texts. Salient points about literary technique, characterization, and thematic content were listed rigorously page-by-page. We can see Kemp's meticulous method of preparation most clearly perhaps in connection with teaching a short story by Joseph Conrad, *The Brute* (1906).[110] Kemp noted: the "casual tone of the beginning"; "the shock of the voice through [the] partition, and [the] reader's uncertainty about who is being spoken of." [111]Kemp's method of *teaching* (what he actually did in the classroom) was to read the story out in class (or get pupils to read in turn) and bring out those features of the text that he had noted down in advance. Reading whole texts in class was obviously important, but pupils could also be relied upon to read at home.

The Brute was one of a series of stories for senior classes. Pupils were expected to annotate their copies of the text before writing their essays for homework. We have matched Kemp's preparation notes with the pupils' annotations. Thus, Kemp writes: "We can now recall the misunderstood murderousness. The fact of personality [is] emphasized." (He is making a point about narrative ordering as well as about the way that the ship is personified.) In a surviving copy of the anthology, we see that the pupil has marked the relevant passage in pencil and written: "[Conrad] brings out ship as [a] personality" thus showing that he has grasped the essential point. Where Kemp comments in his preparation notes, "Tempting providence; we feel something must happen": the pupil writes, "Seems like tempting providence" in his text. It would appear then that during the course of a typical lesson, Kemp would take the class through a close, critical reading of the story and the pupils were invited to adopt Kemp's words and phrases—the teacher's insights and interpretations —rather than attempt a "reading" of their own. This raises intriguing questions about the "authenticity" and "originality" of the pupils' responses—questions that we think Kemp must have considered.

Two additional points: first, Kemp added critical questions and summaries to his listed points, such as, "What point is served by the presence of and character of the North Sea pilot? [...] This seems to me a good and well-planned yarn, [written] with the skill but without the vision of a good writer." He offered detailed judgments that pupils might struggle to produce for themselves. Thus he showed how to produce close readings by exemplary practical demonstrations. These demonstrations were invariably followed by trial essay titles (in preparation for the examination) that corresponded closely to the features of the texts he had already highlighted in class: "How is the ship personified and how does this add to the effect?"

The Brute is a short story, but what about longer texts? When Kemp taught full-length novels his method remained essentially the same. Thus he made systematic notes extending over 95 pages for Conrad's novel, *The Secret Agent*. Additionally, he supplemented his notes with summaries of published criticism. For example, when he prepared, *The Secret Agent*, he drew on *Conrad the Novelist* (1958) by A. J. Guerard as well as *Conrad's Measure of Man* (1954) by P. L. Wiley. However, the choice of texts for study was limited both by the published examination syllabus and the availability of texts.

Tim Dowley suspects that Kemp tended to concentrate on modern works whenever possible: "We never read Dickens or Goldsmith or Austen, or anything like that," he told us.[112] To some extent, Kemp's notebooks bear this out. *A Passage to India*, *To the Lighthouse*, *Portrait of the Artist as a Young Man*, *Brave New World*, and *Lord of the Flies* were each painstakingly prepared, using the method described earlier. But there were many pre-twentieth-century texts too: *Emma*, for example, was annotated with a summary of a published critical commentary. Kemp taught also poetry and drama (Milton, Pope, and Shakespeare) using the same methods. His notes on *Richard II* first appear in an undated MCC notebook, which suggests that they were made early on in the mid-1950s. Later, scene-by-scene notes on *Antony and Cleopatra* were supplemented by readings in Derek Traversi's *Shakespeare: The Roman Plays* (1963) and John Holloway's *The Story of the Night* (1961).[113] Additionally, he made detailed notes on *King Lear* from Derek Traversi's *An Approach to Shakespeare* (1957), and Wilson Knight's *The Wheel of Fire* (1930). Several former pupils mentioned stimulating and enjoyable lessons on Chaucer. *The Franklin's Tale*, *The Pardoner's Tale*, and *The Nun's Priest's Tale* were all painstakingly transposed into modern English.

Our description of Kemp's method of teaching literature may have suggested that he was not interested in eliciting or discussing pupils' own ideas. But this was not the case. Ralph Levinson, a former pupil who attended the school after the 1963 fire, recalled Kemp's style of teaching: "John Kemp was a very considered man, he came over as a deeply intelligent and thoughtful man, and I think all the kids had a lot of respect for him [...] he was a man who was capable of seeing nuances in what people said, and teasing things out, and, you know, waiting for what somebody said and then seeing what... how attitudes differed and being able to sort of bring out contradictions and so on, in a very gentle way."[114]

By the end of our period, especially in his capacity of school librarian, and with help from young colleagues like David Ogilvie, Kemp had broadened the scope of reading in the lower school. By the early 1960s, pupils were being encouraged to read books that were written specifically for young readers, such as *The Silver Sword* and *The Otterbury Incident*. He also compiled extensive lists of suitable texts for lower school reading and pupils copied lists of recommended texts into their exercise books. His reading lists for sixth-formers, especially those preparing for university entrance, were highly regarded.

During the 1960s, Kemp was chiefly instrumental in negotiating changes that led to the school becoming a nonselective comprehensive school. Later, he wrote about what was involved in such changes:

> There was a powerful social purpose in the 1960's comprehensive movement; the idea of failure because of the district where you were born, or the social class you were born into, had to be fought too. The ideal, one can see now, was to change society through the schools – to build ideas of equal respect, co-operation rather than competition, enlightenment, among the children, and then see the changes filtering out in society. The idea, further, was that instead of rescuing some working class children from their origins through the grammar school, we should prepare them, in terms of loyalty and understanding, to stay where they were, to lead and inspire their own areas.[115]

Following the devastating fire in March 1963, Hackney Downs entered negotiations with the LCC with a view to reopening. Expecting a battle over going comprehensive, the authority's officers could not have predicted the course of events. Kemp, who was secretary to the staff common room, prepared the case for turning the grammar school into a nonselective comprehensive. This was a highly unusual move and wholly unexpected by the authority. Brearley was opposed to the proposal, but Roy Dunning who was head of modern languages and a supporter of the comprehensive principle, recognized Kemp's skill in the negotiations that followed: "He [Kemp] prepared his brief extremely well, and made it quite clear what the strengths of the school were, and what we wanted to see preserved. And what we were offering was our resources to a wider section of the community."[116]

After the fire, during the school closure that followed, the unease that some teachers felt about the cost of creaming off the ablest boys in the area came to the surface. Kemp writes, "For a time, the senior school shared premises with a half-empty, run-down secondary modern: and the H.D.S. staff could observe 'how the other half lived.' We often saw lively and alert children in a pretty depressing and limited place, and tended to say, 'We could do a lot for that kid, if only we had him at Hackney Downs.'"[117] The grammar school was exceptionally good at singling out able working-class pupils, developing their abilities and encouraging them to go on to university. However, the ending of selection meant that teachers had to adjust to a new kind of intake with pupils of different abilities, often with low levels of literacy. Perhaps the greatest barrier to progress in English toward meeting pupils' needs was the way the former grammar school teachers overlooked the language and culture of the new entry as a starting point for work in English, when the school became a comprehensive. The level and intensity of literature teaching that characterized English in our period could not be maintained although it was a while before writing displaced it as the central activity. Daily contact with pupils who made up the majority of the school age population set the grammar school teachers thinking, but it would require a radical overhaul of their whole approach before a version of English for all could become a reality.

Chapter 4

Walworth

The School

The village where the painter Samuel Palmer was born in 1805 may have been a "leafy Walworth" with which his later abode in the squalid East End was in "dismaying contrast"[1] but the Walworth in which in 1905 the London County Council (LCC) opened Mina Road Higher Grade School had long been a crowded working-class industrial district. Walworth County Secondary School,[2] the official name of its 1946 incarnation, was an "interim comprehensive school."[3] It was located on a small site between rows of houses in Mina Road, off the Old Kent Road a mile south of the Thames. The school drew its pupils from three neighboring Metropolitan Boroughs, Southwark, Camberwell, and Bermondsey. The poor but long-established population on which Walworth drew was almost entirely working class and was housed in overcrowded and rundown nineteenth-century terraces (typically two families per two-story dwelling) and twentieth-century "council" flats and houses (built by the boroughs and the LCC). There were few immigrants until the arrival in the 1950s of some Greek and Turkish Cypriot families—enough eventually to provide one or two pupils per class in Walworth School. The area had a vigorous street life, especially in its markets and pubs. The bombsites and fire service reservoirs, still widely evident even at the end of our period, provided popular, if dangerous, playgrounds. Male employment was mainly in transport (the docks and railway goods yards) and printing; female in a variety of manufacturing, including biscuit manufacture, and services.

80　English Teachers in a Postwar Democracy

A higher grade school was a selective elementary school with a vocational bias for pupils aged 12 and over, charging fees that ordinary people could afford, unlike the less affordable grammar schools. In 1911, the one in question was renamed Mina Road Central School and in the 1930s, as Walworth Central School, it took over the 1882 elementary school building next door (Figure 4.1).[4]

As explained in chapter two, although the LCC had no comprehensive schools at the end of the war, it had resolved to introduce them across the

Figure 4.1　Walworth School, 1882 building (left), craft block (right). Photo taken apparently in 1950s.

system, rejecting the Spens Report's tripartite scheme. In straitened financial conditions, however, the best that could be done was to establish in 1946 five "interim" or "experimental" comprehensives based on existing central school buildings.[5] One was to be Walworth. These would have to be smaller than was thought desirable and would lack a proper representation of the ablest children who, for the time being—those whose parents could afford the fees or who won an LCC scholarship—would continue to be recruited by the selective grammar schools. Their intake, therefore, was almost entirely of "11 plus failures," so called after the selection test taken at age 11.[6]

Research Considerations, Sources, and Methods

Several considerations determined the selection of Walworth School for a case study: its prominence from 1956 in the proceedings of the London Association for the Teaching of English (LATE); the school's close relationship with the University of London Institute of Education; the publication and widespread adoption of Walworth's course book (*Reflections*)[7]; the subsequent fame of some of the teachers; and a published novel by a pupil,[8] set in the school and neighborhood. In addition one of us (Medway) taught there at the end of our research period and had maintained useful contacts.

A large proportion of our data comes from interviews with former pupils and teachers initially selected from existing contacts and from 60 responses to an appeal on the Friends Reunited website. Postings on a blog and, later, the project's website elicited emails with information and led sometimes to extended exchanges, to written submissions, and to the loan or donation of documents. Our documentary sources include the novel already mentioned which gives a fictional account of the school; exercise books and folders of work; photographs; syllabuses, lesson notes, and mark books; meeting notes; and lists of examination results. In addition we secured some documents when the school closed prior to reopening as an "academy," including weekly staff bulletins for a number of years, school council minutes, and staff lists.[9] A key secondary source has been a 1976 dissertation by Patricia Jones[10] which draws on interviews with teachers and pupils and documents left by her aunt, effectively the first head teacher of Walworth, Anne O'Reilly.[11] In comparison with the two grammar school studies, however, we were disadvantaged by the absence of an old pupils' association that held lists of names and addresses. There is no published school history.

The School 1946–1955[12]

The head teacher initially appointed stayed only briefly. Her successor, Anne Winifrede O'Reilly (1891–1963), who took over before the end of the first year in June 1947, was considered by 1955 to have placed the school on a successful footing despite formidable difficulties. This achievement was attributable to progressive, New Education Fellowship principles combined with determination and, in apparent contradiction with her principles, an authoritarian personality. G. A. (Guy) Rogers (1919–2012), appointed as her deputy in 1952 and later as head teacher, recalled their first meeting: "After being bombarded with a torrent of words for over an hour, somehow I knew that something important had happened to me."[13]

"Some of [the experimental comprehensives] were very much more successful than others... A notable success against the odds was at Walworth where a brilliant headmistress, Miss O'Reilly, proved how much could be done under conditions that were anything but easy."[14] "[H]er coming soon resulted in the school moving in the direction advocated by the L.C.C"[15] which, as formulated by its Chief Inspector, was about developing democratic values as a counter to the threat of totalitarianism.[16]

The "umbrella phrase" that O'Reilly invented "to cover her social aims for the school" and that was picked up by the LCC Inspectors and by Harold Shearman, Chairman of the LCC Education Committee,[17] was "the Walworth Way of Life," characterized in her lectures for teachers (1956–1957) as offering what "'[t]he developing potentialities of the adolescent require, namely a rich social environment which must make provision for them to experience the democratic way of life with opportunities for the interplay of personalities, for free speech and discussion, and for the acceptance of responsibility for the well-being of the school community.'"[18] At Walworth this meant, for instance, weekly minuted form meetings. The stress on social rather than academic development is typical of LCC statements of the time.

The school became well known and by 1954–1955 was so overwhelmed with national and international visitors that O'Reilly was turning even distinguished figures away.[19] Despite never being granted a proportionate share of 11 plus passes, the school acted as if it were a full comprehensive. The curriculum, with the exception of an innovative "social studies" that replaced history and geography, was far more grammar than secondary modern in the range of academic subjects offered and in the rigor of the teaching in the academic stream. Confronted with the grammar school accusation that the comprehensive school risked sacrificing the nation's best brains to a "'post-war cult of mediocrity,'" O'Reilly could answer that

"'I've seen an academic group grow here without forcing it...We see that our best groups are stretched. Without making a great fuss, we see they get the mental discipline they need.'"[20]

In the mid-1960s, after nearly two decades under strong and progressive head teachers, not only the rhetoric but to a significant extent the staff's active commitments were still in line with the 1946 "experimental" brief that was understood to include opportunities for all, an emphasis on personal and social development, and an internationalist, democratic outlook. The school attracted and held progressively minded teachers. Walworth was well regarded locally and heavily oversubscribed, and is regularly recalled with fondness and gratitude.

English at Walworth is most readily considered under a succession of heads of department, all male: Arthur Harvey, Harold Rosen, John Dixon, and Alex McLeod.

English Under Arthur Harvey, 1949–1955

The first English teacher of whom we have substantial knowledge at Walworth is Arthur Edward Harvey (1905[21]–1981), head of English from January 1949 to June 1955,[22] who is remembered more fully than his colleagues, only one of whom, as far as we know, has survived to give his own story. Memories of Harvey's teaching are vivid, those about colleagues in his department both far less extensive and less specific; of some we know little more than their names. The pupils who Harvey taught were the older and abler classes that included most of those who would gain access to higher education and the professions.

Harvey's appointment at 44 or 45 was unconventional and has been noted[23] as typical of the boldness of O'Reilly's policies, in keeping with her understanding of the innovative purpose of the school. In the first place, Harvey had not been a teacher except for a year in a secondary modern school.[24] Secondly, he belonged to a world of high literary and theatrical culture in which the more usual ways of making a living were writing, publishing, broadcasting, and work on the stage. A published poet,[25] he moved in a world that included Louis MacNeice, W. R. Rodgers, and Dylan Thomas. Thirdly, although his Oxford degree had been in English, his life outside poetry and theater had been spent outside that discipline and, from studies at the Sorbonne and years living in France, he could just as well have been a teacher of French, of which he was in fact for a time an inspector in Northern Ireland.

Harvey's teaching was about bringing literary culture to children from an environment not normally regarded as favoring such an endeavor. His version of literary culture differed from that of the traditional grammar school, however, in its emphasis on creative writing as well as on literature and grammar. His idea of comprehensive education seems in practice to have meant giving a chance to children who had narrowly failed the 11 plus test, effectively the Walworth top stream.

From Harvey himself we have two articles[26] and a syllabus that seems so impracticable that it could hardly have been implemented except by himself with his own high-ability classes. An LCC inspection report of 1951 speaks highly of English in the school.[27] We have gathered testimony from six ex-pupils and from John Sparrow who taught with both Harvey and, briefly, his successor, Harold Rosen. One pupil whom we have interviewed, Valerie Noakes (née Avery), who returned to the school as a teacher in 1960, wrote a trilogy of novels,[28] one of them while in Harold Rosen's class, based in part on her experience of being taught by both Harvey and Rosen. We have also been able to examine the work one pupil did for Harvey over four years.[29]

Harvey's teaching is remembered as inspirational and as involving informal as well as timetabled interactions with pupils; at its core were wide exposure to literature, lively discussion in class, prolific writing at home, and formal grammar including clause analysis (Figure 4.2).

Figure 4.2 Arthur Harvey, senior English master, 1949–1955 with sixth form group.

In preparation for the O level English Literature examination he taught classic works by Shakespeare, Austen, Byron, Keats, Dickens, and Conrad. His approach was thorough and lively; he assigned characters to pupils and, in a move that became distinctive of Walworth teaching,

> Elicited comments to get us to relate what we read to personal experience. So the first question on beginning to read *Pride and Prejudice* was something like "Have you ever heard a woman talk as much as Mrs Bennett?" He pretended to think that Lear's daughters' cruelty was impossibly exaggerated, so that we would give him similar examples of cruelty in families, daughters and sons to parents and vice-versa, that were within our experience. He'd then get us to write about them.[30]

Books read in class before the examination year reflected available school editions, though Harvey seems to have ignored the reputable children's literature titles being published from the late 1940s.

In his efforts to persuade his pupils to read he would go far beyond the literary canon and school texts, reading aloud extracts from Simenon (Maigret), Micky Spillane and Hank Jansen, as well as nonfiction works by Beatrice Webb, Rachel Carson, and Margaret Mead.[31] He took pupils to Foyles second-hard department and in the club that he ran after school Harvey claims that pupils discussed Dickens alongside Joyce Cary, Thackeray alongside Nigel Balchin and Angela Thirkell and Margery Allingham alongside Steinbeck and Emily Bronte, though we have no independent pupil accounts of these gatherings.[32]

Harvey's syllabus gives a list of recommended fiction authors of whom Forster and Wells are the most recent, including a subset from whom "Every pupil should have read at least one book before leaving school": Thackeray, Mrs Gaskell, Hardy, Trollope, Stevenson, Kipling, Lamb, Dickens, Austen, Wilkie Collins, Emily Bronte, Jefferies (novels of rural life), Scott, Charlotte Bronte, George Eliot, and Lewis Carroll.[33] What the other teachers read in class with their lower stream and younger classes is largely unknown.

With Harvey, "[we] wrote constantly, in class and out of class, and the 'best' pieces were pinned to the notice board in the corridor."[34] In his articles Harvey expressed a belief in writing as a vehicle for imaginative and emotional development. One reported approach (later described by Harold Rosen as the "bolt from the blue"[35]) was simply to throw out a title: "The Redheaded Man with a Glass Eye,"[36] "Dick Shottat Gets the Diamonds,"[37] "My Wild White Cat"[38] . . . "When we said we didn't know how to start, he said, 'Just write something like "Sausages and Eggs" and go on from there. It'll come.'"[39] Or the subject might arise from a text being studied, such as Gray's 'Elegy': "The composition title he set...was simply: 'Full many a flower is born to blush unseen/And waste its sweetness on the desert air.'"[40] This strikes us as very much the traditional grammar school approach that was discouraged by HMI.[41] According to the pupil who has kept her English exercise book, Harvey's practice was to assign each week a choice of five or six titles[42]; one set (undated) that she wrote down is "Down the river," "Sly as a fox," "Poetry," "Speed," "Papering a room," "Tobacco," and "Spending"; two other sets are quotations from texts being studied, mainly Shakespeare. Other remembered topics related specifically to the pupils' local experience: "Conversation in the fish and chip shop," "At the barber's," "The Nightwatchman," "Guy Fawkes – letting off fireworks," "Observing the weather through the front room window," "Lamp posts," and "Waiting outside the pub."[43]

Qualities Harvey valued in writing are said to have been observation ("He got us to see the Thames in different lights, related this to The Waste Land, and encouraged us to look at the river from the bridges"[44]) and original figurative language, such as "Sun in a mist, like an orange in a fried fish shop"[45] from Joyce Cary's *The Horse's Mouth*:

> Arthur was excited by vivid language, so he was fired into injecting it into his Head of Department meetings and his classes. I think the ice "cracking and growling" in The Ancient Mariner raised his emotional blood pressure just like the...Joyce Cary, and I would bet his classes came away on those mornings in a state of euphoria.[46]

Two of Harvey's pupils won literary competitions in national journals.[47]

Little of the values and enthusiasm ascribed to Harvey is apparent in the work that a member of the top group did for him and that nevertheless attracted his favorable evaluation (a grade or brief comment). It strikes us as run-of-the-mill writing typical of many schools in the period. Almost none of it displays sharp observation of particulars, freshness of language, or frank expression of the writer's feelings and states of mind. In the whole collection only one piece seems unequivocally to relate to a specific experience, a second year account of having her hair shampooed with a bottle of beer stolen from her father.

As reported in chapter two, the teaching of grammar was a cause of contention and generally in decline in our period. Neither applies in the case of Harvey, an enthusiast for clause analysis. Ridout's series[48] was used for comprehension and précis.

Frequently remembered are Harvey's meetings with a favored (male) group after school in the Quick Service Café[49] on the Old Kent Road, a gathering whose formal title was the Manuscript Club.[50] (The biology teacher was the focus of an alternative, perhaps opposed, group in a café across the street.⁵¹) Visits by Louis MacNeice and W. R. Rodgers are recorded.⁵²

Harvey favored free oral exchange in the classroom, assisted by his remarkable rapport with pupils: "He came in, he had a sort of magnetism, and he started asking them questions...and as soon as he got an answer from someone he plunged to one of the others and said, Is that right? Do you agree with that? He had them all arguing like hell within three minutes. It was the way, when he went into a class they were instantly listening, they were there, in the presence. Oh, it was uncanny, uncanny."⁵³

As head of department Harvey was unsatisfactory: "...he didn't give you stuff to work with...so you really had to sort it out for yourself...He was a hopeless organizer...He had no idea what books there were there, I don't think he cared."⁵⁴ He deserved credit on the other hand "for pushing the dept. into loosening up our attitudes to pupil expression. In his departmental meetings he introduced lots of ideas."⁵⁵

Harvey's contemporary as head of mathematics (1949–1952) has left an account of her activities in that role.⁵⁶ The comparison shows what one teacher dedicated to the comprehensive idea thought needed to be done and Harvey conspicuously didn't. Mathematics was not the only subject, she says, to have arrived at a common curriculum for all abilities; she led her own team toward it by a process of consensus arrived at in discussion meetings.

Harvey's philosophy, as he expounds it on paper, is hard to take seriously; the following is typical:

> Intolerance between social groups within a community, between nations, between races...will continue to move inevitably to destruction until creative artists of all kinds, by demonstrating their truth, with all the immense drive at their command, arrest the movement and turn it into constructive channels. The teacher has to be an artist and not just a craftsman. Only the teacher-artist is capable of experiment and of seeing "the truth within his pupils." ⁵⁷

Harvey succeeded in his aim of gaining academic success for "11 plus failures": exactly what an insecure new "experimental" school needed, despite its emphasis on primarily social aims:

> So, he certainly put Walworth on the map as a place where if you went to learn English you would do well. No question about that...at least 12 or 14 of his pupils...left school...went on eventually to do teacher training.⁵⁸

He was an inspiring sixth-form literature teacher and seems to have indeed created a culture of literary aspiration down the Old Kent Road, with certain pupils meeting poets and novelists, winning literary prizes, and ostentatiously carrying copies of Dostoevsky to the gatherings in the café.[59] His exceptional abilities, combined with the idealistic and romantic aspirations expressed in his (hopelessly unrealistic) syllabus, seem to have enabled him to implement a program that would have been beyond the reach of most teachers.

This program was far, however, from being the potential "common curriculum" that was sought elsewhere in London and, in the next period, in Walworth itself. What Harvey wanted for pupils beyond the top stream is far from clear. His ideas had no influence on the English profession in London. "Arthur was not so much like a spearhead for a different English, but more like a non-religious Christ figure sending out missionaries and converts."[60]

Harvey left for a headship in Essex in summer 1955 at the same time as O'Reilly retired, so that the next head of department came in January 1956 into the new regime of Guy Rogers.[61]

Of the members of Harvey's department John Sparrow has told us something of his own teaching, which was clearly inventive and effective once he got established, but we know little of his colleagues' work. Mr Hall was regarded as "boring" by Valerie Noakes but as kind and uncondescending by others.[62] Alex McLeod and Judith Wild (now Richards; she mainly taught social studies) were New Zealanders. The Scottish teacher Pip Porchetta came in 1953 and stayed until retirement in 1976. J. V. (Gus) Grealy (1954–1958) is fondly remembered, particularly for his drama productions, though no details emerge, and Guy Rogers, the head, taught some O level English effectively.

Drama was important in the school throughout our period. It had been there from the start.[63] The LCC inspectors reported that "lively and original class-room plays were seen in a first-year class" in 1951[64]; John Sparrow wrote a play[65] for lower school pupils; and the weekly staff bulletins indicate a thriving tradition of lower school dramatic performances. Some productions took place in public halls, sometimes within drama festivals organized by the local authorities.[66] Harvey was producing Shaw's *St Joan* when he left. In and after Harvey's time visits to the Old Vic[67] for productions of Shakespeare and other classics were frequent. There was as yet no sign of improvised drama as a part of English lessons

English Under Harold Rosen, 1956–1958

Harold Rosen was appointed in January 1956 and stayed until July 1958. The fact that we were able to interview him before he died in 2008 adds a dimension of understanding that we lack for Arthur Harvey. While both were inspiring teachers committed to comprehensive schools,[68] what emerges most forcibly is a sense of how they were different, as people and as teachers and heads of department.

Rosen was a Jewish East End scholarship boy from a poor working-class family; pupils who Rosen took over from Harvey found him a more "ordinary" person who they could imagine playing football with his sons.[69] His university was London and he was an intellectual in a way that Harvey was not, with a literary sensibility that embraced European as well as British literature. He was a member of the Communist Party from his schooldays and this, combined with his own experience at school as a "troublesome boy"[70] patronized by teachers with his Jewish peers, determined his attitude to his pupils in Walworth: on the one hand, commitment to the educability of the working class ("if you can't do something with working-class kids it isn't worthwhile doing. Because they are the hope")[71] and on the other a refusal to conform to the stereotype of communist teachers "as rather stern disciplinarians" for whom working-class culture was no culture at all.

After teacher education at the Institute of Education and military service he taught in a number of grammar schools in Middlesex for 12 or more years and was a founder member of LATE. At Walworth he took seriously the head of department's responsibility to promote the work of the whole department, supplying ideas and detailed help (and taking stocktaking seriously) (Figure 4.3).[72]

Rosen produced a syllabus in 1958 and here we are in a different world from Harvey's.[73] His ideas about English strongly influenced both his successors at Walworth and other teachers in LATE, where they were consistent with the arguments that James Britton and Nancy Martin were putting forward. From the time of Rosen's appointment developments in Walworth were part of a larger, London-wide, experimental scene, the focus of which was LATE. Asked about the effect on his work at Walworth of his membership of LATE, Rosen told us

> Yes, that was LATE, and quite often I took something that someone had outlined and tried it out, or adapted it, for Walworth. So there is no doubt about it, the sense of solidarity. Prior to Walworth there was a terrible sense of isolation... we could help each other, that's the point.[74]

In a strikingly unconventional declaration for 1958, produced just before he left Walworth, Rosen opens his syllabus with the core principle that the pupils' language and the pupils' experience need to be the inseparable starting points.

Figure 4.3 Harold Rosen directing school play, 1956–1958.

> The teaching of English at Walworth calls for a sympathetic understanding of the pupils' environment and temperament. Their language experience is acquired from their environment and from communication with the people who mean most to them. This highly localized language is likely to stand out in their own minds in strong contrast to the language experience being consciously presented in the framework of English lessons in particular, and school work in general. This contrast can all too easily become a conflict, "aversion to poshness" and affectation can easily bedevil the teaching of English. Whatever language the pupils possess, it is this which must be built on rather than driven underground. However narrow the experience of our pupils may be (and it is often wider than we think), it is this experience alone which has given their language meaning. The starting point for English work must be the ability to handle effectively their own experience. Oral work, written work and the discussion of literature must create an atmosphere in which the pupils become confident of the full acceptability of the material of their own experience.[75]

That this is only the "starting point" becomes clear as he goes on: "I just felt that running through what most of us [in LATE] were trying to do was, I remember the phrase...being hospitable to their experience. Not being...anchored in it. But there is no other place to begin."[76] The journey outward from familiar experience and language leads to both "a sort of alien world"—an experience of "foreignness" and "strangeness"[77]—and, in the end, a more "complex form of speech and writing."[78] In the end there could be intellectual breakthrough, a transition into rationality, and a reasoned public discourse, especially its written modes.

Rosen was interested in and appreciated working-class language. Working-class people, for whom argumentative and reflective modes are rarely "well-trodden paths,"[79] "make narrative do a lot of work," which is why Walworth children "took to narrative like ducks to water.[80] So his syllabus specifies that narrative should dominate the writing program in the first and second years, and only in the fourth year should teachers attempt "to steer pupils away from writing solely in narrative." This principle remained a foundation stone of Walworth English for the remainder of our period and contrasts with whatever assumptions underlay Harvey's practice when a high proportion of his assignments involved not the narration of something that happened but the generalized discussion of a topic "as if they were addressing the civilized world".[81]

On spoken language, while fully acknowledging the need for pupils to progress to a language "that...is intelligible to the widest sections of the community" and conforms to "nationally accepted standards of speech and writing,"[82] he is clear about the first priority:

> The teacher at Walworth will inevitably feel a conflict between the lively but often barbaric expression of the pupils and the need to inculcate standards of acceptability...the wish to say something and communicate it should always be seen as basic, and therefore sincerity is the first standard to apply.[83]

When it comes to that more public language that is the eventual aim, the "standards" he refers to "are only part of a complex form of speech and writing. The desire to use this form and understand it must be built up."[84] It is far more than a matter of avoiding error and observing conventions; it means coming to hold the purposes and envisaging the sort of communicative relations that those complex forms evolved to serve.

In an article he wrote on writing while at Walworth Rosen urges, "Keep sending them home—to mum, to dad, to the family; at meals, quarrelling, having a laugh, getting up, going out, buying something." The rationale is straightforward; the article is entitled "What shall I set?" and this is the simplest way to get language going: "Because they know and feel about these things they have the language to write about them. The springs of language are being tapped."[85]

"The ability to handle their own experience" meant in practice a thematic approach and so his syllabus suggested "some possible themes that most of the work could be based on."[86] Topics are listed for each year, organized under themes: under "Out of School," for instance, "Out with the family"; under "The Street," "Someone moves in"; under "Persons, Places, Things," "People observed – a docker, a teacher, a conductress, etc."

Rosen's approach involved consulting pupils' interests and enthusiasms, not by asking them but by trying a range of things and seeing what worked. Thus he discovered that "Dickens is their author" and they "take to" certain of Shakespeare's plays, like *Antony and Cleopatra* (which he produced, with a troublesome girl in the lead role), and not to others.[87] Given the limitations of what was available in school editions in the mid-1950s Rosen found it necessary to draw on texts that no English teacher would have studied at college or university, including European works and adult novels never intended for a juvenile readership. Examples of the former are works by Maxim Gorki[88] and *The Good Soldier Schweik* and of the latter Greene's novel, *The Quiet American*, with which he satisfied, from his own collection, a pupil who denied that anything in the class library could ever interest him.

Taking the pupils' experience as the essential starting point meant using it to help them make sense of potentially off-putting texts:

> So we would take all the scenes from Julius Caesar which were about the lads, you know, the lynching of Cinna, "tear him for his verses," and it's a gang, very recognizable for them, and once I had put them in that direction, they could find similar situations.[89]

Rosen concedes the usefulness of textbooks but knows none that are satisfactory: "Ideally teachers should duplicate material needed in class, but it is recognized that difficulties often prevent this."[90] A current popular textbook already in the school with which Rosen was dissatisfied was Ridout.[91] He persuaded County Hall to take them back and in return supply some new poetry anthologies. (His successor, however, claims to remember Ridout as still being there when he came, and disposing of them himself.)

A striking feature of Rosen's syllabus is the format he proposes for the pupils' thematic written work:

> [W]hat I wanted [the staff] to do was get kids freed from their exercise books, those terrible books, and to get them making books instead, of a whole term's work. And quite a few of us...did that. And I can remember

we had a parents' day at the end of the first term, and every kid had on their desk a book that they had made. And it could be all the written work that they'd set them, poems they liked, diary entries, a real sort of medley, if you like, and needless to say, they decorated them.[92]

In the syllabus he refers to these collections as "magazines," of which the contents would be "best" work, "written up" from regular composition pieces, which pupils would have an incentive to correct and improve.[93] "Strong emphasis...on presentation, illustration, etc...should be linked with the fact that the magazines are intended for circulation." Progression involves, in the second year, more "re-shaping, pruning, re-writing" and inclusion of dialogue, which in the fourth year will involve "much more adult themes" and "efforts...to steer pupils away from writing solely in narrative."

When it came to grammar, Rosen was far from being a true believer like Harvey.

The place of Grammar in the secondary school syllabus is a matter of violent controversy. This syllabus does not pretend to solve the problem. It represents an uneasy compromise between certain modern trends in the teaching of Grammar, and the demands of various public examinations. It is not included in the belief that it is a means of correcting common errors, which must be treated as they arise.[94]

"Serious and regular treatment" of spelling was required.[95] Quite unlike the impression commonly given of "progressive" English teaching in the 1960s and 1970s, Rosen and his successors took the technical aspects of English very seriously.

There are no vivid pupil recollections of Rosen's teaching but a student teacher observed a lesson with a low-ability group:

[T]he door would come open, and there'd be Harold, all goggly-eyed, looking around, and slightly smiley, as though, "Right chaps, now we'll get going!" And it was amazing...Basically he got them...I can't sort of imitate, but he said– [I] want to talk about, we are going to talk about today...your neighborhood, where you live, who are the people you know, the neighbors who come in, all these kinds of things, the interaction with people, you and the neighborhood. And these kids were absolutely jumping with stories about the people who lived...And the lesson was packed with the excitement of all this experience that they had. It was wonderful, and then, of course, eventually, they wrote up their pieces, we heard their pieces, and it was astounding to me.[96]

Of Harvey's former department, Judith Wild and Alex McLeod continued under Rosen. Pip Porchetta stayed for the rest of her career, John Sparrow and Mr Hall for a few more months. A significant new arrival was Andrew Salkey, a black Caribbean writer and poet[97] who regularly broadcast on the BBC World Service. Although a well-liked and effective English teacher who changed racial stereotypes in some pupils' minds, he opted before long for writing over teaching, to the disappointment of his colleagues.

The cases of Harvey and Rosen throw up an interesting issue about interpreting the data. If we were going solely by the two teachers' writing from the time, and particularly their syllabuses, Rosen would appear immeasurably superior on almost every count, an evaluation that would be confirmed by his impressive interviews. From Harvey we have no interview, but we do have a substantial body of pupil testimony on the strength of his teaching. While the one set of pupil work we have seen hardly corroborates that testimony, his undoubted achievements in getting pupils into teacher training colleges and instilling a lifelong love of literature support it. For Rosen, who was of course there for only two years and two terms as against six years, we have been able to recover no pupil work and very little pupil testimony of substance. When we examine the powerful sense we have of Rosen's effectiveness, we have to ask as researchers whether in the end that is based on anything much beyond his own words and our knowledge of his later distinguished contribution. We are still hoping that his pupils will come forward and supply the sort of memories and saved work that will enable us to make up our minds with some confidence.

The School 1958–1965

In 1959, the school began to receive its share of "grammar school" pupils, although only 10 percent in the area reached the standard, rather than the 20 percent who the school would have been allowed to accept. Streaming was reduced to a threefold division, 1:4:1, the minimum in view of "the number of young, inexperienced teachers who had to be recruited every year."[98]

In 1962, Walworth amalgamated with Nelson secondary modern school, taking over its pupils (third year—age 13, and older), its building a mile away that became the lower school, and some staff, including an English teacher, Brenda Harvey. The intake increased from six forms to eight.

English Under Dixon and McLeod, 1959–1965

By the time Harold Rosen was about to leave he had got to know John Dixon through LATE and suggested he apply for the job. Dixon took over in January 1959. With his arrival we can plausibly speak for the first time of English as being developed by the department rather than simply its head. For this period we have more knowledge of other teachers, and so need say less about Dixon's own teaching. We also have a substantial body of pupils' work.

While Dixon's biography and previous (and subsequent) career are of great interest, it will suffice here to record that from being a scholarship boy in a small Cumberland grammar school, he had gone in 1951 from Oxford, military service and the Institute of Education to Holloway Boys Grammar School, an LCC school that became comprehensive in 1955. Over the following four years before moving to Walworth Dixon learned alongside colleagues how, in particular, to teach the "secondary modern pupils" and contributed to developing a common syllabus for all streams, a process undertaken by several departments. [99] Where Rosen had been a communist, Dixon was, in his own words, "an active member of a strong group of Labour [Party] Teachers in London, in my case radicalized by my experience of the Holloway boys, the inadequacy of their curriculum and their environment, and also by the fallacies of 11 plus selection."[100]

Teachers in the second half of the 1950s were operating in a changed climate that created exciting new visions for those who were attuned to it and perhaps sharpened the divide between them and the others who lacked that awareness. Politically the shocks of Suez and Hungary (1956) had undermined both nationalistic assumptions about the scope and virtuous role of British power, with educational consequences for attitudes to celebrations of the "great British story," and left-wing convictions about the USSR as a model. Both may have enhanced the attractiveness of working with the strengths and culture of British working people and their daily lives, a turn that was reinforced by a range of cultural developments including, as two Walworth teachers have told us, the British documentaries being shown at the National Film Theatre (including Karel Reitz's, *We are the Lambeth Boys*), plays about working-class life at the Royal Court Theatre, planning ideas in the *Architectural Review*, new painting and photography at the Institute of Contemporary Arts, research by the Institute of Community Studies into East London people and the meetings around the *Universities and Left Review*.[101]

Under John Dixon and his successor Alex McLeod the department became more cohesive, not least with the appointment of two committed new teachers,[102] with two more joining later. Individual initiatives led to intensive collaborative development and innovation. A common approach was developed by Dixon and his newer colleagues, although others, while not hostile, remained unpersuaded.

Of the newcomers, Leslie Stratta was a working-class Londoner who had been a mature student at training college, while Simon Clements—public school and history at Oxford—was appointed by Guy Rogers on one day's notice each way; he stayed six years, one more than Stratta. Valerie Noakes, who as Valerie Avery had been a pupil of Harvey and Rosen, came from Goldsmiths College in 1960. Charles Stuart Jervis, after six months in the school, was sent by Rogers in 1961 to work in the Nelson for a year to prepare for amalgamation. He identified Brenda Harvey as a teacher who should be invited to join Walworth, which she did in 1962 (thus finally bringing about a reasonable balance of men and women in the department); he left in summer 1963 while she stayed for the rest of her career, gaining respect and affection for her strict but inspiring teaching and her drama productions. Of teachers continuing from earlier periods, Pip Porchetta, while disagreeing with Dixon's wish to reduce grammar to a minimum, was respected by colleagues for her dedication and humanity.

Although not part of Dixon's team until the final six months before taking over as head of department, Alex McLeod can be mentioned here. He first came to Walworth in 1952, returned to New Zealand from 1958 to January 1963 and then rejoined the staff, to succeed Dixon that September. Despite the five-year gap he is a crucial figure in the development of Walworth English, respecting Harvey and becoming Rosen's key ally and the exponent of a distinctively "Walworth" pedagogy that he resumed and developed on his return.

In what became an exceptionally strong department, the innovative core was Dixon, Stratta, and Clements. According to Dixon a new syllabus (which has not been found) resulted from a series of department meetings, one of which (in the summer holidays) drew up the fourth-year course, the materials from which were published in 1963 as *Reflections* with comments and suggestions for work in an accompanying *Teacher's Book*. Dixon explains that while he and Clements had much to learn about South London working-class pupils, Stratta "felt for working-class kids directly in a way that we couldn't"[103] and while he and Stratta were pedagogically cautious, Clements was a risk-taking innovator, spontaneously deciding, for instance, to ask Rogers if he could produce *Twelfth Night* after seeing it at the Old Vic and making a film with a third-year class.[104] Clements learned many things from Stratta including, from observation, how to write words and phrases on the blackboard while a class discussion was progressing, as notes of emerging themes and ideas, and then to ask: "What have we got here? What does this add up to?" thus leading the class into more abstract and general reflections and preparing the ground for writing—an example of the department's stress on intellectual as well as purely literary development (Figure 4.4).[105] This new style of intradepartmental cooperation was crucial to Walworth's development. Clements says, "I have often thought of my years at Walworth"—involvement with the department and, beyond it, LATE and the Institute of Education—"as a second university."[106] The department felt excitement and pride at what was being achieved, and a sense of possibilities yet to be realized. Listening to tapes of young children at an LATE meeting, Dixon says—in a remark that could stand for the spirit of the new approach to English—"We thought, 'Good God, what are we doing in school? We've got these amazing kids.'"[107]

As the department's work developed over several years and was recognized in London, "Walworth English" became a substantial reality and the significant increase in surviving pupil work enables us to describe its distinctive features with some confidence, begin to evaluate its significance, and identify where it came from.

Figure 4.4 Simon Clements supervises his third-year class while they film a bombsite scene for their "Two Bob's Worth of Trouble" in 1962.

There are difficulties in evaluating the Walworth achievement. Although the unreliability of the 11 plus assessment meant some children in top streams might as easily have ended up in grammar schools, where we know something in general about the English teaching, there is little evidence of what most would have experienced if they had gone to secondary modern schools. Comparison with grammar school achievement is made difficult by the fact that many Walworth children left school at the end of the term in which they were 15, which might mean Christmas in the fourth year, while only around half stayed into a fifth year (though 60% was achieved in a good year) and many fewer again for a sixth.

Rosen's vision of the English curriculum became a reality and the fragmented English of traditional textbooks, exercises, essays, and literature, organized as unconnected elements, was replaced by a three-part simplification: spoken language (including improvised drama), written language, and literature. These would often flow into each other without clear demarcation. Moreover,

> So far as writing is concerned we had moved a step on from Harold [Rosen], by proposing that writing over a term or year should have continuities – like the Charlie/Eleanor stories in the first year [see later in this chapter], or the human themes from the fourth on. By selecting those themes...we'd given a kind of unity to a variety of thinking, investigating, talking and writing, which could stretch on for a month or more. That was a very significant break away from the current models. It all coheres, I believe.[108]

As always, however, innovatory impulses came up against the inherited book stock and lack of money. While it appears no new textbooks were ordered by Dixon and McLeod (except *Reflections*, considered a "course book" rather than a textbook), books recorded by Rosen and others as still held in 1958 included one entitled *Précis and Comprehension* (which could be either of two publications from 1947 and 1953),[109] O'Malley and Thompson's *English Three*,[110] and Ridout's *English Today*, Books 2–4, bought but eventually mistrusted by Harvey, though still in use in Rosen's time at least by supply teachers. In the 1960s two books rated highly by teachers were in use: Cedric Austin's *Read to Write*, with its integrated approach that Dixon had found useful at Holloway, and Nancy Martin's book of comprehension passages, *Understanding and Enjoyment*.[111]

A poetry book recalled as in use in the 1950s was Methuen's *An Anthology of Modern Verse*.[112] This had been up-to-date when it was published in 1921, with a heavy representation of Georgians (De La Mare, Davies) but also Yeats, First World War poets and even T. S. Eliot. For one pupil in later years the gateway to poetry was opened with a lasting impact by a collection bought by Dixon or McLeod, the *Albemarle Book of Modern Verse*.[113]

The place of spoken language—"talk"—was prized as it had been under Rosen: "before they're thoroughly impregnated with literary texts—so impregnated with them that it is second nature to them—then their natural resource is their oral language and that will show through and it should be really the basis from which they start."[114] The concept of working-class children from families with little education coming to school with resources rather than a deficit to be remedied was distinctive of the new English developed at Walworth and in LATE.

Discussion lessons, the value of which was discovered by Dixon at Holloway, became a special accomplishment of Walworth English teachers. As Clements explains it,

> I think I knew that the children had experience, which our job as a teacher would be, if you like, to get it out of them. So if a boy or girl started talking…you would go on [i.e. stay with that pupil, not move on to someone else]. And I was actually having to learn to develop a skill of…the nearest I have come to it is…radio interviewers who…have been amazing at getting stories out of people…So that the English lesson would be that suddenly a clue came, there was an experience: "Come on, Peter, tell me more. Where were you?" And so you started to fill in…and then you were watching the rest of the class to see that they were listening. And usually they were, because it was a child talking…And I hadn't made it a philosophy, but somewhere I knew that that is what mattered.[115]

From the pupil's point of view the experience might be as follows (this example from Alex McLeod's fourth- and fifth-year teaching):

> He never treated us as children, or teenagers, he just talked to us like we were young men and women, which led to discussions, and sometimes it could be uproarious – some people had a lot to say! – but he would involve us, he would make us look at something and think about it, he would ask questions, searching questions, he would ask you to think about things, and it was just so completely different.[116]

Part of the spoken language experience was improvised drama, an impetus for which came from a demonstration at LATE by a junior school teacher with his pupils. Dixon recalls two of his first-year pupils "doing the Deputy Head…interviewing them" for admission to the school, and a boy on the way to the hall for a drama lesson asking if they could act Beowulf which they had been reading—Dixon had to improvise in a hurry. "And that was my first awakening to the fact that actually the things you are reading in literature are probably going to be jolly good things for moving into your improvised drama as well [as the pupils' experience]."[117]

Progression in the curriculum for writing, with spoken language activity around it, followed Rosen's syllabus in being based on themes that lent themselves in the earlier stages to descriptive and imaginative work that drew heavily on everyday experiences of people and situations, and in the later ones to more generalized reflection on social issues. Throughout, it was the "personal voice" that was sought, the sense that it was the pupil's own experience, thoughts, and responses that were being put into words.

The elements of a pupil's typical writing curriculum were as follows.

First-year pupils wrote pieces describing familiar scenes such as the family watching television or "The Tramp." After perhaps a term they embarked on a series of "Charlie stories" about "a kid from the area," male or female, who is "meaning well but always getting into trouble...you'd have Charlie up the park, Charlie mucking about on the canal."[118] After being marked, with some read out and discussed in class, the stories were copied into a special book with contents page and illustrations.

A pupil in Robert Thornbury's first-year "remedial" (bottom stream) class wrote "Charlie got a job":

> One day when Charlie was laying about indoors his mother said:
> "Why don't you go and get yourself a job instead of laying about indoors all the time?"
> So Charlie said: "I'll think about it."
> "Yes," said his mother, "that's all you ever do is think, isn't it?"
> So Charlie got up from the settee and put on his coat and said:
> "Oh well, I might as well go and try to get a suitable job."
> Soon after, his mother went down the market as it was Saturday. As she was walking down the market, to her astonishment she saw Charlie working on a vegetable stall. She went up to Charlie and said: "Can I have 4lb of potatoes and 2lb of greens?"
> Charlie took the money and gave her the same amount of change! Then she went home.
> When Charlie got home that evening, his mother said, "Good boy, son."
> Charlie said: "Yes, and I get three pounds–and it's only for the weekends."[119]

This is the piece referred to by Thornbury when he says the potential for "succinctness, conceptual adroitness" in language needed only to be triggered "under pressure and emotion," so that it can be left unspoken that Charlie let his mother get away without paying.[120]

Second-year work was serial stories which by 1963–1964 had settled on "The Street," about the characters and families in a street of a type familiar from everyday experience. The connection is evident with the village projects described in Hackney Downs (chapter three) but the implicit acknowledgment—finally!—that the pupils' environment was urban not rural is significant, though so is another switch from writing from imagination about lives you don't know about to describing ones you do. Development from the first year seems, in work we have seen from a very able class, to have been away from picaresque into sharper social and psychological observation. Thus in one chapter the mother of a mentally handicapped teenage son tries to comfort a pregnant neighbor whose baby is expected to be similarly disadvantaged; other episodes are knockabout comedy though with accurately represented dialogue, like the family in which the father is looking forward to a betting shop opening in the street and the mother puts him right on his anticipation of gambling the housekeeping money.

The core of third-year written work seems to have been a novel. The pupil whose second-year serial on the street we have just described went on in the third year to write a story in chapters, "Black Coffee," in which she takes on the persona of an 18-year-old who has left home and is at work north of the river; little of the situation described is drawn from experience of the social world she knew at first hand. Her teacher, Brenda Harvey, came from a different background from the "core" of teachers who were there when she arrived, with her own sense of what was important, and it is hard to know how far her colleagues would have agreed with fostering this sort of departure from the pupils' direct experience.

The fourth-year course was drafted in the summer of 1960 and began to be taught by a strong year team "with a cohesive feeling."[121] While half the time is said to have been devoted, as it was throughout the years, to "poems, plays and novels,"[122] the other half was based on social themes drawing on sources from pupils' own experience (parents and teenagers) and that of the sort of people they knew or were aware of (old people) to newspapers and television and thence to public issues such as crime, war, and world peace, an approach that gave scope for a "movement between concrete experiences and more generalized discussion."[123] The social themes material was eventually published in 1963 as *Reflections*, and reprinted twice in 1964.[124]

In Shayer's history[125] the authors of *Reflections* are implied to be acting as "part-time sociologists," "absorbing English work into an unholy alliance with the social sciences." If Dewey, arguing for "knowledge of society, its structures and workings," had insisted on the equal "importance of imaginative experience," some recent English work including *Reflections* had neglected the latter in favor of the former.[126] This, however, misunderstands *Reflections* in more than one way. While it is true that, as Robert Thornbury recently pointed out, the section headings were not unlike those of a first-year sociology textbook and the book could be said to be "raising consciousness, sociologically," social studies at Walworth "wasn't sociologically alert"[127] (it was simply combined history and geography) and an educational gap existed, which any politically conscious English teacher would have seen as needing to be addressed. More relevantly to Shayer's criticism, however, a glance at the Teacher's Book[128] or at pupils' fourth-year English folders will reveal that there was plenty of imaginative work, particularly the writing of stories; what *Reflections* did, moreover, was nothing like social science (which in any case was rarely available in schools as a subject)—both in the sense that it dealt with the experience and texture of everyday life, not least through imaginative work, and in the sense that it paid less regard than sociology to academic knowledge and concepts; if there was a possible criticism it would be a quite different one from Shayer's, that imagining what it would be like to be a soldier in X war was no substitute for historical knowledge about the war; it was precisely the absence of a social science grounding that might be seen as the problem. In fact the authors' mission as set out in the Teacher's Book leans far more toward moral than sociological education.

The book was innovative in several ways: in the quality of its production (good paper, typography, and photographs) and the absence from the main text of the customary comprehension exercises and instruction about usage.[129] Only about half the writing was literary in nature, the rest being by specialists in disciplines such as planning, cultural and media commentators, and journalists. Testifying to its influence, Geoffrey Summerfield commented that no upper school English course could now justifiably neglect "social themes." *Reflections* "has been followed by a motley crowd of imitators, most of which have been strenuously camouflaged to ensure that they do not fall prey to the odium that attaches to the unabashed text-book"—an odium to which the Walworth book had been a large contributor.[130]

Fifth-year and sixth-form work was partly determined by the syllabuses for public examinations, but staff had "a freer rein [with] the large group of non-GCE candidates" with whom *Reflections* approaches could sometimes be continued.[131]

Class and school magazines reveal that poems, not necessarily related to the themes, were also being written in all years (and certainly featured largely toward the end of our period). Many involved rhyme (rarely handled with skill). A frequent preference was for dramatic or enactive presentations through syntactically simple clauses, one per short line, conveying a single experience or impression in rhetorically heightened or portentous form. Some more literary third- and fourth-year pupils wrote what is thought of as typically adolescent verse, sometimes on postapocalyptic themes ("Has all that, too, departed...?")[132]; some intensely imagined narratives and vignettes are laid out as verse for no obvious reason or apparently because that lent an air of significance and licensed an escape from everyday speech patterns into high-flown statements that would otherwise have come across as pretentious. Poems often have one feature evidently identified with "poetry" such as rhyme, linear structure, or frequency of adjectives and adverbs while conveying little sense of being poetry.

The most sophisticated poems comprised page-long stretches of blank verse, often in three or four sections, with lines of varying length some of which were in effect prose with an extra charge of figurative language (adjectives, adverbs, and similes); others were Whitmanesque or Lawrentian ("Snake") in their attempts to capture a single sight or feeling or impression. A fourth-year poem, "The Bombsite," that, though the lines are not long, represents the genre at its most developed begins "Out of a wood of flowering hawthorn/Rose a chimney."[133]

A problem with interpreting adolescent poetry, however, as Michael Baldwin pointed out in 1962, is that young people who eventually turn out to be good poets go—necessarily, it seems—through many experimental iterations, some of them highly derivative of a genre or a particular poet, the results of which can often seem simply bad.[134] Another is that a poem may have met a personal need without being good poetry. Poetrywriting is an area to which conventional ideas of "standards" seem particularly ill-suited. The writing of pupils of 13 and above, not just poetry, can afford a vehicle in which to explore the adolescent state, very much in line, in Walworth's case, with the personal development aims of both the school and its English teaching (as laid out in the *Teacher's Book* for *Reflections*). Thus Brenda Ives' short poem "The Sea and Him,"[135] in which the poet watches a small boy "lost in his wonder-world/Alone, all alone on the breakwater...It's just the sea and him," seems to be savoring the writer's leaving behind of childhood. Robert Long in "Friends and Foes" rebukes human folly as if from a view outside humanity.[136] (It must also be said that there are instances of the type of knowing and whimsical writing that Walworth teachers associated with grammar schools: "This genial mortal [the conductor of the "omnibus"] will approach you and render the traditional grunt, which is the cue for the passenger to state his fare."[137] This ran, of course, exactly counter to that "sincerity" that Rosen had stressed in his syllabus and that Dixon and colleagues valued as a personal voice coming through.)

The *Reflections* course, beside its social and moral awareness aims, sought to develop competence in reflective and argumentative writing. This was demonstrably achieved with at least some pupils, as for instance in the third- and fourth-year work that the top stream pupil showed us, and was in the process of happening also in some writing from slightly lower groups.

Teachers would use a lesson between the writing of first and second versions to give pupils the chance to listen to examples of each other's writing and to promote critical reflection. Dixon learned how to make the handing-back lesson effective:

> But anyway, they'd do these pieces and you'd have probably a whole lesson for handing back…And I used to read paragraphs or sometimes whole sections…and then I'd say, "What do you think?" And they'd say, "That's good." And I'd say, "Can you tell me three things you particularly liked, or three things you particularly remember?" So I was building up this notion that they are becoming the appreciative critics of their own writing…the idea of self-evaluation and group evaluation, as you go on, in an appreciative way, that builds up unconscious criteria for what you are after, you know?[138]

Dissemination of writing was regarded as important, via noticeboards, readings in assemblies and duplicated magazines.

Most pupils in the fourth year were apparently able to write several pages with few enough errors for reading to be relatively unimpeded and in the fifth with enough competence for about half (not only top stream) to meet O level English Language requirements and for the rest to be entered for the more vocationally oriented City and Guilds or Royal Society of Arts examinations. A recent review by John Dixon and Jenny Leach Dixon of essays written in 1963 by the 40 percent who would be leaving in the summer revealed only a handful (some of whom had come in the fourth year from the amalgamated Nelson secondary modern) for whom "the written medium as a whole was still alien."[139] The technical capability this involved was fostered in part by weekly lessons devoted to what were called "Standards." These comprised systematic instruction and practice in the most important features of spelling and punctuation[140] on lines developed by John Dixon at Holloway. Formal exercises in grammar and details of usage had been abandoned[141] but it is worth stressing, in view of later stereotypes of falling standards, that attention to technical aspects of writing remained important at Walworth throughout our period. A list of "standards" for each year was pinned up in all form rooms.[142] "Standards" work was included in the *Teacher's Book* for *Reflections* and went into a draft booklet, *With Your Reader in Mind*, which the authors were persuaded by James Britton not to publish—to Dixon's later regret, because had it been published English teachers could not so easily have been accused of disregarding grammar and punctuation.[143]

The Character of Walworth English

It appears that the treatment of class readers, private reading, and poetry in Walworth was not notably different from what was regarded as good practice generally. A growth in the publication of school editions of both juvenile and contemporary fiction led to a broadening of the offering. We have testimony from some individuals that their English lessons induced a lasting habit of reading; thus Margaret Barton née Langhelt who left in 1958 ascribes her continuing love of reading to Harold Rosen, with whom in the fourth year she enjoyed *The Kon-Tiki Expedition* and *Julius Caesar*.[144]

In October 1958, Guy Rogers, who as head teacher was acting as head of department in the term after Rosen and before Dixon, sent to all parents a letter and a two-page reading list of titles organized in three sections: Section A, 27 books of which pupils should try to read "ALL" and including the familiar children's classics (*Tom Sawyer, Wind in the Willows, Heidi, Tarka the Otter*) as well as five volumes of folk and fairy tales from the British Isles; Section 2, "a long list" among which pupils were expected to find some they like and including titles by Geoffrey Trease, C. Day-Lewis, Noel Streatfield, and Mary Norton; and Section C, nonfiction, of which "only a few (12) [from the library] are selected" including five on scientists. Finally there is a paragraph on buying books for yourself that recommends "Puffin Story Books (2/6 each)" and, for those with a generous benefactor, the 12 volumes of the *Oxford Junior Encyclopedia* at 30/- each.

In evaluating the depth and subtlety of the response to literature that children developed at Walworth our evidence is inadequate. Recollections in interview after so many years are unlikely to recapture the precise experience of a text or to go beyond broad responses such as boredom or absorption and excitement; and the genres of associated written work either give evidence only indirectly of the reading experience (imagining being in a situation parallel to that of a character in the novel) or, in the essays preparing for O level, achievable without much penetration or feeling by assiduously following a more or less explicit template and reproducing the teacher's commentary.

In the following, although we make reference to instances, we also to some extent go beyond the data in an attempt to reconstruct general positions and attitudes. Here we must acknowledge that we may unconsciously be drawing in part on Medway's own memories of the school from 1964–1971 and of Rosen's PGCE teaching in 1963–1964.

Over the years at Walworth there was a move away from the teaching of language—from *instruction*—to reliance on motivating its production, most obviously in the elicitation of writing. Arthur Harvey encouraged writing to flow but is also remembered as having taught writing in the sense that he showed his pupils that the texts they were producing were artifacts as well as expression. It is claimed that he would take a section of a pupil's piece, write it on the board and with the class edit it to make it more effective, a matter not of correct grammar but of the arrangement or engineering of the words and ideas, an approach that stemmed historically from the classical rhetorical tradition. Whether Rosen worked in this way is unclear, though we know that he used the blackboard to help attain conceptual clarity in the discussions that led to writing, as did Stratta and Clements and doubtless Dixon.

In contrast with Harvey, in the practice of, certainly, Simon Clements in the lower school (years one and two) and Alex McLeod in the upper school, instruction in "rhetorical engineering" seems to have fallen away. For them the secret of good writing, as for Ted Hughes and the earlier advocates of "creative writing,"[145] was precise observation and recollection together with concrete particularity. Teaching writing was directing attention to what happened and could be seen, not eliciting or imparting vocabulary as in the celebrated film clip of Peter Emmens blowing bubbles in a secondary modern school and giving the class the word iridescent to use in their essays.[146]

A further stress might be termed "anti-formal." Clements, according to a pupil, "fostered the idea that there was no right way or wrong way to do it which was liberating. It was all about ideas. The important thing was telling the story, including dialogue and descriptions of characters."[147] Within the climate of English teaching at the time, and in view of the teaching experienced by Walworth children in rather formal junior schools, the emphasis on motivated writing free of worry about possible censure, as opposed to contrived efforts that avoided risk, was no doubt a necessary countermove.

If one emphasis of Walworth English was opening up the channels of communication to expression that was relatively uninhibited by prescription and instruction, a second was the centrality of the children's own experience. The importance of this is explicitly asserted in the *Teacher's Book* for *Reflections*, while in a Schools Council booklet written not much later by Dixon and Britton with Summerfield the English classroom is unambiguously "a place where people meet to share their experience of life"[148]—not, as many would have argued, of literature or language. When, however, the "emphasis in *Reflections* on the possibility of eliciting children's own experience running parallel with whatever the text was" was brought up in our interview, Dixon pointed out that he later learned, "partly through college, which had wonderful drama, how drama and simulation can get you into situations which are outside of your experience... against using always personal experience... And I could have changed *Reflections* that way."[149] Such a change might have been appreciated by those pupils who preferred *The Hunchback of Notre Dame* to what one of them called less "imaginative" material and for whom everyday and social themes failed to stimulate their imagination.[150]

Lower school English seems always to have catered more to the imagination. Classes read *Beowulf*, *Children on the Oregon Trail*, and *The Hobbit*, while teachers who taught both English and social studies (combined history and geography) were getting a quite different sort of writing and drama out of canoeing down to the St Lawrence in 1700 and the landscape of the outback—some distance away from "personal experience."

A final emphasis, as we have seen, was on spoken language, now acknowledged as a full third leg of the curriculum, as Walworth assessment procedures began to acknowledge.[151] Talk as discussion was at the heart of many lessons; dramatic speech featured in improvised plays, and one-to-one teacher-pupil conversation was the method in experimental oral examinations.

Beyond the core trio—themselves quite different—the department, though in most respects pulling together, ranged from the formal Scottish style of Pip Porchetta to Alex McLeod's easy approachability and understanding which were appreciated, during his earlier stay at the school, by two boys of the new "working-class bohemian" type[152] who read widely and found school regimes unsympathetic. Pete Jones and Tony Maclean had their own "existentialist corner" on the noticeboards of McLeod's classroom; Maclean describes the experience of his teaching style (never shouting) as like being taught by a Buddhist monk.[153] McLeod seems to have been particularly attuned to the emerging teenager of the late 1950s and 1960s. "He liked the pupils, regarding them as vital and interesting. Particularly he contrasted them with his New Zealand pupils whom he regarded as boring and dull. He learned about London pupils' music and language."[154] A later pupil of the same type (representatives of which from other schools were the fictional Absolute Beginner and the actual photographers David Bailey, Terence Donovan, and Brian Duffy) to whom McLeod was equally sympathetic, was Brian Catling who, discovered in the library reading *Gargantua and Pantagruel*, was "rescued" from the bottom stream just in time by Porchetta and McLeod when about to "fall off the cliff" into early leaving. He became an eccentric arty sixth former, gaining A level English, and is now professor in the Oxford University Ruskin School of Drawing, thanks ultimately, he claims, to his teachers' recognition of an imagination in need of being fired.

Different again was the formidable and effective Brenda Harvey who had moved with a cohort of pupils from Nelson secondary modern on amalgamation in 1962 and who, without her colleagues' history of socialization into the theory and assumptions of Walworth English, adopted aspects of it and combined them with practices that her teacher's experience and common sense had taught her were needed, such as a more thorough correction of error than was the norm with the some of the department—though her red ink was selective and not excessive—and instruction and practice in devising metaphors.[155]

Valerie Noakes'[156] first-year class in 1961–1962 was reading Wolf Mankowitz's *A Kid for Two Farthings* which is set around the Petticoat Lane market in the East End. Patrick Kingwell's grandmother worked in the rag trade so that

> When this book came along, which was all set in Petticoat Lane around Aldgate, that just really gripped our imaginations. And I remember going with [a friend; we got] got Red Rovers [bus passes] and actually went over to Aldgate and the East End, and we did maps of the streets and we did listings of all the clothing companies and the rag trade people...and this was all stemmed from reading that book. And I remember we did a project and I gave it in to Mrs Noakes...and she was quite pleased about it. Because we hadn't been asked to...but that was the impact of the teaching...And it was a great thing to be opened up to.[157]

Conclusion

When Walworth started there nowhere existed any model of English for the comprehensive school—that is, a way of teaching English that would be effective across the range of ability. By the early 1960s there did. The Walworth version, developed for a specific London context had, on the evidence of sales of *Reflections*, proved effective elsewhere too. This chapter has sketched the stages by which that version was arrived at. It remains to speculate further on how and why it came about as it did.

Walworth English was neither grammar school nor secondary modern school English. It might have been closer to some secondary modern versions in its attention to social themes and relationships, but was akin to grammar school studies in the intellectual seriousness of its purposes, its ambition, and its assumptions about the potential of its pupils.

A significant factor in Walworth English, as in other subjects too, was the nature of the particular school. A grammar school English teacher (like Harold Rosen before he came to Walworth) might move from school to school without his teaching having to change much. In Walworth, on the other hand, some teachers taught their subject and comported themselves as teachers in ways that reflected the aims and ideology of that school. Not only was Walworth designated an experimental comprehensive but its affirmation of the worth and educability of its working-class pupils, far from being promotional rhetoric, was actively subscribed to by a significant section of the staff. There was little distance at Walworth between the liberalism of the English department and the official ethos of the school. To an extent that took us by surprise, Walworth English belongs to the history not just of a subject but of a school and was in part an attempt to realize the ideals of democratic relationships, responsible conduct, and self-respect that Anne O'Reilly had espoused from 1947.

The ethos and atmosphere of the school were in turn affected by factors specific to London, not least the attraction the capital held for able young teachers from elsewhere who socialized with each other after work and engaged in animated talk about education and their pupils. To the latter they were plainly a distinct group from their more established colleagues and aspects of their cultural tastes were by the 1960s closer to those of the younger generation. This was true of teachers across the subjects, and in their recollections, even though they know our interest is in English, former pupils consistently talk about "the school" or "the teachers," with the implication that English was one case among several with which they were able to enjoy fruitful and respectful relations. Peter Johnson who started at Walworth in 1962 writes in his blog:

> The most immediate difference in my new school was the teachers. It was evident from the first day, that these were a different breed from the ones that I had known before [in primary school]...At Walworth...[the teachers] fell into two distinct categories. There were the older ones, the sort you expected to get. Big on discipline, somewhat jaded, mostly unmarried,[158] not great communicators. Then there were the younger ones, some of whom were only 10 years older than us. They wore relatively fashionable clothes, they were interested in music and films, they talked to you as if you were

a person in your own right, and they gave you personal responsibility, not just a list of rules. They genuinely made you feel valued, far from just being a face in a crowd. Perhaps more importantly, for children from a working-class background, they had expectations of you, and a hope that you would do well...After all, we [presumably the boys!] were destined to be the Dock-Workers, Printers, Tradesmen, and Manual Labourers of Society, so the rest was of little consequence. Suddenly, all that had changed. We had a purpose, our future was important, we could do anything we wanted, be the best that we could be, and this new breed of teacher was there to make it happen...you must believe me when I say that this was life changing. I would certainly not be writing this blog, or reflecting on a relatively successful life, were it not for those few teachers.[159]

Among the incomers the significant contingent of New Zealanders is felt to have had an effect, coming as they did from what they felt to be a less class-ridden society and a better, more egalitarian school system. They gave glowing reports of Walworth on returning to New Zealand, "against all of these gloom and doom missionaries who were...telling them what awful schools there were in London."[160]

Asked some year ago by a researcher "what it was like in the early comprehensives" Robert Thornbury had answered, "very distinctive experience, absolutely halcyon days, a joy to be born each day to go to school .. There was scope for innovation in the curriculum...People were very tolerant of experiment and excitement of experiment was there."[161] When Simon Clements was leaving in 1964, a colleague told him, to his lasting satisfaction, "For me you represent the spirit of Walworth"; the belief that there was such a thing was widespread.

Walworth English was, belatedly, influenced (through LATE) by new movements in primary education and particularly the "free writing and expression work, including the writing of poetry" that expressed "much of the aims of the new methods—the release of the inner resources of the children and the search for ways of enabling them to capitalize on their own organized and unorganized experience."[162] The cultural studies of Richard Hoggart, Raymond Williams, and Stuart Hall became an important confirmation of a belief in the value and potential of working-class culture.

Subsequent Careers

Harold Rosen taught in a training college, then at the Institute of Education, eventually as professor; Alex McLeod left Walworth in 1967 to become a member of the Writing Research team and then a lecturer at the Institute of Education; the *Reflections* authors continued to publish, together and separately, and to disseminate the new English abroad, particularly in Canada, Australia, and New Zealand; John Dixon, from a Northern college of education, chaired the Schools Council English Committee and wrote the key text, *Growth through English*.

Chapter 5

Minchenden

Minchenden Grammar School was in suburban outer London, beyond the London County Council's administrative area in the County of Middlesex (the education authority) and in the borough of Southgate, but effectively in London in terms of transport, employment, and other criteria.[1] Southgate was a largely middle-class community, home to a relatively prosperous, albeit mixed, population. During the interwar years Southgate had experienced substantial housing development, especially with the extension of the Piccadilly Line underground railway in 1933.[2] The borough's population continued rising in mid-century as a result of wartime and postwar population dispersal from inner-city areas, thereafter remaining unchanged over the next decade. Southgate was well connected to central London through underground, rail, and—until 1961—trolleybus services.[3] The fathers of many Minchenden pupils "went up to London" each day to work in white-collar office jobs. In 1955, the Mayor of Southgate reflected that the borough "has grown from what some of our residents knew as a rural area, to a suburb which is second to none in its set up."[4] The Council prided itself on sensitive town planning and provision of many parks, playgrounds, and other recreational facilities, where organized activities included gramophone recitals, fishing competitions, and tennis tournaments.[5] Teachers at Minchenden sought to instill pupils with a sense of local civic pride through instruction in the workings of local democracy by regular visits to Council meetings. From the 1930s, pupils were well aware of living through important changes. An editorial in the 1934 school magazine on the new suburb of Old Southgate reflected on this expansion:

> New houses are being sold to parents of children who will come to be part of our School. Vigour and adventure are typified in the Underground Station and in the new shopping center.[6]

Despite its proximity to London, Southgate culture was suburban and, according to the poet James Kirkup who taught at Minchenden in the late 1940s, "deadly dull."[7] Peter Blakebrough, a pupil at the school in the 1950s, echoed this view:

> [Southgate] was very, very staid. When my parents moved there it was '54, my grandmother, who was a working-class woman, little education, described it as "kippers and curtains." I don't know if you know the phrase, but curtains for keeping up appearances, and kippers for not having the money to do it.[8]

"Southgate values" were "an exaggerated respect for education...a fear of running into debt, a respectability, a chip on the shoulder with employers."[9]

In the 1950s and 1960s there was a flourishing associational culture in Southgate centered on such largely lower middle-class and middle-class groups as sports clubs, branches of the Townswomen's Guild, allotment and horticultural societies, Chambers of Commerce, ratepayers' associations, and owner-occupiers' associations,[10] and for young people several companies of the Church Lads' and Girls' Brigades, a large number of Girl Guide packs and Scout troops, a branch of the Junior Red Cross and five of the St John Ambulance Cadets, two units of the Sea Cadets, a number of church youth groups, a youth orchestra, and a council-run Coffee Bar Club.[11] There were five cinemas, a music hall, and two dance venues.[12]

Southgate was a safe Conservative parliamentary seat and Minchenden pupils' politics tended to reflect this conservative tone, at least in the early period of our study: in the school's mock election in 1945—the year of Labour's landslide victory in the general election—the "Socialist" candidate came third. Evidence from pupils suggests that later the school's political alignment was more with the Campaign for Nuclear Disarmament (CND), the Anti-Apartheid Movement and the New Left.

Southgate was religiously mixed with nine Anglican and three Roman Catholic churches as well as 22 nonconformist chapels, halls, and meeting houses in 1956.[13] During the 1920s and 1930s a significant Jewish population built up as families moved out from inner London districts including Hackney and Shoreditch for a better future, as well as through fresh refugees from Germany and Eastern Europe.[14] The first synagogue in Southgate was founded in 1926.

Minchenden School

Minchenden School was founded immediately after the Great War. A severe shortage of schools in the district had resulted from the population growth following the extension of the railway out of London around the turn of the century. In 1919, a new coeducational grammar school, originally known as Tottenhall Road School, Edmonton, opened with 90 pupils. In 1924, this school purchased an eighteenth-century mansion and grounds, Southgate House, and was renamed Minchenden School, after the famous "Minchenden Oak," an 800-year-old tree that stood next to the local parish church. Adapting the house for school use proved challenging; "uncomfortable cosiness" was how the school magazine described it.[15] In 1933 the school was extended with a new building that included science laboratories and a gymnasium. The old building was still the heart of the school, however, and being educated in such grand surroundings made a strong impression on generations of pupils. At the opening of the new buildings, it was suggested:

> The boys and girls who came here would have as fine traditions to look back on as the public schoolboy under his Gothic towers. He would be reminded of and live again that great soldiering family, the Lawrences [former residents]. He would be reminded again of that fine sporting family, the Walkers [likewise], and would learn, like them, to play our great national game of cricket.[16]

Minchenden built up a reputation for academic excellence in the interwar period. A number of the teachers wrote textbooks or acted as examiners. English teacher Miss Crossley, for instance, was a University of London-appointed Assistant Examiner for the Matriculation and General School Examinations. Geography teacher James Stewart published *An Economic Geography of the British Empire Overseas* in 1933 and Sydney Wells and Percy Packer each produced several German and French course books and readers. Modern language teaching was particularly strong in the school from the 1920s to the 1960s, seemingly at the expense of Latin.

The school was three-form entry until the later part of our period when it became four-form entry (There were 614 pupils on roll in 1958.) After the first year, the school was streamed by ability with the top set taking German in addition to French, the second set studying Spanish as well as French and the bottom "A" and "B" sets taking no additional language. In the 1930s German language and culture exerted a strong pull on the school. A "German soirée" was held annually and a 1936 school visit to Nazi Germany featured as its highlight sing-songs and social evenings with a branch of the Hitler Youth.[17]

Minchenden was not evacuated during the Second World War, although the school suffered the disruption of air raids and a curtailment of extracurricular activities.[18] In fact the school roll grew as it received additional pupils who had not been evacuated and in the early part of the war pressure on space meant a part-time timetable was introduced with pupils taking work home. Pupils managed to aid the war effort in various ways, for example, sending parcels to former pupils held as prisoners of war in Europe. The girls established a Junior Red Cross branch, while the older boys volunteered on annual harvest camps arranged in Gloucestershire. In 1945, a pupil reflected on the experience of war:

> We spent much of our time in the cold and gloomy concrete trenches and work was again interrupted. The news from Europe was grim; there were no out of school activities; homework had to be done to the accompaniment of air-raids, and many of the school gave up their leisure time to pre-Service training.[19]

Following the 1944 Education Act, Middlesex maintained three secondary moderns and two grammar schools in Southgate and supported selected pupils to attend public boarding schools or art and technical schools; interviewees recall friends and siblings who took up this opportunity.[20] In 1945 the school, though not seriously damaged despite a bomb landing on the playground in 1941, was nevertheless in a state of dilapidation and disrepair owing to a labor shortage. At the end of war a group of older pupils got up a party to clean up the drive and weed and returf the grass verges.[21] The school also faced a severe shortage of teachers, which it alleviated with the help of trainees from the Institute of Education and the newly established Emergency Training College at nearby Trent Park. It seems that these young teachers brought a variety of new perspectives into Minchenden classrooms. They included a trainee teacher from Nigeria, a concentration camp survivor from Germany, and a PE specialist from Homerton College, Cambridge. The Nigerian student apparently won pupils' "interest and sympathy" through talks about his own schooling in Africa.[22] Some ex-servicemen also joined the staff, including a mathematics teacher who had been a navigator in the RAF and made a strong impression on pupils.[23]

The school's grand buildings and parkland setting impressed generations of pupils and its excellent reputation encouraged families to choose Minchenden over other grammar schools. Valerie Whittle, a pupil in the 1940s, recalled that other grammar schools in the area were "not a patch on ours. We were the best."[24] Likewise the cookery writer Marion Kane noted, "My parents chose [Minchenden] over local ones because of its reputation for high academic standards and an enlightened headmaster."[25] The 1958 HM Inspectors' report confirms that Minchenden was indeed a "first choice" school.[26] From a later period, the 1960s, another pupil reported, "The guy up the road, who was considered very bright, went to

Minchenden, and it had a good reputation at the time. So I thought I'll go there then."[27] Prestige was attached to passing having passed the 11 plus to get to grammar school, and students at Southgate Technical College were seen as "greaser boys, [with] leather jackets, motorcycles, and they are regarded as the 'techs,' and beyond the pale."[28]

While the social profile of Minchenden pupils was broadly middle class, there were also pupils from poorer backgrounds and many whose parents had originally been working class but were moving up the social scale. Pupils in 1958 were drawn from 66 different primary schools.[29] A pupil at the school from 1943 described living south of Arnos Grove tube station as living on the "wrong side of the tracks."[30] This area had been heavily bombed and in the 1950s Southgate began building new council estates, including the first tower blocks, completed in 1960. Minchenden pupils came from small rented flats and maisonettes in this area as well as from the semi-detached 1930s houses closer to the school. Some also came from the large detached houses in Winchmore Hill in the north of the borough. One pupil at the school in the 1940s recalled that a few parents of her schoolmates owned cars, a sure sign of wealth in postwar London. Parents tended to be employed in white-collar occupations in city firms or to be small business owners such as printers, bookbinders, paint manufacturers, and tradesmen. One pupil recalled that a pupil whose father was a journalist for a national paper stood out as different, as did one whose father was a bus driver. Pupils described this social mix with pride: "I mean my parents had no money, and lots of other people's parents had no money, but we were in the best grammar school in the area."[31]

At the start of the period the school's sixth form was small, consisting of 57 pupils out of a total roll of 586.[32] In the late 1950s around more than half of the pupils left the school at the end of the fifth form, with about 40 pupils staying on each year who were joined by a few new pupils in the sixth form; the sixth form expanded further in the early 1960s. In the 1950s most sixth formers took a two-year A level course, although around a third of the group stayed on to take S ("Scholarship") level. In 1958, 17 students won a university place and several others went to technical colleges. The sixth form was divided into Arts and Science "sides." English was the most popular Arts subject, with 24 entries in 1964 and 22 in 1965.[33]

Pressure on classroom space meant that in 1960, Minchenden was split across two sites, with the first two years housed in the "Fox Lane" annex, a mile down the road in the former buildings of Southgate County Grammar. In 1967, the new Enfield LEA produced a scheme for comprehensive education and Minchenden became a nonselective comprehensive school, merging with Arnos Grove School in 1984 to become Broomfield

School. The former Minchenden School building is now occupied by a further education college, Southgate College.

English at Minchenden Before 1959

The English department at Minchenden was selected for this study because Douglas Barnes, head of department from 1959 to 1966, played a key role in advancing the ideas and practices of the new-style English that had been developing within the London Association for the Teaching of English (LATE). The department became a showcase of English teaching in London with influential overseas educationalists and trainee teachers—not to mention the head of English from Eton College—regularly arriving to observe lessons. Before Barnes' arrival, it was felt that the English department at Minchenden offered a staid experience of English, with a focus typical of many grammar schools of the period on the teaching of grammar, literature, and composition. There is evidence however that the Minchenden English department under previous heads of department was, if not "progressive," at least well regarded by outsiders, forward looking in its own way and offering a good educational experience to pupils.

The school began to build a strong reputation for English teaching in the 1930s when its senior English master was Francis Isaac Venables. On his leaving for promotion to a headship in 1941, the school magazine—in an admittedly panegyric piece—recorded that Venables' leadership meant it was no "small wonder that English prospered and many visitors came attracted by its fame."[34] Venables was responsible for starting a strong tradition of Shakespeare productions at the school and initiated an annual Stratford-on-Avon visit "to pay homage to Shakespeare and to have a good time." [35] Mr Venables was also an active member of an association known as the Society for Teachers of English, which was formed in the interwar period, "to advance the standard of English teaching," and included leading commentators on English and education including Percival Gurrey, W. R. Niblett, Kenneth Muir, and A. A. Evans.[36] Venables also wrote the school song. Like other Minchenden teachers he was responsible for published textbooks. Working with D. C. Whimster, English teacher at Harrow, the famous public school, Venables put together a four-volume course book called *English for Schools: A Planned Course in Comprehension and Expression*, which was originally published in 1939 and reissued in a revised edition in 1958–1960. The book was timely, meeting a need identified in the 1938 Spens Report for "anthologies containing passages of good thought or narrative well expressed, both in prose and verse" to be widely used in schools.[37] On initial publication *English for Schools* received largely favorable reviews for its "well-chosen prose and verse passages for class study" and "useful subject-analysis chart, whereby easy reference can be made to passages and exercises illustrating particular forms of speech"[38]; a 1949 report of an LATE study group on textbooks included *English for Schools* in a list of books which members had found helpful[39] and by 1951 it had been reprinted six times. By the 1961 second edition, however, sentiment had changed, with a negative review of the "disappointingly pedestrian" language exercises.[40]

Minchenden's reputation for excellence in English teaching was consolidated in the 1940s and 1950s under a new head of department and further developed by the new headmaster, English specialist Dr J. H. Walters. Miss Crossley was head of English from Venables' departure in 1941 until her retirement in summer 1959. A Birkbeck College graduate, she had been teaching at the school since the late 1920s. At the time of the HMI visit in 1948 there were four women teachers of English under her, reflecting the shortage of male teachers after the war, although only two taught English full-time and not all were English specialists. Miss Hill, for example, taught English, religious education, and mathematics, while a Miss Russell had joined in 1945 to help in English and History departments.[41] Miss Amiot, the school's music teacher, also taught first-year English. The department's work was aided by a steady supply of trainee English teachers from both Trent Park and the Institute of Education.[42] The 1948 HMI report noted "the staff is academically well qualified, and works together harmoniously and with great enthusiasm."[43] The school had just lost James Kirkup, already a published poet, whose experience of what he called "teaching hell" at Minchenden in 1946–1947 nearly resulted in a nervous breakdown, but did at least give rise to a poem, "In a London Schoolroom," first published in the BBC magazine *The Listener*.[44] The Inspectors in 1948 recommended the appointment of a male teacher and in the early 1950s a number of men were recruited by Miss Crossley. These included John Kemp, who started his teaching career at Minchenden in 1953 before transferring to Hackney Downs, and John Wilkes, who left in summer 1958. Mike Riddle had grown up in nearby Finchley and attended a Catholic training college, St Mary's in Twickenham, before spending his national service with the Army Education Corps in Kenya and Somalia. While teaching physical education in London at an all-standards school in the early 1950s Riddle studied for an English degree at Birkbeck College, enabling him to move into grammar school teaching. Interviewed in 2009 Riddle felt his appointment in 1955 was largely due to the fact that he was, like Miss Crossley, a Birkbeck graduate.[45] Two new teachers, Yvonne Redman (afterwards Bradbury) and Mike Whittaker, originally from New Zealand, were recruited in 1958, just before Barnes joined the staff.

Appointed headmaster in 1947, Dr Walters was a softly spoken academic who was an editor of classroom editions of Shakespeare but also liked to keep his hand in at classroom teaching. The 1958 HMI report recorded he took one fourth-year English set and several pupils we interviewed remember being taught by him.[46] Walters introduced some key innovations to Minchenden, notably a six-day timetable that included one afternoon a week for games and one for a range of other extracurricular activities and hobbies such as English country dancing or play reading.[47] Walters' modern and instructive Player's editions of Shakespeare for Heinemann were routinely well-received, with one reviewer considering his *Twelfth Night* the "best school edition I have seen."[48] A later review noted that "Dr Walters' asking of questions rather than answering them implies an awareness of pedagogical method, unusual enough in school editions."[49] Indeed, this appears to differ from the methods of Crossley who, remembers one pupil, would not ask questions about texts but told pupils the answers straight off.

Although under Barnes and later Dennis Roberts the English department developed a strong collegial atmosphere, there is little evidence that this existed before Barnes' arrival. Indeed the term "department" may be anachronistic for this earlier period. Toward the end of her period in the late 1950s Miss Crossley was suffering ill health and reportedly rarely left her room at the top of the school.[50] In the mid to late 1950s at least, the English teachers seem to have had little to do with one another, with no departmental meetings or discussions. Mike Riddle, certainly, found Crossley uncongenial and possessive, and was annoyed that she repeatedly rejected his requests to teach sixth-form English. There was little shared practice or planning before Barnes took over. (Riddle didn't believe in preparing lessons in any case.) Yvonne Redman had little to do with Crossley or other colleagues in the department and doesn't remember talking to anyone about teaching in her first year at the school: the focus of her life at this point was outside the school with the New Left Review and CND.[51] It is perhaps not surprising that both Redman and Riddle sought support through membership of LATE. In fact both eventually took up leadership roles in LATE, with Riddle serving on the LATE Committee 1956–1958 and Redman from 1961.

Whatever her relations with her colleagues, pupils studying English for Higher School Certificate and later for A level found Miss Crossley's teaching inspirational and HMI praised her in both the 1948 and 1958 reports. She taught her advanced classes in small discussion groups in her room in the old servants' quarters at top of the school, which Terry Hearing (at the school 1941–1948) remembers with "great pleasure" as "an enjoyable experience."[52] Crossley took her pupils to see plays such as T. S. Eliot's *Murder in the Cathedral* at the Mercury Theatre in Notting Hill. In 1958, she was praised for maintaining the strong tradition in English studies in the school and for overseeing a "well-balanced curriculum."[53]

Under Venables there had been a strong theatrical tradition but during the war and immediate postwar years there were no school plays, until the tradition was revived with Miss Richardson's production of *The Winter's Tale* in 1951.[54] In the mid-1950s John Wilkes directed *The Boy with a Cart* and *She Stoops to Conquer*, later Yvonne Redman put on *Much Ado About Nothing* and *As You Like It*, and in the 1960s Robert Hardman directed *The Misanthrope* and *A Resounding Tinkle*.[55] However a play-reading society was started in 1946 to enable pupils to select and enjoy a wider range of plays, including modern plays, than they would come across in lessons. Plays read between 1946 and 1950 included Priestley's *When We Are Married*, Coward's *Blithe Spirit*, Capek's *R.U.R*, Eden Philpotts' *Yellow Sands,*, Bax's *A Rose without a Thorn*, and Shaw's *Androcles and the Lion*. All these plays were available in French's Acting Editions published in the 1930s, cheap paperback publications intended for reading aloud. Moreover pupils' choice may have been influenced by radio and film productions of these plays—and they are strikingly similar to the plays read at the Hackney Downs play reading group at the same date. *Blithe Spirit*, for example, was a popular West End show, which was turned into a film in 1945. There were also a number of annual interhouse verse reading and poetry competitions with which the English staff became involved in this period. In the mid-1950s English teachers Wilkes and Riddle helped run the school's Literary and Debating Society, which organized debates, "Brains Trusts," and discussions of films, books, and plays.[56] In 1958–1959 a new Dramatic Society was formed, with 60–70 members at the inaugural meeting. HMI felt this wider literary culture aided classroom English teaching.[57]

At Minchenden School in the 1940s and 1950s, as at many grammar schools, the English curriculum was arranged on traditional lines with the elements such as grammar and literature taught in separate classes. There was more space for English teaching in the first-year curriculum before the introduction of a second foreign language for most pupils after the second year, although there was also an option in the fourth and fifth year for pupils in the lower streams to take extra English. As was common in many schools, the A level English course attracted more girls than boys. Madeline Salter, already quoted, at school in the 1940s, remembered "we had different subjects, we had English grammar and English literature lessons in the 1940s, and you had a different teachers for them," though not all remembered having separate lesson. In this period individual Minchenden teachers operated fairly independently and were free to shape their lessons as they wanted. Mike Riddle described how he arranged his teaching week in the mid-1950s:

> I divided up my week. One was the drama class, and the other was the grammar class, and then there was the précis and comprehension class, and then there were the literature classes, I can't remember exactly what the balance was. And that made [for] a lot of variety.[58]

The 1948 HMI report found that "A very satisfactory syllabus has been prepared, covering all sides of English work, and a careful development from year to year is planned."[59] Although it was difficult for pupils of this period to remember the exact content of lessons or homework, we do have evidence from several exercise books from the 1940s and 1950s, which, combined with analysis of the course books used, can help us to reconstruct schemes of work. As one pupil recalled "we did a lot of grammar!"[60] This is a claim backed up by the exercise books, which contain regular clause analysis exercises for homework. Analysis of three different pupils' books from junior forms in 1949, 1952, and 1954 shows that the main course book used in the first two forms of the school was Venables and Whimster's 1939 *English for Schools*.[61] It seems likely that this course formed the core curriculum of English in the lower part of the school from the late 1930s until the mid-1950s. Certainly Venables tried out both the approach and the individual exercises on his pupils in the 1930s, who are thanked in his introduction for their "unwitting help." The idea of the course was to "base all the varying types of work done in English lessons on a common foundation, that of reading and understanding."[62]

The prose selections in *English for Schools* were largely taken from children's classics like the *Wind in the Willows*, *Tom Sawyer*, *Little Women*, and *Black Beauty*, and the poetry included Tennyson, Hardy, Spenser, and Nash, and historical tales such as "'Tracks of our Forefathers." Also included were several excerpts from Lamb's *Tales from Shakespeare* followed by a short extract of the original play, including *The Merchant of Venice* and *A Midsummer Night's Dream*. While such choices were intended as appealing and accessible for 12- and 13-year-olds, they perhaps reveal a reluctance to engage with more contemporary works. Much of the work was intended to be done orally, rather than for written homework, after the selections of text had been read aloud by the teacher or silently by the class. Each section of prose or poetry was followed by a series of comprehension questions followed by questions on use of language and grammar. Additional exercises asked pupils to rewrite stories as a play, to read bible passages or poems with similar themes, or to draw scenes from the stories. However what is noticeable from analysis of the pupils' exercise books is that while the topics are often those in *English for Schools*, the exact readings or questions set varied, suggesting teachers used the course book for inspiration rather than slavishly following the course. For example, one exercise undertaken by pupil Daphne Chitty was to retell a scene from *Merchant of Venice*, a set question in *English for Schools*, but the scene prescribed was not that printed, suggesting that the pupils read at least part of the original play. Nonetheless, perhaps it was reliance on this course book that led the 1948 inspectors to conclude that "the approach in the junior Forms is not as spontaneous and natural as could be wished."[63]

Literature appears to have been a long-standing strength of Minchenden English. The 1948 HMI report recorded that an "unusually wide range" of prose texts, which were "well suited to the age and ability of the pupils," was introduced, and the whole scheme was centered round the school library. Yet we have little other evidence of this range. Pupils from the 1940s and 1950s recalled a great deal of Shakespeare being taught, even in the lower forms. Valerie Whittle, at school in the 1940s, believed that she studied eight different Shakespeare plays over the five years before she took her School Certificate. This reflects both the prevalence of Shakespeare on examination syllabuses of the time and the influence of Shakespeare scholar Walters, whose own editions were, unsurprisingly, widely used in the school. Indeed a later teacher, Robert Hardman, remembers that Walters' texts remained very good for use in school because they were clearly laid out and encouraged pupil discussion, recalling that in the 1960s he "used them again and again."[64] The poetry reader Whittle remembered was *An Anthology of Modern Verse*, a very widely used and popular school textbook published by Methuen in many editions between 1921 and 1949. This anthology made such an impression on her that she bought her own copy of the book on leaving school.[65] Pupils who remembered Miss Crossley felt that she encouraged a love of literature in her pupils. As in other schools, the choice of literature higher up in the school was dictated by the School Certificate during the 1940s and by the O and A level examinations after 1951. Pupils of Crossley's period recalled studying such classic fiction and dramatic texts as Dickens, Hardy, Austen, Browning, Bernard Shaw, and Chaucer alongside Shakespeare.

Perhaps in part because of the influence of the *English in Schools* textbook great value was attached to classroom discussion at Minchenden. Pupils from the 1940s and 1950s recall a strong tradition of teacher-led discussion, especially around literature. Madeline Salter, for instance, remembered her literature classes with Crossley, noting "I'm sure there was discussion, and I feel we were encouraged to be confident speakers."[66]

Confirming this view, the 1948 HMI inspectors noted the school's strength in classroom oral work:

> Oral English and speech training receive careful attention, and a wide range of activities, debates, discussions and lectures is carried on. In general the pupils talk with confidence, and express their ideas with clarity and point. Based on the oral preparation a sound scheme of written work is laid down, though it is recommended that more opportunity should be given to the pupils to write about their own experiences and interests.[67]

Drama, debate, and discussion remained important in the 1950s. Mike Riddle recalled "I would talk about anything," although some of his pupils remembered that he led class discussion in a very controlled way. As one suggested, Riddle would ask, "What do you think this character meant? What do you think about that?" Riddle mentioned an encounter with one pupil who "used to talk and talk and talk, and it was always interesting, and in the end we had a running battle on nuclear disarmament."[68] According to pupils of this period, John Wilkes stood out as "both an engaging teacher and one who wanted to promote learning by doing":

> Drama, story-reading and debates were his main vehicles. He liked to get us to move all the classroom furniture to make space for practical activities. The maths teacher who followed our lesson (Mr Bullen) used to complain that we got too light-headed and failed to restore the furniture properly.[69]

Later, there was a more general shift away from teacher-led discussions to small group work. Mike Riddle recalled that boys and girls would sit on opposite sides of the classroom when he first started, and mixing them up, so that a pair of girls sat with a pair of boys to form a group, was controversial among older staff. These early attempts at "group work" became a common aspect of English teaching later in the school's history. Interestingly, Riddle suggested that he learnt the "secret of getting the pupils to help themselves in a group to learn" while teaching PE at an all standards (all age) school in the early 1950s. One pupil, reflecting on the subtly different approaches to talk in the classroom after Barnes' arrival in 1959, suggested that while teachers such as Whittaker and Riddle "really wanted to engage the class, it was question and answer and they would be happy to talk for fifteen or twenty minutes before they allowed us in, whereas Douglas was a much more dialogue based tutorial teacher."[70]

Another key element of the changing English curriculum in the 1950s was the gradual introduction of a wider range of novels, plays, and poems as well as a shift in the approach to teaching literature in the classroom. Interestingly, this change appears to have been under way in the mid-1950s before Barnes' appointment, although our evidence for this is constrained by pupils' ability to remember what they read. For instance, Riddle noted that George Orwell's *Animal Farm* (published in 1945) was the one of the first literature texts he taught at Minchenden and argued it was effective because it prompted long discussions with pupils. Riddle also encouraged his pupils to read widely outside the set texts. Pupils recalled his technique of asking them to choose a fiction book and then submit it for his approval. In the late 1950s, for example, Peter Borrows chose the recently published *Doctor Zhivago* in order "to impress him, more than anything else. I never actually finished it. Don't think I got beyond chapter one, to be honest with you."[71] Other pupils remember Riddle and Whittaker teaching late nineteenth- and early twentieth-century poets like Gerard Manley Hopkins and T. S. Eliot, and Norman Ellis, at the school 1954–1962, remembered Walters talking to the class about railways and discussing the Bradshaw railway guide as a way into the Edward Thomas poem "Adlestrop." Ellis noted that although he was not very good at English literature some of the books he read did make a lasting impression, identifying these as *Jane Eyre* by Charlotte Brontë, *The History of Mr Polly* by H. G. Wells, and *A Pattern of Islands* by Arthur Grimble, published in 1952.[72] The 1958 HM Inspectors' report commended the "vigour and zest" of the English course and noted it was based on the encouragement of independent reading and sound literary study.

Peter Boot, who left Minchenden in 1960 to study engineering, felt that the literature curriculum lower down the school and for O level was dominated by Shakespeare, but remembers an extra English class that was offered to the science sixth form consisting of:

> One hour a week, and there we were basically encouraged, not forced, but encouraged to read modern novels. That was much nicer, and I enjoyed it. And we all enjoyed it, and we read Orwell, and we read Huxley, and we read Evelyn Waugh and people like that, and it introduced me to stuff I still value.[73]

Such a scheme of extra English for the science sixth had been recommended by the HMI report of 1958 and Boot must have been one of the first to experience it.

The 1948 HMI report regretted a lack of opportunities for pupils to write about their own "experiences and interests." The perception is corroborated by evidence from exercise books of the late 1940s and early 1950s. Creative writing homework tasks of this period tended to involve a pupil writing in the first person as a character in various historical or fictional settings in the past, such as a ship's boy or soldier in the Napoleonic wars. Nature was another strong theme in pupils' compositions. Examples from the surviving books include Roger Dean on "the noble humble bee" and "May" (written in winter) or Monica Meadows on "A Hot Summer's Day" (also written in winter). Even titles such as "My favourite sport" did not prompt personal writing but romanticized descriptions such as "I think there is nothing better than to lie under the shade of a tree in a quiet village and watch the local cricket match." These descriptions were perhaps influenced more by books such as A. G. Street's *Country Days* (a series of broadcast talks published in 1933), of which Roger Dean wrote a review in 1953, than by the actual experiences of suburban schoolchildren. A round up of poetry submitted to the school magazine noted that in the first two forms nature poems such as "Dawn in Palmers Green" or "Spring Comes to Potters Bar" were common.[74] Other influences include popular series of adventure or mystery stories for children. For instance, Monica Meadows' first-year exercise book contains several exciting stories of children discovering hidden caves on their holidays. The books also include regular précis homework exercises on passages about the finding of Alexander Selkirk, the escape of Charles II, and the like. Yet, more explicit suburban themes do crop up in the surviving work. For example, in 1950 a Minchenden pupil Elaine Ratcliff won the (national) Poetry Society's Junior Verse Competition with a poem that was judged to be a "remarkable piece of work for a child of 13 and no other poem had reached so high a level." It appears at first glance to be a standard, derivative nature poem about a brook with "waters calm, unsullied," but the final three lines bring the reader sharply back to a suburban London park with a "business man, with brief-case under arm" hurrying homewards "With scarce a sideways glance at all this charm."

Overall the 1958 HM Inspectors felt that English literature teaching was more effective than language teaching in the school. The inspectors praised the wide variety of literature on offer, which ranged from legends and children's classics to works by contemporary writers.[75] However, reflecting the underlying tensions in the department outlined earlier, the report noted that the choice of literary texts and approaches to teaching varied greatly among the English staff. Such variations of practice were potentially disruptive and confusing for pupils. Therefore despite their support for the breadth and depth of the English course, the inspectors noted that standards in the first two years did not always measure up to pupils' potential. In the third and fourth years improvements in literature teaching and composition led to "promising developments." On the whole the average standard of attainment in English was judged "very satisfactory and that reached by the ablest pupils is very good."[76] It seems that by the late 1950s, despite strong traditions in English, some innovative practice and a few new staff, there was room for increased consistency in English provision across the school and there was an opportunity for a strong head of department to make a mark.

The Minchenden English Department After 1959

Douglas Barnes was appointed head of English at Minchenden in 1959. After grammar school in Kent, Barnes read English at Cambridge under F. R. Leavis before taking a Certificate in Education at the Cambridge Department of Education, and started teaching in 1949. At Minchenden Barnes found himself head of a department composed of six or seven teachers and felt a clear need to "offer some kind of leadership" to a group that had not experienced this before. [77] Barnes later offered an analysis of the English teaching he found when he arrived at the school: "I succeeded a woman who retired, who was extremely backward-looking... I think the head wasn't sorry to appoint me. I think he'd had enough of her."[78] Although Barnes' goal was to build up a strong and mutually supportive team of English teachers, the transition was difficult at first because one or two of the teachers he inherited "thoroughly objected to what I was doing" such as stopping the "old fashioned grammar teaching."[79] This lack of cohesion appears to have been obvious to pupils, two of whom recall "the Douglas Barnes team we knew [in 1959/61] was not a tight team – they had different styles and, we imagine, different values."[80] While Barnes immediately established a rapport with Yvonne Bradbury (née Redman), he found it harder to get along with Mike Riddle and Mike Whittaker. Under Miss Crossley Riddle seems to have been used to doing as he liked in the classroom, enjoying the freedom not to plan lessons but to rely on his personality to engage pupils with particular topics or activities. Yvonne Bradbury, who remembered the transition from Crossley to Barnes, felt that the atmosphere changed and there was lots of new material and ways of using it, although she didn't feel it affected the way she taught.[81]

When first Whittaker and later Riddle moved on, Barnes was able to begin building his own team, recruiting new teachers through his contacts with the English department at the Institute of Education and LATE. A key consideration for Barnes, as earlier for Crossley, was to recruit as many men as possible, because he "didn't want English to turn into a girls' option."[82] Robert Hardman and Elizabeth Stuttard (afterwards Hardman) were two newly qualified teachers who found their first jobs at Minchenden under Barnes after training at the Institute in 1963 and 1964, respectively. Elizabeth Stuttard had attended a Methodist boarding school in Yorkshire followed by a degree at Oxford. Robert Hardman went to grammar school in the northern city of Warrington and avoided the sales job at a local factory his mother had lined up for him by staying on into the sixth form. After winning a place at Cambridge, Hardman spent his national service being trained as a Russian interpreter at the Joint Services School for Linguists on the east coast of Scotland.

Dennis Roberts, who joined the team in 1962, was originally from South Africa and had attended a boys' boarding school in Durban before taking a four-year liberal arts degree at the University of Natal, where he specialized in history and English and took a taster course for teaching. He came to Britain in 1957 in part because of his increasing concern about living under the apartheid regime. Finding his South African degree didn't count for much in the United Kingdom he enrolled for a masters degree in English Literature at Birkbeck taught by the inspiring lecturer, Barbara Hardy, while teaching by day at a secondary modern school in Northolt. Barnes later noted he had appointed Roberts because he "came with a very strong reference from Barbara Hardy... he had obviously impressed her."[83] Although London was a huge culture shock because nothing had prepared him for the existence of "working-class white people," Roberts later recalled that his South African background was helpful in teaching as it meant he could not be identified as belonging to a specific social class in England and therefore pupils couldn't place him so easily. There were several other English teachers in the department at this period that we were unable to speak with, including Redman and her replacement Enid Aisthorpe, but we did interview several teachers who taught at Minchenden slightly later than the period of our study, including Jean Dunning, recruited at the end of Barnes' period in 1966, Jenny Lewis and Barbara Platt who both joined in 1969 and Mike Benton who was head of department in the 1970s.

One of Barnes' first steps was to start regular departmental meetings, a move greeted by existing staff as a welcome change from the old regime. Through the meetings, either held in the school or more often in Barnes' own home, teachers worked together to develop the English curriculum and discuss methods of teaching and this led over time to the group becoming a tightly knit team. Much time at such meetings was given over to discussing and selecting fiction, poetry, or other reading books. Barnes summarized:

> We used to have these meetings, and I would ask one member of the department to introduce something about, say, personal writing, or poetry, and we would take off from there into a general discussion, and I would be taking notes, and I would type it up, and it would become a revision or an

addition to the English syllabus. We all had files in which we put sheets of the curriculum as it developed. [84]

These meetings were of central importance to all the English teachers we interviewed. The English staff also supported one another informally, exchanging advice on how to manage classes and how to prepare lessons. Many of the teachers in the early 1960s lived near each other in Muswell Hill or neighboring suburbs of North London. This proximity encouraged a strong social life among the younger teachers, revolving around drinks in the pub, playing tennis, and wine and cheese parties. Elizabeth Hardman (née Stuttard) characterized the teachers:

> The department was full of larger than life characters – even I, when I gained confidence. We were all self-opinionated, passionate in argument, widely read, interested in things outside school and English, e.g. theatre, art, opera, music. There was a lot of discussion, some heated...If you weren't 100 per cent committed you were out of the group – it was a clique.[85]

The collegial/cliquey atmosphere was reinforced by the involvement of most Minchenden English teachers in LATE, involving London meetings and residential conference weekends. This was in part because Douglas Barnes was a leading member who edited two widely used volumes of short stories published by LATE.[86] Barnes played a key role in the Dartmouth Seminar in the summer of 1966, drafting a report on drama teaching in schools. The importance of LATE to members of the Minchenden English department comes across strongly in interviews. The meetings and weekend conferences brought London school teachers into contact with the main teacher educators and English teaching specialists of the day, notably the Institute's English team, James Britton, Nancy Martin, and Harold Rosen. Dennis Roberts pinpointed attending LATE meetings as a formative experience for his own development as an English teacher: "Just imagine spending time with people like that: Rosen and Britton and Nancy Martin. Wonderful people."[87]

Interviews with former pupils reveal a great deal of affection and respect for this generation of English teachers, particularly because they felt many of them related to pupils as adults. Being taught by Roberts was a "seminal experience" in the mid-1960s for Sandra Newton, who had vivid memories of studying *Macbeth* with pupils acting out parts. She noted "he didn't sort of talk down to us, he engaged us, and somehow he just opened up the text."[88] Irving Finkel recalled that in the early 1960s there was a "coterie" of people who were good at English and wanted to be writers and who were very responsive to the new English that Barnes and others were bringing into the school:

> I was very secure in English because I had an extremely mature vocabulary, I was really interested in English literature, I read a lot, and I wanted to be one of them, you know what I mean. There was a little bit of this patronage from [Enid] Aisthorpe, and there was certainly a strong sense of it from Douglas Barnes.[89]

Though it was unusual for teachers to have much contact with pupils they did not teach, some like Yvonne Redman were exceptions. As one pupil noted:

> She's the one that related very well to the students, and we used to, I'm sure it was her who helped to organize all these visits to the theatre and I don't know, I can't remember, I remember Dan Jacobson, the novelist, came to see us after, when we were in the sixth form, to talk about his work, and we read his book.[90]

In interviews and his memoir Douglas Barnes recalls that his development as a teacher in this period was closely influenced by Minchenden colleagues both inside and outside the English department. The increasing popularity of English in the 1960s led to a degree of friction between the English teachers and some other staff members, particularly in mathematics and science. Barnes claimed that the science teachers resented English because "we became very popular with the kids who wanted to spend all their time reading and writing, and that was one of things that this group who objected to us were saying. We were taking too much of the attention and enthusiasm of the kids, who ought to have been working hard on their science."[91] Although there were colleagues at Minchenden who did not wholly approve of the direction the English staff were taking, other teachers of history, geography, and classics became interested in the ideas about language development and new teaching techniques, which were emanating from the English department. Pupils from the 1959–1961 period identified "some overlap between the interests of the Douglas Barnes-led English team and a few other humanities teachers."[92]

One teacher who was particularly influenced in the early 1960s was Margaret Bradley, a young geography teacher who later married Dennis Roberts. She described in an interview how she was drawn into the English department:

> In our corner [of the staffroom] we'd just have educational discussions of the kind, I'm not sure if they still go on in staffrooms now, but we had

quite – and again it was kind of a cross-curricular group…and I, I just experimented. I was told I could do what I liked, so years one, two, and three I just did what I wanted, to bring things alive. So I started using extracts from books, travel books, anthropology.[93]

Supported and mentored by Barnes, Margaret encouraged her pupils to write poems or songs in response to the topics they covered in geography and developed a cross-curricular project on Japan with Robert Hardman. Picking up on other techniques from English she got pupils to undertake extended projects on topics such as koala bears or Aboriginal art, which would be presented in bound project books. Moreover, finding her own subject association uncongenial, Bradley was drawn into attendance at LATE meetings. Robert Hardman also taught history to first and second years and introduced the new English approach to his classes teaching history through drama, poems, and "ballads."[94]

English teachers continued to make a strong contribution to the wider school culture, although as head of English, Barnes was less involved with this side of the work than were other teachers.[95] In 1959–1960 Mike Riddle, "horrified to learn about the somewhat low general level of culture" of his lower sixth English class, started a new society called the Culture Vultures.[96] Although a voluntary group, apparently most members of his English sets regularly went on the group's excursions which included seeing plays like the *Lily-White Boys*, *The Caretaker*, *The Playboy of the Western World*, and *Rosmersholm*, the Picasso exhibition at the Tate, *The Marriage of Figaro* at Sadlers Wells, and a concert at the Royal Festival Hall.[97] By the early 1960s raising money for charities such as Oxfam had become an important part of the school's ethos. For example, in 1961 the school's UNICEF committee was particularly active, raising money through cake sales, a staff baby photography competition, a boxing match, and Halloween party. English teachers like Riddle contributed by writing humorous reviews as fundraisers. Robert Hardman was involved with a Record Club as well as the Film Club, and recalls taking pupils to see the famous Russian *Hamlet* in 1964. Dennis Roberts and his new wife Margaret took pupils on ski trips. English teachers in the early 1960s also contributed heavily to the General Studies and extraEnglish courses offered to sixth formers. The latter were programs of talks by English teachers and outside speakers as well as excursions. They did not lead to an examination or follow a set curriculum, allowing teachers to speak on topics of interest to them such as the press, current affairs, and parliament. Margaret Roberts remembered organizing a term's work on South Africa "where Doug did literature, Dennis did some politics, I did some geography of apartheid" and speakers were invited from both the Anti-Apartheid Movement and South Africa House.[98]

Under Barnes, teachers at Minchenden enjoyed a new freedom to develop collaboratively the school's English curriculum and its internal examinations. Through LATE and NATE they were also able to influence national development in both. Minchenden teachers were closely involved, too, with other educational associations such as the Enfield Association for the Advancement of State Education (AASE), one of a number of such associations formed in the 1960s under a loose federation. Douglas Barnes convened Enfield AASE's 1965 lecture series on the topic of "Talking, making and writing," which included talks by Nancy Martin and Connie Rosen as well as Margaret Roberts from Minchenden. The Nuffield Foundation Resources for Learning project was also strongly influenced by ideas developing at Minchenden, as both Elizabeth Stuttard and Margaret Roberts left "to work for [the project] with our ideas full of Minchenden."[99] Margaret Roberts was also part of a group who drafted the final chapter of the Barnes, Britton, and Rosen volume *Language, the Learner and the School* (1969).

Toward a New English Curriculum?

One of the first and more controversial moves by Barnes was to end separate grammar teaching as part of a move to a unified English curriculum. He later wrote "The LATE view was that clause analysis and parts of speech, however they were taught, contributed nothing to young people's control over written language, and that they added little to their understanding of language in general."[100] This change was introduced only slowly; when Dennis Roberts started in the school in 1962, he recalled that the staff were "still doing some traditional English teaching at Minchenden. In the early days Ridout was the bible."[101] The abandonment of formal grammar was accepted reluctantly by some other members of the department, who enjoyed that part of the work and who were proud of their ingenuity in making such compulsory lessons enjoyable for pupils. Apparently Mike Whittaker was the teacher most opposed to this change and would lie in wait for Barnes each morning and engage him in "a sequence of energetic arguments" before lessons began.[102] Certainly some pupils recalled that they enjoyed learning parts of speech while others noted that while they remember having them they couldn't remember how such grammar lessons were taught.[103]

Barnes' abolition of formal grammar lessons was accompanied by changes in internal English examinations, starting with end-of-year exams for first- and second-year pupils.[104] The new exams, "designed to help pupils write well," omitted grammar and skills tests out of context, leaving simply a series of "invitations to writing" as Barnes noted in a 1965 article.[105] There was no set number of questions. Pupils could produce up to five shorter pieces of writing or concentrate on one longer essay during the two-hour exam. The next step was the adoption of a new O level paper in English Language, which related the teaching of language to the teaching of literature.[106] This London Examinations Council examination had been sponsored by LATE, and was one of several alternative English language examination papers developed by examination boards in the early 1960s.[107] Barnes was supported in this by some of the newer and younger members of his team; later recruits to the department committed themselves to the move away from grammar teaching. Pupils of a later period recalled that they were aware of this shift, which was most obvious in the way they "experienced texts."[108] Other pupils contrasted their experience with what they perceived to have been that of pupils a few years before: "English was boring, wasn't it? English was parsing, English was précis, English was reading tough novels."[109]

Barnes' attempts to introduce new linguistics-based grammar teaching at Minchenden were, however, less than successful. His fourth-year class were bewildered by the nonsense language of C. C. Fries and his structural analyses.[110] His colleague Elizabeth Hardman was critical of such methods, which she suggested were "flavour of the month" in LATE at the time.[111] However these experiments did not amount to an abandonment of all rules. Barnes recalled:

> I was concerned that my pupils should conform to normal practice in spelling and punctuation, and that when it was appropriate they should use the forms and structures normal in standard written English...However like many other teachers in the fifties I came to believe that exercises did little to eradicate the errors pupils made when writing.[112]

There is a marked contrast in attitudes to grammar between teachers of the earlier period and those of a later one, with Barbara Brooks—a young teacher who started at Minchenden in 1969—outlining her position succinctly: "no way was I going to do bloody parsing and bloody clause analysis."[113] The unified approach to English became part of Minchenden teachers' routine practice which they took with them to later appointments.[114] For example, Yvonne Redman, writing just after leaving Minchenden, described as "representative" of her teaching a week's lessons on the topic of child discipline, which involved "All the aspects of English teaching – literature of fact and imagination, drama, discussion, reading aloud, comprehension, précis, essay and story writing so often taught in isolation."[115] Robert Hardman suggested:

> We always tried to relate everything at Minchenden, so you didn't do things in isolation. So the writing would come out of what you'd been reading, talking about, they were never just sent home with a topic to write about. It always arose out of some activity, it could have been some free drama, it could have been a book we'd read.[116]

Part of the shift away from grammar involved a reassessment of the textbooks and materials pupils used. Key to all Barnes' innovations was his concept of a "rolling curriculum" in which an English syllabus was continually developed by the English staff through meetings and discussion. Central to the new English teaching as it emerged in Minchenden as in some other postwar London schools was the idea that English lessons should encourage language development in pupils of all ages. Douglas Barnes suggests that the major shift in his own pedagogy was the move, over 15 years, from "seeing my central task as introducing pupils to literature to that of encouraging them to develop the use of their own language resources."[117] Dennis Roberts likewise described his own transition toward encouraging pupils' language development, and noted the formative influence of LATE and the translation of Vygotsky and Luria from Russian to English in this process:

> Luria and Vygotsky and language development made you realize that… language development was absolutely crucial in children, and your job was to facilitate language development by exposing them to as many different language experiences as possible, whether you are reading, whether you are talking, whether you are acting, or watching a film, or whatever you are doing, that's language experience, and that the wider range of stuff that you are providing a person, the more the language develops.

Pupils' language development was promoted in a number of ways at Minchenden. These included exposing them to a wide range of prose and poetry, including nonfiction in newspapers and magazines; a strong emphasis on talk and drama in the classroom; a "social studies" influenced approach to topic selection; and encouragement of writing and talking about their own experience. In a very useful document, a paper given to the Enfield AASE in 1965, Barnes outlined his philosophy of education as it stood near the end of his time at Minchenden. He argued that secondary pupils need to be given opportunities to "use language to explore in talk and writing their own experience, to find out what they feel and think, and how it relates to what other people feel and think."[118] As the lessons had to deal with the pupils' world as they see it, "the teacher cannot really choose this for them." Thus pupils' self-determination implied a good deal of work in small groups that would encourage "honest talk and writing that ranges widely over what is important to them."

The new English curriculum as it developed at Minchenden over the period 1959–1965 was interpreted by the individual teachers in different ways. However, the "rolling curriculum" that teachers developed together in department meetings and through shared resources in the English room, meant there came to be many common elements. There was a focus for younger pupils on everyday experiences: "family, parents, friends, school, boy-girl relations, and moving, and death too came up occasionally," as Barnes recalled.[119] Typical writing activities included tasks such as asking first formers to prepare leaflets describing "what they would want to tell the kids who were coming up from the junior school" or descriptions of family members and friends. Other popular writing tasks included "On the Island" projects and pupils interviewing relatives about their memories.[120] The examination questions for first- and second-year pupils asked them to write on topics such as a shopping expedition with "your mother for something you don't want to have bought for you," "turning out my cupboard," "what things in your junior school do you miss at Minchenden," and "taking care of a pet" and "playground games."[121]

The shift to personal writing, both fictional and nonfictional, can also be traced in the surviving pupil work we have collected. Jean Dunning remembered the main activity she did with the younger forms in the mid-1960s was autobiographical writing of various kinds, although she did start to find that pupils had done similar activities at primary school. We have a copy of an illustrated literary magazine called *Fox Lane Extra* compiled by first- and second-year pupils with the assistance of Elizabeth Stuttard. This includes many examples of the personal writing that had been developed in lesson-time, with poems and stories about family members, school, scout camp, moving house, and the local area. Examples include short descriptions of local characters like Dudley, a black porter at Sainsbury's self-service store in Southgate, and a story about a girl "rocker" who changes allegiance to become a "mod."

There was also use of the "stimulus and response" style of teaching. At the end of her second year Margaret Brookes (afterwards Butt), a pupil who started school in September 1966, described her very first English lesson at the school: "our teacher came in and asked us to describe an apple she had taken a bite out of."[122] Margaret Brookes' surviving English exercise books are dominated by autobiographical writing, and although these date from just outside our period, other pupil reminiscences suggest they are fairly typical of mid-1960s English teaching at Minchenden.

What differs most from the earlier period is this personal style of writing, the absence of grammar or comprehension exercises, and the nature of the teachers' response to homework. Most of the tasks assigned invite a personal response, including descriptions of family members, memories of home and school, and reviews of favorite books. Her essay "A perfect summer's day" is not a pastiche of nature writing in the vein of the 1950s examples mentioned earlier, but a fantastical description of a day in London, shopping on Carnaby Street, and a trip to see the Monkees pop group in concert (she wrote the piece before attending the concert!). A piece on her younger brother she recalls was a "a sort of obituary, an imagined obituary, and I can remember writing it, and weeping over it as I wrote it. Bizarre thing, what we were asked to do God knows!" In her third year Margaret produced a 12-page autobiography. Rather than a simple grade and one word comment as is common in the books from the 1940s and 1950s, in the mid-1960s exercise book the teacher enters into a dialogue with the pupil, asking questions which Margaret then responds to. Other pupils at the school in the 1960s recalled receiving no marks on written assignments, just three or four lines of comments, a process Peter Blakebrough described as "communion with your teacher." He recalled eloquently:

> English creative writing homework was sacred to me...the bit that was the heart of you, the core of you. I would go home, and I would sit at my dining room table, I've probably still got some of them, or I might have thrown them out now, but bits I wrote, two or three sides of...I remember writing one thing about, lyrical stuff, a description of my street, and how it looked. It's making me emotional just to talk about it, it's emotional, it's absurd. Writing this kind of stuff about the place that you lived, stuff that was important to you.[123]

Under Barnes, the shift toward contemporary authors begun in the later 1950s was consolidated and approaches to teaching texts were made more uniform across the school. In Barnes' 1965 paper to the Enfield AASE, he argued that teachers should choose stories, poems, and extracts that "honestly explore experiences that the children recognize as important," forgetting any preconceptions they might bring from their own education about what constituted "classics."[124] A key realization was recognition of the validity of children's responses to stories and poems: "I had to accept that a poem would often speak quite differently to a twelve year old – or even to a sixteen year old – than it would to me."[125] The personal nature of pupils' responses to literature in no way implied a diminution in its importance for Barnes and his colleagues because without it pupils "were left within the bounds of their own experience," whereas stories and poems could give new perspective to their own lives and present experiences they had not had. As Barnes later outlined, this represented an important shift from his own earlier thinking where he would start with literature and move out into experience. By 1965 Minchenden teachers were starting with experiences and then moving to literature.

The selection of appropriate stories, poems, and extracts required team effort and was one central focus of discussion in meetings. Together, English teachers drew up a reading list and purchased short sets of these novels and nonfiction books so that pupils could work in small groups of three or four on a text. The department also created class libraries, which were boxes filled with individual copies or short sets of a range of different books. As Robert Hardman recalled, "you encouraged the kids to, on Friday afternoon, to choose their books."[126] Jean Dunning recalls how important these carefully chosen books were for her teaching in the mid-1960s. She remembers Frank O'Connor's *My Oedipus Complex and Other Stories* and Alan Sillitoe's *The Loneliness of the Long Distance Runner*. Several of the teachers began to base their teaching in the lower forms on the new children's books that were published in the 1950s and early 1960s in series such as the Heinemann New Windmill, which began publication in 1950, and included books like *The Silver Sword, The Family from One End Street*, and *The Grudge Fight*. As Elizabeth Hardman reflected these were "modern books, and they tended to be about teenage children, or slightly older, in situations. There was a definite feel that these books are ones that children can and should respond to."[127] Dennis Roberts noted that Tolkien's *The Hobbit* and Golding's *The Lord of the Flies* were used with lower forms. Authors like Doris Lessing from other Anglophone countries were introduced.[128] Short stories were often taught and the two volumes edited by Barnes were used by teachers in the school—*Short Stories of Our Time* in particular was used with the fourth year.[129] In fact as Barnes later acknowledged it was Yvonne Redman who suggested many of the stories chosen for the volume which she had found to work well with Minchenden classes.[130] O level set texts included *Strife* (Galsworthy), and at A level *Luther* (Osborne) and *A Man for All Seasons* (Bolt).[131] Emerging from LATE there was also strong encouragement of the idea of introducing pupils to modern nonfiction books such as Gerald Durrell's *My Family and Other Animals* and Thor Heyerdahl's *Kon-Tiki Expedition*.[132] The new criteria applied to selection of literature represented a break from past practice in Minchenden and the current practice of more traditional schools. Elizabeth Hardman recalled a job interview in 1968 at a South London girls' grammar school where she "really got up their nose because I said I wouldn't teach Shakespeare to eleven year olds, and I wouldn't do this, and I wouldn't do that, I was a sort of Minchenden progressive."[133]

Although, as for the earlier period, it was difficult to get pupils to recall specific examples of literature, we do have some evidence of the impact of these choices. For example, Irving Finkel recalled Barnes "making a lot of fuss" about his second-year class needing to read Chinua Achebe's *Things Fall Apart*, a relatively new novel published in 1958.[134] Pupils discussed the book in small groups in the classroom and afterwards wrote an essay about it. Although Finkel, who was keen on English and from "a very bookish family," enjoyed the book he discovered that the rest of his group found it "really boring"—a fact he pointed out in his essay. In contrast Finkel, like some others we interviewed, hated books like the *The Hobbit,* recalling "we had to write essays on *The Hobbit*, and I wouldn't do them. I once wrote a poem about *The Hobbit*, which was about three lines long, and I got a very low mark for my homework." Barnes recalls that Whittaker's selection of "kids' fantasy stuff" like *The Hobbit* and also Tolkien's *Farmer Giles of Ham* did not go down well with the pupils.[135] Other pupils remember books like Beverly Clearly's 1956 novel *Fifteen* about teenage girls, which was reviewed by Margaret Brookes for one English homework. In her later interview she described it as having a "startling" effect because it was so different to other books she had read at school.[136]

Barnes encouraged group work as a method of learning, describing an experiment of recording pupils which revealed that "discussion of serious topics when not directed by an adult released hidden strengths – of personality as well as speech."[137] Again, this was an element that teachers took with them to later schools. Robert Harman recounted his approach to English in his next school, a boys' technical high school in Kent, where he "had them sitting around in groups" discussing work. This was a move that made him unpopular with the rest of the staff, but "the boys took to my teaching just like ducks to water, and they loved it."[138] The use of tape recorders reflects a more general integration of new technologies into the classroom over the 20-year period. The 1958 HMI report recorded that "The school has an interesting collection of gramophone records of spoken literature, and this merits the provision of an adequate record-player for the use of the English department."[139] From the late 1950s and early 1960s pupils recall teachers not just playing recordings of poetry but recording pupils as well and this process had important effects on pedagogical practice, such as highlighting the value of small group talk.[140] Barnes and others regularly listened to pupils' recorded discussions on poetry or other topics. Margaret Roberts got her classes to devise tape recorded radio broadcasts based on the popular show *Down Your Way*. Barnes recalled that Minchenden teachers and others were also very influenced by the radio ballads of Charles Parker, who spoke about his work at an LATE meeting:

> We were very impressed. I think, too impressed. Because, looking back, putting different pieces of people's speech together is not allowing them to talk. Imposing your message on their voices. But it seemed enlightened, somehow new in those days.[141]

Recording in the classroom could inspire pupils, as Steve Butters recalled:

> Somewhere along the line doing poems Riddle wanted to use tape recorders, and the thing weighed a hundredweight, it was this big, reel-to-reel recorder... But gradually we learnt to use one of his tape recorders, and he let us borrow one, we took it down to the biology lab... So we fetched this enormous heavy tape recorder down to the biology lab, and practiced recording *Paradise Lost*.[142]

There are a number of similar recollections from the 1950s and 1960s, which testify to the lasting significance for pupils of using new such technology inside and outside the classroom.

A further aspect of the evolving English curriculum was a new priority accorded to unscripted drama at Minchenden in the 1960s. Douglas Barnes recalled that his interest in this stemmed from attending conferences on improvisation and from his reading, particularly of Rose Bruford's books on speech, drama, and mime. He encouraged teachers to use the school hall or playing fields for drama and experimented with team teaching. Barnes described his methods:

> You started off with having them doing individual work... And then you started them in pairs, doing various activities, then moving them around, then having them in threes. You did a lot of this before you expected them to start adding language to it and acting roles, apart from the sort of role that you could do alone... If you put them straight into groups and told them to act out so and so it was often very disorganized and ill matched, whereas if you got them working up to actually using their bodies as well as their voices, and collaborating with others in movements and speech, you got better results when you did put them in the groups.[143]

Under Douglas Barnes the English curriculum at Minchenden was related not just to "pupils' private concerns but to social issues that were important at the time."[144] A typical approach for pupils in the third or fourth years was a sort of social studies and English fusion which was in tune with developments at other schools—including Walworth—and the ideas that were becoming widespread within LATE. Such wider concerns developed out of the focus on home, school, and family that dominated the lower forms. Teachers would start with a piece of information or literature and then ask pupils to imagine themselves in various situations related to the reading, to relate the topic to their own lives and then to give their opinions. Topics might be chosen from literature or other writing that teachers brought into classrooms such as newspaper and magazine articles, often drawn from Sunday supplements or *The Listener*. Dennis Roberts remembered talking in lessons about the Beatles and the Cuban Missile Crisis. He noted:

> We were careful not to indoctrinate, but to encourage discussion of issues on each side of the question. Sort of debating kind of things, capital punishment and all that. We very much, as I say, we were watching television and bringing that into the classroom, news, newspapers.[145]

For example, Barnes recalled using a D. J. Enright poem as a way into discussion of the Vietnam War, looking at the commercial aspects of Christmas, and talking about CND and nuclear bombs.[146] Pupils similarly remembered discussing topics such as nuclear war, civil rights problems in America, newspapers, and the media during O level English classes.[147] Dennis Roberts argued that he encouraged much work on the media, for example, taking a story covered by several newspapers and analyzing how the papers "used language to do the same thing."[148] He continued:

> We all felt that you could analyse film and television in the same way that you can analyse Lawrence, Shakespeare or anything else, it's all language...So instead of just staying with English literature, language happens in newspapers and language happens in films.[149]

Part of this work would be done in class discussion, part as written homework, perhaps based on cyclostyled worksheets with questions and writing topics. Elizabeth Hardman recalled using *Reflections*, the Walworth course book published in 1963: "It was something you could use very freely, it wasn't a comprehension book...it was the nearest thing we had to a textbook, really."[150] Barnes however asserted that although there were copies of *Reflections* around it was not used much at Minchenden because "we took the view that as English teachers we should be selecting passages for our own use."[151] It is probable that *Reflections* was not followed as a course book but used selectively as one resource among others. Some of its techniques were certainly used in the school, though adapted to the suburban concerns of Minchenden pupils. For example, for one English homework exercise Margaret Brookes wrote a letter to the Southgate Civic Society protesting about the proposed destruction of Georgian houses on the Southgate village green. The shift away from textbooks that occurred under Barnes makes the actual topics or sequences of work hard to reconstruct through loss of material. One fragment of a cyclostyled worksheet containing an essay topic survives in the archives and closely echoes similar questions asked in *Reflections*:

> Have you ever lived, or stayed for a time with your grandparents? Write an honest account of how you got on with them, including opinions on the causes of any "friction" between you?[152]

Conclusions

By 1965 Minchenden School was famous in London for its English teaching. High profile visiting educationalists as well as trainee teachers included Minchenden on their tours of schools and a dynamic and collegiate department worked closely to improve the experience of learning English for a broad range of pupils. Pupils enjoyed being addressed as adults and relished discussion of topics of relevance to their everyday lives in the early years as well as wider social and political concerns as they moved up the school. The innovative curriculum, strong commitment from teachers combined with a grammar school intake of pupils most of whom were highly motivated translated into good rates of success in public examinations. At O level, pass rates for English Language were 87 percent in 1964 and 94 percent in 1965 and for English Literature slightly lower at 65 percent in 1964 and 74 percent in 1965.[153]

During the period 1945–1965 Minchenden was a largely middle-class, suburban grammar school. Teachers we interviewed for this study noted that the middle-class background of most pupils did affect the teaching methods they used. Indeed, as Barnes later reflected, teachers can be more influenced by their pupils than they sometimes admit.[154] Writing of Minchenden he noted that "boys and girls came to school with a tacit understanding of what was required, and a predisposition to please."[155] This meant that the group-based teaching style he developed in the early 1960s was implemented without difficulty. Robert Hardman recalled that pupils were "lively, gifted, engaged and responsive to me" and that "many of them brought a lot *with* them; and I learned from them, e.g. about Jewish history and culture." [156] Dennis Roberts, however, argued that the techniques developed by Barnes and colleagues would have "worked anywhere," asserting "Well, it did work anywhere, because I went on to teach all over the place, after Minchenden."[157] In particular the influence of the significant Jewish minority was perceptible to teachers and other pupils at the school. Teachers felt that they were especially rewarding to teach. As Barnes recalled:

> Amongst the most lively and interested kids were a very large proportion of Jewish kids... Wonderful kids to teach. This sense that Jews often have, of being under pressure and needing to work hard to get this security. And also a support of cultured, middle-class Jewish families.[158]

There was a relatively small group of students who were particularly responsive to the new English teaching at Minchenden and who forged strong personal relationships with their English teachers in the classroom as well as through extra A or S level classes and reading groups which met in teachers' homes and through extracurricular activities. For others, notably those who specialized in science in the sixth form, English was less memorable. The English teaching developed at Minchenden had a wider influence on the teaching profession more broadly through teachers' subsequent roles, talks, and conference presentations and publications.

Chapter 6

The Three Schools—What We Have Learned

In this chapter, we first summarize the story of English in each school between 1945 and 1965 and then consider the picture in terms of aspects of English rather than school by school, both elements that changed and ones that stayed the same. Moving beyond curriculum and pedagogy we next address school English departments and associations outside the school. We review our findings in terms of the national picture we presented in chapter two and comment on how far they reflect what the histories of English teaching say about the period. Finally we describe in a more general way the character of the changes we have reported, and speculate briefly on connections between the changing or stable nature of English and social and cultural change.

Our three schools were different from one another in ways that allow of three pairings. The institutional, demographic, and locational differences were explained in chapter one. In terms of their approaches to teaching English, the schools also fall into pairs, at least if we consider the later period, from the mid-1950s, separately. English at Hackney Downs, and at Minchenden before 1959, evolved within well-established grammar school traditions; Walworth, especially after 1956, developed a new approach, in which it was joined from 1959 by Minchenden, thus forming a new pairing, strongly aligned with a current of thinking and practice in LATE.

English at Hackney Downs School was above all *cerebral*. It was the intellect that counted: knowledge of a wide range of literature, the articulation of ideas, dedication to the life of the mind within a broad, humanist view of education—such were the ideals cherished by a succession of outstanding teachers, most of them heads of department (senior English masters), who had themselves been pupils in grammar schools and with whom the most promising boys entered a master–apprentice relationship. The study of English literature was central, literary criticism replacing literary appreciation and scholarship during our period as the means considered best suited to attaining the teachers' ideals. The switch involved changing methods and reordering priorities without disturbing the grammar school ethos.

However, while regarding their subject as the intensive study of literature, teachers also, to what was perhaps an exceptionally high degree in grammar schools, valued pupils' creative productions in writing, including poetry, and dramatic performance—as well as their mastering of the genres of academic writing. At the same time, it is fair to say that the cultural and linguistic background of the pupils was overlooked as a potential starting point and resource for work in English.

As was true in most grammar schools, the subject was framed by public examinations and the syllabus could have continued largely unchanged if the school had been picked up and set down in a country town.[1] On the other hand, the pupils' *experience* of lessons beyond the curricular content, and particularly that part in which interaction featured, was strongly affected by the character of the locality and of the population of pupils drawn from it, which after the war was increasingly working-class and Jewish. The spoken contributions of these London working-class (cockney) and Jewish groups lent a vibrancy to any lesson that involved discussion and debate.

The school curriculum as a whole was intended as a preparation for continuing education at university and entry into the professions. While for the top streams, and especially the sixth form, English provided an intellectually stimulating environment, this highly academic orientation was, as might be expected, inappropriate for many pupils in the lower streams—though it should be remembered that all had passed the 11 plus and thus belonged to the top quarter or so of the population by measured ability. The lower stream groups were not expected to continue in school beyond the age of 16 and the English teaching they received could be boring and ineffective. It was resented by some individuals who felt they were not given opportunities to develop particularly their creative abilities. Yet this was by no means always the case because the English experience offered by some teachers was lively, while the practical support they provided to pupils from poor homes was appreciated. In general, however, the school's concentration on exam preparation meant that the intellectual and expressive capabilities of lower-stream pupils were rarely exploited as relevant resources for English work. The prevailing view that the cultural and linguistic resources that working-class pupils brought with them were inadequate for progression in education placed the school at a disadvantage when it eventually became a comprehensive. For the most talented pupils, however, many of them from working-class and second and third generation immigrant homes, English offered an exhilarating intellectual experience from which some—most famously Harold Pinter—were able to succeed in fields where their studies in school made a huge contribution.

Walworth was a new type of school, a comprehensive or, more accurately, an *interim* comprehensive—a school that was set up with a view to becoming fully comprehensive. It was envisaged that in due course it would receive those boys and girls who for the time being (in the event, for most of our period) continued to pass the 11 plus and be accepted into grammar schools. The school's headteachers were committed to the comprehensive ideal and they ran the school in anticipation of attaining fully comprehensive status by implementing a curriculum that was designed for pupils of all abilities. The less academically gifted pupils would not, as was so often the case in the former senior elementary schools and was still so in many secondary moderns, receive a restrictive education that denied them the possibility of progression. The first relatively long-lasting head of English (1949–1955), Arthur Harvey, was appointed by the school's pioneering headteacher expressly, it seems, to further the principles they both espoused. Yet, while Harvey was committed to comprehensive education in principle, in practice he ran what was essentially a grammar school English course for his high-ability classes. He made no appreciable effort to adapt the course for the remainder of the pupils or to coordinate the work of the department. As was common at the time, members of the department went their own way using a variety of traditional and imaginative methods.

Real change came with the appointment of Harold Rosen as head of department who gave concentrated thought to the education of all children. Rosen and his successors encouraged the department to act as a body and, working in a new collaborative way, they made a radical break with traditional practice by setting up an English program that placed heavy reliance on the children's motivation to express themselves on topics close to their own lives. They took it for granted that curriculum development and thinking were central aspects of their work. The theory was—and it was to a significant extent made to work—that in content pupils would move from personal and local to societywide matters, and in language from modes close to the self (especially personal and narrative writing) to abstract and reflective discourse. None of this was necessarily to the neglect of literature. The Walworth approach, with which the work of a number of other schools (many of them in the provinces) came to have much in common, was widely thought to be the much-needed, viable model for English in the comprehensive school.

For much of our period, English at Minchenden was characterized (certainly for the top streams) by inherited grammar school practice, being geared primarily to public examinations and relying heavily on textbooks. Then, from 1959, with a new head of department, Douglas Barnes, and some new English staff, an overhaul of practices along LATE (and Walworth) lines began in earnest. This came about not because the school was about to go comprehensive (though many teachers were in favor of such a move) or out of concern about the impoverished version of English offered to the lower streams, but rather from a sense that English as it existed was ineffective in developing boys' and girls' thinking, their sensibilities, and their language. A perception grew among teachers at Minchenden that English was failing to engage profitably with what most concerned the pupils themselves—a perception that was remarkably similar to that of teachers at Walworth. However, at issue at Minchenden was not so much social justice—how to make equal provision for all pupils, including those from working-class backgrounds—as a liberal view of education as a process that was personal as much as intellectual. Although the English program at Minchenden became progressively less reliant upon inherited approaches, it did not stop being intellectually stimulating. It broadened its appeal by taking seriously pupils' interests and by taking advantage of the wider range of literature that had become available in the late fifties. Toward the end of our period, the notion of fostering both children's language and personal development supplanted the structures and strictures of disciplinary studies that derived their methods and values from English in the universities.

Some Trends, Common and Divergent

When we proceed to pick out some broad trends, first we note a growing dissatisfaction with teaching based on the available textbooks, the majority published before the war. These typically contained exercises in précis, comprehension, and grammar and their place was secured by their role in preparation for the School Certificate and, later, O level English Language examinations. In the eyes of some teachers they killed the spirit of the subject. The carryover from the prewar period into the 1950s is unsurprising in view of printing restrictions and financial stringencies. In some lessons there were not enough copies of a book to go round the class. New textbooks did appear, notably Ronald Ridout's series *English Today*, which appeared between 1946 and 1950 and was used in Walworth and Minchenden. As Harold Rosen was quick to see, despite its more modern presentation, the book perpetuated many of the shortcomings prevalent in prewar textbooks, as later did many others.

Deficiencies in the passages for study provided in the textbooks tended to be compensated for less through the purchase of new textbooks than with sheets of extracts and poems typed and duplicated by teachers (with, if they were lucky, the assistance of office staff). Improvements in the educational publishing scene were reflected in the schools not so much in new textbooks as in new texts for class reading and for library and private use. As we described in chapter two, contemporary or at least twentieth century works came into use, including recent children's literature, a field that saw a flourishing of new writers and publications in the 1950s and 1960s. The private reading the schools encouraged included recent adult fiction, including, for one pupil at Hackney Downs, John Wain's *Hurry on Down*, Alan Sillitoe's *The Loneliness of the Long Distance Runner*, Kingsley Amis' *Lucky Jim*, and J. D. Salinger's *The Catcher in the Rye*.[2] In the late 1950s John Kemp introduced more appealing titles for younger pupils into the school library, such as *The Silver Sword* and *The Otterbury Incident*. The pattern at Walworth and Minchenden was broadly the same, except that Guy Rogers at Walworth felt it necessary, for his entirely working-class (and non-Jewish) parent body to accompany his list of recommended reading with explicit guidance, such as was evidently deemed unnecessary in the grammar school, about also *buying* books. His list included nothing like *Hurry on Down* or *Lucky Jim*: their references to university life might have made some sense to grammar school pupils for whom university was constantly presented as the destination most to be sought, but would have meant little in Walworth. Rosen had found that a different sort of adult book, *The Quiet American* by Graham Greene, apparently *did* make sense to one sophisticated but reluctant reader, with its world of sex, colonialism, and international relations that because of films and television news were more familiar than the common rooms and soirées of provincial academics.

LATE was active in reviewing books for school use and produced two collections of short stories under the leadership of Minchenden's Douglas Barnes. Minchenden also contributed to a new approach to class reading by giving a small group of pupils a "short set" of copies of a novel to read, discuss, and use as the basis of whole class presentations or homework tasks. This method enabled more books to be read each term and more pupils to engage actively in discussion, the small group context being less intimidating than the whole class. This model, though it was endorsed by LATE and was used at Walworth, does not appear in the evidence from Hackney Downs

A further development in "methods" was the adoption of activities that extended over a number of lessons, or even several weeks—a departure from the system of one lesson, one topic and task. This changed the nature of teachers' work by requiring a different sort of planning. As explained in chapter three, a blueprint was provided by Britton's prewar course book, *English on the Anvil,* which replaced separate lessons on grammar points by an extended island project that linked activities including imaginative and descriptive writing, as well as grammar, across a number of lessons. Another Britton project, "The Village," was commended in *The Use of English* in 1953 and adopted by Kemp in Hackney Downs, while at Walworth from the late 1950s second-year classes wrote a series of linked stories about a street in a neighborhood like their own. Exercise books from Minchenden reveal, there too, a move toward sequences of lessons that reflected a preference for a curriculum that "flowed." A new pattern of lesson emerged that started with the reading of a passage and might lead on to a related comprehension task and an extended discussion, giving rise in turn to a piece of writing that, marked and handed back in another lesson, might suggest to the teacher further reading which he or she would feel free to pursue—all in an improvisatory spirit released from rigid pre-programming. Coherence across such sequences tended to be provided by a theme, such as those Harold Rosen proposed in his Walworth syllabus of 1958 (described in chapter four).

Two schools paid decreasing attention to the teaching of formal grammar, the topic being largely reduced to spelling, punctuation, and paragraphing. No traditional grammar teaching was proposed in the Walworth course book, *Reflections,* but the accompanying *Teacher's Book* included short writing exercises on punctuation and the like, topics that were also addressed in lessons that were weekly in the younger years. English teachers at Minchenden maintained formal grammar teaching for longer but eventually abandoned it. At Hackney Downs, however, the weekly grammar lesson continued throughout our period.

English in two schools began by design to reflect the lives and experience of London pupils. For the majority of working-class children in a school of the 1940s and 1950s the subject matter of English lessons tended to be distant from their experience, while the language they were expected to speak and write was outside their familiar usage. After the breaks that came with new heads of department in 1956 and 1959, English teachers in Walworth and Minchenden came to believe that a condition for their pupils' fuller engagement was bringing a sense of—from the pupils' point of view—*reality* into English. They therefore made changes to both curriculum and pedagogy, making the pupils' lives and experiences the starting point of lessons and encouraging them to talk, using whatever language and forms of expression "came naturally," under the immediate need or desire to communicate. It was no longer the case that school work involved leaving outside the classroom door both everything you knew from your life and your accustomed ways of talking about things. Pupils were positively encouraged to speak and write about the world they knew, the former at least using their own language. This led to a lesson structure in which after 20 minutes or more of lively discussion—predominantly the recounting of experiences—pupils were found to take readily to writing. Often what resulted was not good writing by the standards of an older grammar school teacher, an examination board or a professional employer, but the work produced was nevertheless believed to be the best basis for enlarging language capabilities, since writing willingly undertaken about content that mattered to the writer tapped, in Rosen's phrase, "the springs of language."[3] The crucial insight—not Rosen's alone—was that the development that children have achieved by the age of 11 had been achieved in language learned and used in home and community, and that a language that was more versatile and capacious could only come by development from what was there already.

In their testimony from Walworth and Minchenden, teachers made clear their belief that it radically affected pupils' experience of English, and their willingness to participate in it, when the use of ordinary, familiar language became acceptable in the classroom. In a change that would have made more difference to working-class than to some middle-class pupils, individuals found themselves able to use the language that came spontaneously to them, even when it contrasted with the language of their teachers. (Yet, although there were pupils who spoke other languages besides English, we found no evidence of efforts by English teachers to take account of language diversity, although this was a feature of many pupils' daily lives.)

Where the impulse toward greater realism of content took hold, an immediate and obvious target for criticism was the rural bias in textbooks and anthologies (as discussed in chapter two.) As Medway discovered in his review of textbooks published in 1958, the world evoked was by default rural; scenes represented or referred to were typically drawn from countryside or country town. It was the world of Methuen's 1921 *Anthology of Modern Verse*,[4] still prescribed for O level in the 1950s and in use in all three schools. In asserting its more realist slant, Walworth responded to what might be described as a "rediscovery" of the working class by writers, filmmakers, and sociologists of the 1940s and 1950s. In chapter four, we described how Patrick Kingwell and a friend had travelled independently to the East End (no mean undertaking for a child living south of the river) where *A Kid for Two Farthings*, the 1953 novel by Wolf Mankowitz (later made into a feature film) was set. In Mankowitz, who came from a Jewish background similar to Harold Rosen's, a Cambridge education and teaching by Leavis were followed by a career whose implicit values were quite different from those of many Leavisite teachers in that he chose to write a popular novel set in the working-class East End of London. It perhaps tells us something interesting about grammar school English that *A Kid for Two Farthings*, while eagerly taken up at Walworth, received no mention from former Hackney Downs pupils, many of whom travelled to school daily from Mankowitz's East End.

The approach to English in which children's language and local experience were favored was endorsed by a significant group in LATE and supported by James Britton and Nancy Martin at the Institute of Education, themselves partly responsible for the ideas on which these practices were based. Traditional pedagogy regarding children's writing meant a mixture of teaching them to do it better—instruction—and a great deal of practice. Instruction meant giving rules, those of prescriptive grammar being the main set, stylistic guidance, and models. Pupils' essays were judged by educated literary standards. Composition tasks were, precisely, "practice"—"dummy runs"[5] as preparation for the challenges of the real thing at some indefinite point in the future, but also more immediately in the O level examination. For Walworth and Minchenden teachers after the new regimes took over in the second half of the 1950s, however, as for James Britton and like-minded colleagues in LATE, speaking and writing in the English lesson were not just "practice." Rosen's decisive move at Walworth was to begin to make the classroom more of a "real" world environment—a domain in which communication was valued for *what* it communicated as much as for the manner of its accomplishment. This was not a curriculum that put a premium on the "creativity" of the child (though few teachers have matched Rosen as a defender of the creative possibilities of working-class children's language). Rather it was concerned with broadening opportunities for children to use the resources they already possessed for real communication to or for listeners or readers who would respond to it as such (and not as a display exercise), whether the utterance or text was recounting experiences or telling invented stories. Motivated, engaged, or impelled uses of language (frequently occurring terms in the writings of Britton and his Institute colleagues) were the aim. Thus the teacher's responsibility shifted from intervention and correction toward fostering expression. One did not, for instance, like Peter Emmens in the famous film, gather "good vocabulary" on the board before setting them to write; rather one got them to write from a desire to write, relying on the stock of language they already possessed and were constantly expanding through their English work, including their reading. It is right to place on record that as far as we can see, in the years after the war Harold Rosen was the first practicing teacher who was an intellectually well-grounded thinker to give his mind, and then to commit himself in practice, to the education of the majority. Education in the elementary and secondary modern schools had rarely been a topic that engaged the attention of those with an education that qualified them to teach in grammar schools; nor even, it seems, had the situation of working-class children in the lower streams of grammar schools.

Changes in the ways that English was studied in the universities affected the school subject in some places. English teachers in all three of our schools were influenced by Leavis' ideas, although not all in the same way. Joe Brearley and Douglas Barnes had both been taught by Leavis at Cambridge—Brearley before the war and Barnes after it—though Barnes considered he had ceased to be a Leavisite well before he reached Minchenden. The particular appeal of Leavis was for grammar school teachers who could count on a high degree of literate competence in their pupils and for whom sixth-form teaching was the most rewarding aspect of their work. Indeed, Leavis' collaborator, Denys Thompson, foresaw difficulties in extending literary criticism to pupils in the modern schools (and by implication the lower streams of comprehensives) who were less competent readers.[6] Brearley emphasized the importance of literary criticism as a training in discrimination, rather than the literary scholarship favored by some predecessors. John Kemp had read Leavis' criticism in his final year at King's College, London. Brearley, Kemp, and Barnes all carried the *Scrutiny* ethos of intellectual and moral seriousness into their teaching, though Barnes moved the center away from literary criticism toward developing children's language resources, the main alternative articulated position that was available in the 1950s and 1960s.

At Walworth no teacher until Graham Reid (1964–1965) had been to Cambridge or been taught by Leavis or his followers; Harvey, Dixon, and Clements had gone to Oxford, Rosen to London where in his undergraduate course at UCL, with its heavy emphasis on traditional scholarship and premodern literature, he could recall not even a mention of Leavis. Together with the key Walworth teachers after him, Rosen found more relevant the concentration on the active processes involved in pupils' reading, writing, and talking that we find in Gurrey, Britton, and their associates at the Institute of Education, as we explained in chapter two.

But the influence of Leavis was pervasive in the literary culture of the time and is unlikely to have left any well-read and alert young English teacher unaffected. A recent writer has claimed that, even for those who find and found Leavis irrelevant (the likes of Rosen, perhaps) he "reshaped the value of reading so completely that we do not notice it."[7] The way that

Leavis' ideas and values showed in Walworth and Minchenden was in the conviction less that essential aspects of life were to be found in literature than that it was to these that pupils' writing and talking should be giving expression. Of the thinkers who persuaded teachers that English should be regarded as a central educational pursuit, Leavis must be among the first. For the London teachers we have been discussing, English was much more than a matter of *taste* and was believed to bear profoundly on one's sense of life, not least in its moral and political aspects. Hence Leavis was partly and indirectly responsible, alongside Gurrey and Britton, for reshaping the value of *writing* and for putting *personal* writing, about *experience*, at the center of the new English curriculum—not least in John Dixon's definitive 1967 text, *Growth through English*.

The Professional Context: Departments and LATE

We reported in chapter two that, at least in London, English teachers in schools began to be organized as English *departments*: meetings began to be held and senior English teachers increasingly took responsibility for influencing and guiding the teaching practices of their colleagues, typically through collective consultation. We found this development in Walworth and Minchenden, though not in Hackney Downs, where teachers continued to plan their work independently. Before the mid-1950s Arthur Harvey at Walworth did hold brief meetings but offered little in the way of departmental leadership or support to colleagues. Miss Crossley at Minchenden presided over a set of teachers who operated, it seems, entirely as individuals, until 1959 when Douglas Barnes introduced department meetings where teachers would choose the books, plan activities, and collaboratively develop a "rolling curriculum" with shared resources.

Speaking of a "traditional grammar school," which was not Hackney Downs although it could well have been, John Harris noted that there was "no overall concept of English teaching [held in common within a department] but respect for each other's opinions."[8] In Medcalf's department at Hackney Downs the commitment of Brearley and Kemp to literary criticism constituted an implicit challenge to Medcalf's largely prewar assumptions about literary appreciation and scholarship, but we found no evidence of actual conflict. Conversations in the staff room tended to be literary, about novels, plays, and poetry, and not pedagogical; there was rarely discussion of pupils' learning or lesson planning, and little need was seen for regular departmental meetings. There was neither scope nor perceived need for internal development of curriculum or methods in a school where the syllabus that counted was set externally by examination boards and where lessons relied on published textbooks—though Kemp brought into his teaching, without attempting to promulgate them, methods that he had learned on his PGCE course at King's, supplemented by later reading in professional literature, especially the *Use of English*.

At Walworth the role of the head of department expanded to include curriculum leadership and planning, and also mediating current theoretical ideas for members of the department. Rosen and Dixon organized and gave practical support to the members of their departments who also supported each other, and planned lessons and made materials together. This was a world away from Hackney Downs. Collaboration extended to the design, development, and eventual publication of the fourth year English course as *Reflections*. Cooperation was not confined to meetings: Margaret Hewitt, a young teacher at Walworth, reported that the most helpful aspect of her department was informal discussion over coffee in which "members of staff exchanged not advice but experience."[9] At Walworth and Minchenden new patterns of collaborative working included meeting in one another's homes to plan lessons or mark work, in a new combination of professional with social relationships.

Despite the continuance of older models, Rosen concluded the 1966 LATE conference on English departments by suggesting that the "Head of Department, as source of all wisdom is finished" and that the future of the department was a "sort of non-stop seminar-cum-club, a miniature LATE, rather than as the officers' mess which it could easily become."[10]

Our story, in any case, is not just of departments but of exceptional individuals making striking impacts, about some of whom a salient fact seems to be that they had had little or no teacher training. Joe Brearley had not done PGCE and looked back to Cambridge for his sense of what English was for. It was partly through not having been inducted into the teaching profession, but instead having long experience of other relevant activities including work with young people, that Harvey at Walworth could bring fresh thinking to the teaching of English at a new kind of school. Both were essentially solo operators, depending little on the support of colleagues. Simon Clements, with a public school education, a history degree, no PGCE, and an ambition initially to become an architect, was burdened with few preconceptions about what English—or a state school classroom—should be. Indeed he claimed he would not have been nearly so bold in his practice if he had taken the PGCE before coming to Walworth. For him, however, unlike Brearley and Harvey, joining a dynamic team of English teachers who appreciated and supported his ideas and shared their own was crucial. Also crucial, he affirms, was participation in and support from LATE, as they had been for Rosen. The association, in which Britton and Martin (and in the early days Gurrey, its founding spirit) were deeply involved, with its meetings, working parties, research groups, and publications, was a powerful influence on new teaching in London. Not on Hackney Downs teachers, however, although Kemp owned and valued Gurrey's *The Teaching of Written English* and knew James Britton. While not active in LATE, Kemp was keenly aware of the intellectual currents that were reshaping English.

The Case Studies in Relation to the National Picture

Our findings from the three schools afford a specific perspective on the national picture that we presented in chapter two, drawing on miscellaneous sources that were often partial or tendentious. Although local and circumscribed studies like ours cannot be expected to throw much light on the general countrywide scene, findings that are strikingly at odds are worth commenting on. One such instance immediately calls for discussion. Writers, themselves skeptical, reported a wave of enthusiasm for the publication of the series *English through Experience* by Rowe and Emmens.[11] There was no sign of this in the three schools; the books are never even mentioned. The phenomenon appears to indicate the existence of a new trend in English that our schools had no part in. The work of the authors of *English through Experience* was associated particularly with a belief in eliciting responses to "happenings" (Summerfield's "ad hoc excitements"), such as Emmens himself was seen deploying on TV with his bubble-blowing lesson. When commentators in the mid-1960s reviewed the English scene nationally, what most stood out for them as characteristic of new tendencies prominent in English departments and teacher training was not the innovations we have noted in two of the three schools—reflective and enactive narrative based on the pupils' lives and experience—but approaches resembling that of Emmens. Summerfield and Hollins were worried that the influence of the latter was potentially harmful. Our case studies show plainly that this was not the only alternative to the tired tradition of parsing and recitation.

On the other hand, the widespread adoption, though not in Hackney Downs or Minchenden, of Walworth's *Reflections* is evidence of the popularity of what some misleadingly called the "social studies" approach to English.

Our three schools—or at least the two that developed a radically new approach to English—do not indicate the adoption of the Emmens approach, but nor can we say with confidence that the teachers' planning and decisions were actively shaped by James Britton's idea that children should be helped through writing to reflect on, bring order to, and make sense of experience, though they would certainly have been exposed to it and have taken it in, and perhaps used it as justification without it being the impelling force. But if Britton's theory had indeed primarily informed teachers' practice, it would hardly have been apparent to us in the resulting products, which would look very similar if the reason that teachers had evoked reflection on experience was that that was known to be a way to get better writing from pupils. We are in no position to judge because we have very little direct evidence, from the time, of teachers' beliefs and have to rely on interpreting documentary traces, where, rarely, we have them, such as mark books and lesson plans, and on whatever is recalled or reconstructed in later writings and interviews. Statements from the time (e.g., Arthur Harvey's two articles) are in any case poor indicators of the assumptions that actually guided teaching day by day, while extrapolating from, and attempting to give discursive statement to, the ideas that underlay practice is hazardous. Whereas we know that John Kemp at Hackney Downs owned, read, and seemed impressed by Gurrey's book on teaching writing, we have no evidence that he applied in his teaching what the book argued about the processes involved in the development of writing abilities—the interconnectedness of reading, writing, and talking. The *Teacher's Book* accompanying *Reflections* does give some insight into at least the verbally endorsed ideas of its three Walworth authors. But while their statements are compatible with the claim that in their spontaneous use of language children are "giving order to the inner life," as Shayer put it (see below), the writing we have seen from the schools seems hardly to reflect that intention.

Another instance of a report in the histories that found no echo in our findings is the observation reported from a visiting delegation of American English teachers that English teaching in England was characterized by a pervasive anti-intellectualism (see chapter two). This was far from the case in any of our schools, where it seems to us that intellectual development was a consistent aim.

Of the existing histories relating to English between 1945 and 1965 we find David Shayer's chapter five, "1940–70 The New English – priorities and purpose in a democratic society," the most adequate and sympathetic, though there are particular aspects with which we disagree.[12] He proposes that a label such as "the New English" (though we have avoided the term as potentially confusing) might appropriately be applied to the state of the subject as it emerged by the early 1970s.[13]

The limitations on the relevance of Shayer's account to our findings are, first, that the type of data we have gathered—concerning practice in specific schools—is not such as would relate naturally to the printed sources he relies on, and, second, that despite having taught at William Ellis School he reveals little familiarity with the London scene or the influence of either the Institute of Education's English Department[14] or LATE.[15] Yet both have been central to our story in two of the schools, and undoubtedly more important than the pioneering "method books" that Shayer apparently regards as the sources of new practice; for instance, few of the teachers we interviewed mentioned being influenced by Holbrook.[16]

Our sort of data do not enable us to comment on David Shayer's initial claim that it was the influence of new ideas about child art that led to a parallel emphasis on children's natural ability to write with poetic *intensity*, a notion introduced to English teachers by Marjorie Hourd's 1949 *The Education of the Poetic Spirit*.[17] From this there came into English, Shayer claims, a new criterion for evaluating children's poetry and writing more generally—"intensity of expression."[18] We agree in finding this criterion operative in much of the commentary on creative writing, as in Alec Clegg's 1964 *The Excitement of Writing* and Ted Hughes' 1967 *Poetry in the Making*, nor do we deny that the influence of progressive spirits like Hourd was felt by English teachers in London, or that a debt to Hourd was acknowledged by Britton, but we do not find it prominent in thinking about English in our schools. Rosen, Dixon, and their colleagues at Walworth and Barnes' team at Minchenden valued something rather different: honesty and sincerity of expression or the pupil's "individual voice."

At Hackney Downs, Kemp painstakingly elicited first-hand responses to texts even from some of his least able pupils and in his teaching and that of colleagues the considered response was the order of the day. "Intensity" as such does not appear as a value in our schools (it was perhaps more associated with the Emmens style of teaching, and the primary school achievements reported by Clegg), and while there is an abundance of writing that seems sincere and has the feel of the pupil speaking, we have found disappointingly little good children's poetry. Indeed, it could be argued that values of straightforward honesty and sincerity could be at odds with the writing of "intense" poetry.

We find plausible Shayer's suggestion that teachers in our period were impressed by the case for relying less on instruction and more on processes analogous to children's early language acquisition, as described by psychologists and linguists along with the claims that language is learned by use and that premature attempts to impose adult models are doomed to failure. At least their practices were consistent with such a position. Emerging, according to Shayer, along with the discovery of children's natural creativity was the conviction among teachers that in giving expression to their feelings and experience, often necessarily in symbolic form where direct statement was impossible, young writers were giving "order to the inner life"[19] and "coming to terms" with existence as they found it. These views were certainly voiced by Gurrey and Britton whose work, as discussed in chapter two, we know impressed some of our influential teachers.

Shayer, concentrating on books and published materials, attributes to them the spread of important ideas. Thus from Holbrook and Hourd came the notion that vivid writing did not depend on IQ but was a common capability in all children. When we look at what was going on in the schools we find that the ways in which these ideas were enacted in practice can hardly be ascribed to a few key authors. Thus O'Reilly, the earlier of the Walworth head teachers and not an English teacher, told a reporter in 1951 that the areas in which the majority weren't educable were only a small part of the curriculum: "After all, remember, we don't have election meetings, radio, cinemas and the rest of it for the able and the less able. We find that in the Comprehensive School the less able children thrive immensely."[20] Similarly, David Holbrook's "real breakthrough" in starting not from existing ideas of English but from "the pupil's needs in a particular society" was already there in Rosen's 1957 Walworth syllabus that stressed the pupils' talking and writing about coping with living where they lived, and in the even earlier work of teachers including John Dixon at Holloway.

The term "creativity" is regularly attached to commentary on the emphases in English teaching of the 1960s and 1970s, but in our schools we rarely encountered it, while "creative" was found only in phrases like "creative writing." The key thinkers involved in reshaping English regarded the opposition of creative versus cognitive or intellectual as a false dichotomy, particularly as they learned via Richards from Coleridge (and German philosophy) that *reading* literature—not just writing it—was a creative activity and that the use of imagination involved all the mental functions. Nor does Mathieson's "shift of emphasis...from the cognitive to the affective" apply in our schools, for similar reasons, though it might apply to work on Emmens lines. "Affective," or its more everyday alternative "emotional," occurs only rarely, since the governing notion is development or "growth," which embraces the person as *both* feeling *and* thinking. *Reflections* is about "coming to terms" as a person and social being with the world as it is encountered and, in the same processes of discussion and writing, moving into the ways of public rational discourse. Douglas Barnes, though coming from a Leavisite literary formation, is no less committed to the cognitive, as his subsequent work on learning *across the curriculum*—including the nonliterary "knowledge subjects"—demonstrates. In none of our schools do we recognize the anti-intellectualism reported by US observers (see chapter two), nor can we agree with Shayer's paraphrase of another writer's view (it is uncertain whether this is his own position—"Be that as it may"), that "as education is sacrificed on the altar of egalitarianism so English is sacrificed on the altar of pupil-centered creativity with its mixture of self-expression and *Reflections*-like 'social awareness.'"[21]

The consensus appears to be that English in the 1940s and 1950s was essentially a continuation of prewar practice, even, as one HMI wrote, "in a state of suspended animation which had hardly changed over forty years [before 1960]."[22] We have found plenty of confirmation of that continuity in aspects of the work in our three schools in the first half of our period, not least in the continued use of the same or similar textbooks and works of literature within the same sort of weekly pattern of unlinked lessons. However, our project was designed to pick up evidence not of continuity but of instances, which we assumed would be exceptional, of *change;* we selected for our case studies three schools that were believed to have been influential within English teaching in London precisely because they were doing something *new*, pioneering new approaches. From the mid-1950s we have indeed found evidence of change—though not always "pioneering" change—such as the impact of practical criticism on the teaching of literature in Hackney Downs. One of our initial hypotheses, which does relate to "pioneering change," was framed in the light of our knowledge of what happened toward and after the end of our period, namely the widespread and officially promoted version of English that replaced the traditional model of *instruction and practice* in language with one about the encouragement of language *use* around topics that were relevant to the pupils' *interests and experience*. Our sense was that this development was well under way before the 1960s to which it has often been ascribed. We had this in mind when we spoke of "innovation."

There is less to say with reference to Mathieson (see chapter two), since it is hard to relate our data to the particular history of ideas that she traces. The fact that teachers rarely referred to them does not, of course, mean that they had no influence on English teaching in our period. The legacy of Matthew Arnold and the notion of a secular clerisy was probably strongest at Hackney Downs in the teaching of Joe Brearley, who drew explicitly on Arnold, Leavis and the tradition Mathieson describes as "Cambridge English,"[23] but it would be wrong to speak about him belonging to a definite "school." John Kemp saw the appeal of the notion of Literature as a substitute for religion, but looking back he spoke perceptively about the self-deception involved in his own case: "I think what happened was, to some extent, [my] self-deception about what literature could or could not do is the same as Holbrook's, and that is why I found it attractive." He continues: "There was kind of intensity almost to the point of faith, which you saw towards literature and in Holbrook it was almost like a religious thing, almost like the idea of receiving the light, almost like the idea of acquiring a virtue from revelation, and the literature is revelation."[24] The notion of Literature as a unique source of values, a substitute for religion, had minimal appeal for Rosen, Dixon, and the Walworth department.

Stability and Change in the Three Schools

Our hypothesis was confirmed that a new type of English did indeed emerge in the 1950s, although it happened in only two of our three schools and in only the second half of the decade. On the one hand, the picture conveyed in the standard histories could be said to have been by and large corroborated; practice in Minchenden until 1959 and in Hackney Downs throughout displayed more essential continuity with the 1930s than we had thought and underwent nothing like the "paradigm shift" or radical break that was initiated by Rosen in Walworth in 1956 and by Barnes in Minchenden in 1959. Nevertheless, within that broad-brush confirmation of the picture from earlier accounts, their accounts of grammar school practice are not an accurate reflection of what was going on even in those schools where "pioneering" change did not occur, Hackney Downs and, for most of our period, Minchenden. Certainly, what was happening in our grammar schools could by no means be referred to as "suspended animation." Ways of teaching English that were arrived at between the wars were being not simply repeated but developed and adapted in new circumstances for current conditions—for instance, by embracing contemporary literature and media analysis. One of these versions of English, which its practitioners would certainly have regarded as up-to-date and enlightened, was that derived from the continuing innovations in university literary studies associated with Richards, Leavis, and *Scrutiny*. The mainstream grammar school tradition (literary appreciation) continued to develop in lively postwar schools, including, perhaps, in the new interim comprehensive school, where the Oxonian Arthur Harvey taught an essentially grammar school English up to 1955.

Although Hackney Downs teachers, and most of the 1950s staff of Minchenden, were not involved in LATE, our impression of the grammar school version of English that was superseded from 1959 in Minchenden and maintained in Hackney Downs was that it was neither static nor ineffective, though it would doubtless have been far less effective if moved to a comprehensive school. A good proportion of working-class pupils thrived on it, especially when taught by able and committed teachers. A familiar critique ran that school was a different world from home and was experienced as especially alien by working-class pupils, but the domain of experience accessed through literature and the discoveries and creations that could be made in writing essays could be profoundly exciting for them—as could indeed, for some, its simple dissociation from home; some, mainly in the top streams, were led into a lifetime's engagement with literature.

Moreover, while English in two of our schools changed radically, it cannot be claimed that teaching in Hackney Downs was static, although change there was incremental, not like what we saw in Rosen's Walworth syllabus and the curriculum that gave rise to *Reflections*. For instance, John Kemp, for all that he was steeped in canonical literature and Leavis' literary criticism, modernized his teaching by introducing innovative methods, new fiction and contemporary poetry, and led the way in taking pupils' talk and writing seriously. Although English generally in the school continued to be dominated by grammar lessons, in pupils' exercise books we found instances when teaching about Standard English involved studying changes in usage and not merely learning the "correct" version. Pupils' speech was, moreover, rarely corrected and highly able teachers sometimes taught lower streams—both departures from what we had understood to be standard grammar school practice. It changed because the society, culture, and profession, as well as educational resources, were changing; and because some teachers were dissatisfied with existing practice and individually persuaded of the value of, for instance, extended, relatively free writing, the case for which they saw argued in *The Use of English*. It is also worth saying that the direction of the gradual changes in Hackney Downs was not *contrary* to that of the radical changes in Walworth; both were based on a shift away from instruction and exercises toward extending the scope for pupils' expression and their involvement in meaningful activities rather than mere exercises (though more of those survived in Hackney Downs). The telling difference between the two grammar schools was that the model adopted at Minchenden which put the pupils' lives and experiences at the center of much work in English left the school more ready for going comprehensive, its approach being better suited to a wide range of ability.

A key difference between Walworth and Minchenden was that English in Walworth, because it was a comprehensive school, was specifically designed to work with the majority of children, which especially in that locality meant working-class children. English took the pupil's language and culture as a starting point and saw their urban environment and community as the essential content and medium around which activity needed to be based. Minchenden didn't face the challenge of teaching working-class pupils to the same extent, and while Hackney Downs by the late 1950s had a majority of pupils who were both urban and working class, the English department didn't see that as a challenge needing to be specifically addressed. Since one of the salient characteristics of grammar schools was their dedication to the subject rather than the "needs of the pupils," it is not surprising that Hackney Downs did not find the kind of English developed in Walworth appealing.

It is all the more surprising, then, that Minchenden after 1959 did. Why would a respected grammar school, in a largely middle-class suburb, with high academic standards and good exam results, choose to switch from teaching literature and well-constructed essays, the familiar stock-in-trade that guaranteed the subject's status alongside classics, physics, chemistry, history, and modern languages, to a concern with pupils' personal development and "language resources?" What had that, they might have been expected to ask, got to do with a grammar school? From the perspective of the time it must have seemed a strange and unexpected development. (How unusual it was nationally we cannot say, but those of us in the research team who attended grammar schools in the 1950s and 1960s recall few lessons or tasks designed to relate in the Minchenden way to our experiences, family, neighborhood or relationships.) Since the English teaching that had been there since 1945 was, by the usual standards, doing the job and none of the basic features of the school or examination system had changed, what lay behind the change seems likely to have been Barnes' ideas (shared with many others) about education and English, as indeed his own accounts tell us.

Nowhere did we find a consistency of position so well defined that it could be called a "school": the history of how English was maintained and changed has to have regard to affiliations, friendships, sympathies, and chance influences—in short, conjunctures of circumstances.

When we revisit, in the light of our findings, the assumptions, questions, and hypotheses with which we embarked on our study, we conclude:

- this was a far more active period than the outward signs would suggest (these included the fact that the national government for most of the 1950s was opposed to change, there were few new school buildings, and it was only late in the day that comprehensivization got going on any scale in London—and then without wholesale closure of grammar schools);

- a significant group of teachers were actively combining in organizations and campaigns, giving up evenings and weekends to work for educational change;
- the principles and pedagogical strategies on which a wholesale reconstruction of English from the 1960s (say from the 1964 Labour government and the establishment of Schools Council in 1964) had been worked out and had developed up to a decade earlier in schools, if only locally and in a few places;
- as against our expectations, much of what could be regarded as continuous with prewar grammar school practice in its essential aims and assumptions was by no means simply the routine maintenance of established ways but was imaginative and in many ways original teaching, actively involving the pupils; it was carried out with commitment and personal investment and was educationally effective: there were not a few grammar school classrooms where education "worked," changing pupils' lives, giving them access to worlds and discourses well beyond those available in their homes and communities—and providing the basis (along with the growth of white collar jobs) for an unprecedented expansion of social mobility. If education was the state's or society's means of turning the children that home and community produced into adults with sophisticated and specialized intellectual resources, then the English curriculum in the grammar schools showed itself capable of producing readers, writers, thinkers, and participants in public discourse.

One feature of our teacher interviews struck us forcibly. By the time they reached our three schools, the pupils had already been in school for at least six years; and yet the teachers who took them over at eleven seem to have felt that they were starting from scratch. Certainly the pupils' primary school experiences were very varied; the Walworth intake was said to be drawn from some 40 different primary schools; we know from interviews with former pupils from all three schools that some of their junior schools had instilled the makings of a lifelong interest in reading and an enjoyment of writing that would last at least through their secondary school years, while others had been demoralizing, boring, or worse. Although in many pupils' existing accomplishments in reading and writing there was clearly much that could be built on, and in fact was built on without the teachers' having much knowledge of how it had got there, we heard of no attempts to set up cooperation with feeder schools in the interests of shaping a common principle of development in English work. Nor indeed, given conditions in the profession and the school system, would such cooperation have been feasible. LATE made an effort to inform itself about good work in primary schools, not least through the influence of Connie Rosen, a primary school teacher, and Harold Rosen with another primary teacher, Martyn Richards from Hertfordshire, jointly planned a weekend conference on "Talk and Talkers," but that was as late as 1968. We suspect that LATE members in our three schools learned more about work in the West Riding of Yorkshire than what was going on in the junior school next door. It is a sad reflection that the sort of approaches that Rosen and Dixon's team developed for their first-year classes would have worked well with nine- and ten-year-olds too, and who knows what children who had been taught continuously in that way from the age of nine might not have accomplished as speakers, writers, readers, and thinkers.

Society, Culture, and English

Medway (1990)[25] proposed a possible connection between change in the economy toward a new emphasis on consumption, indicating the desirability in the population of consumer rather than producer qualities, and what seemed a corresponding change in English toward self-expression and individuation. While this was speculation, what suggested it was a no less speculative account in the sociological literature that viewed the 1960s counterculture as related to those economic developments; education seemed to be in a parallel relationship. As far as we are aware no one has addressed this idea, to pursue it further, critique it, or suggest an alternative. The problem with it is, of course, identifying the "drive belts" between large economic trends and teachers' decisions in individual classrooms. We have no instance of a banker seeking out a teacher to explain what he would like to see in English, nor of any teacher training course inculcating the need for practice to be based on the "needs of the economy." It is therefore not surprising that there is little in our case studies tending either to confirm or refute the hypothesis. At best we could only point to consonances between tendencies in English and the values that it would suit business to have inculcated in a population that would thereby be rendered more eager to borrow and spend. At school level, there always seem to be other explanations. Thus the development of a new English in Walworth can be explained in part by an intake that was difficult to teach effectively—increasingly so, as it seems—and in part by a new climate, to which some teachers were responsive, supportive of the principle that the education of all children should be taken as seriously as that of the grammar school top stream. But while they may explain the advantages for English teachers of doing business, as it were, with pupils' language and interests, and of valuing "honest" expression above formal correctness, those reasons would not as readily account for the social issues content of the upper school course.

The situation is perhaps clearer when we consider the relationship between how English was taught and other areas of social and cultural change. Speculating about what lay behind development at Hackney Downs, we note first that there was social change in the school's catchment area, with a postwar demographic shift toward a more cosmopolitan, particularly Jewish, population. We have discussed in chapter three how Jewish pupils, including working-class children, enjoyed parental support and were academically ambitious, intellectually engaged and articulate. A shift to a new generation of teachers—another aspect of social change, as discussed also in relation to Walworth in chapter four—represented notably by Brearley and Kemp, meant the effective disappearance of anti-Semitic attitudes and class prejudice among English teachers. We quoted Henry Grinberg, a former pupil at Hackney Downs, on what he saw as the role of new plays and books in changing thought and feeling in postwar Britain. Indeed, across the three schools an influence on the work of our most original and resourceful teachers was their engagement with the culture, and often the politics, of the time. They were fiercely interested in new work at the Royal Court as well as the Old Vic theaters, attended the National Film Theatre to see international as well as British films, visited international and British shows at the Whitechapel Gallery, and took part in meetings of Labour Teachers and the group around what became the *New Left Review*. Cultural and political experiences worked their way into English at Hackney Downs, in the way drama became a focus of creative endeavor and in teachers' support for debates. This, along with an argumentative oral culture, gave rise to a new confidence that drove academic success in working-class pupils. Change in this school, therefore, seems attributable in part to a happy conjunction of a lively cultural ambience in London, a pupil body—at least in the upper levels—exceptionally receptive to new cultural phenomena, and an English staff responsive both to the culture and to the pupils' responsiveness to it.

It can plausibly be argued that changes in the public discourse of the late 1950s and 1960s affected the teaching of English, in the direction of both new attitudes to pupil expression and new content. Speech and writing in the wider society became less stuffy, deference declined, and new types of individual, not least from the working class, began to be successful, notably in music, television, photography, and journalism; established cultural hierarchies were challenged; teenagers had more scope to express themselves, for instance, in choice of clothes and through having new places (coffee bars) to meet and talk. Talking became a more prominent part of English, the literature studied drew closer to what pupils were choosing to read for themselves, and the study of material other than literature—newspapers and advertising—continued to increase, though the case for it had been made by Leavis and Thompson as long ago as 1933.

One more aspect of social change seems relevant, that of generations, mentioned briefly earlier, and in particular generations of teachers. A newer generation, including those of us who entered teaching in the 1960s and 1970s, were likely to have experienced, or been exposed to in our friends, a more relaxed style of child-rearing, one dependent less on traditional norms of adult-child relationships, less on positional than personal authority,[26] and entailing less formal and less role-governed interactions. As a consequence, that generation of teachers were less inclined than their predecessors to make demands by authority rather than to seek to secure assent by reason, and by earned respect and trust. In their own grammar schools they had experienced plenty of traditional authority exercised in a curriculum and pedagogy that often made little sense, and, like Rosen before us, had had enough of it and were resolved to work in a different way. Peter Johnson, an ex-pupil at Walworth, expressed how he liked, got on with, and gained from associating with the young generation of teachers he encountered:

> I was conscious of it immediately, from the age of eleven, that these teachers were different, these teachers were allowing us to be something that a previous generation would never have been...as opposed to...the old, pre-war kind of, you know, three Rs, go and get a job in the Post Office, be grateful you've employment, do your tie up and say nice things to policemen...and they [the young teachers] said no, you don't have to do this, you can read that, that doesn't make you weak if you read that, that doesn't make you different if you say this, and you can use that word, and you can study this foreign language, and you can eat this food, and you can have a dinner party with an older person and it doesn't have to seem strange...And they did this in stages, you know...you suddenly opened up a little bit, then you were reading more serious stuff, then they were expecting you to go to the theatre on your own and come back and write a comment about it, and then they were loading you with this tremendous workload that you previously would never have contemplated, but they had the confidence that you could do it, and you wanted to do it for them. You felt you owed them a debt for believing in you. No-one used to believe in you before...I mean...do we want to hang around with these grumpy old maths teachers that hit you

around the head with a ruler, or do we want to hang around with these people that let you—encouraged you—to play records, read non-syllabus books, and asked you around for tea at the weekend?[27]

While acknowledging the role of social and cultural factors in affecting the teaching of English, we emerge from this study with a strong sense of the effect of *ideas*. In particular, as a result of the convergence of notions from diverse sources, a theory was gradually attaining currency among some teachers in our schools and LATE, or, in less articulate form, a *sense* that ultimately, or potentially, had theory behind it, about education as a matter of *development* as much as of learning through instruction, and with it a belief that the provision of an environment that fostered active language use was critical. Gurrey's precept that it was "wrong to separate language from real life" and that "the best language teaching must concern itself with the [whole] life of the pupil"[28] was readily assented to and extended by Harold Rosen, a former student in his department at the Institute, for whom daily contact with lively London working-class children encouraged an open response to urban realities south of the river. From the outset, Rosen was politically predisposed to find positive value in working-class language and culture. How much he was able to achieve at Walworth in a stay of less than three years we do not know, but John Dixon with a core group of newly appointed imaginative teachers whole-heartedly took up Rosen's syllabus and made it a working reality. Douglas Barnes, who was similarly fortunate in working with a fresh influx of young teachers, contributed his own original thinking to the ideas circulating in LATE about the place of language and literature in pupils' development, working them out in fresh ways in Minchenden. (Such ideas never struck root in Hackney Downs, however.) Generally, the focus of key teachers' attention shifted from the contents of the school subject and methods of instruction toward the nature and purposes of learning.

Thus to describe developments in English as changes in *methods* is misleading, if convenient (both the Newbolt Report of 1921 and the Spens Report of 1938 had made much of the need to develop English "methods"). They were changes in *aims* as much as in methods, a matter of working toward different *ends* and a different notion of what English was *for*. From a political sense of social justice focused initially by the postwar desire to build a fairer and more equal society through "education for all" came a widespread conviction that pupils of all abilities should be treated as responsible social agents. Misguided assumptions about the innate capacities of different types of child that lay behind the 11 plus testing arrangements and the tripartite school system were incompatible with a growing belief that what children could achieve depended on their motivations and purposes—on educational experience making sense to them—and was in principle undetermined in advance by a doubtfully relevant IQ. From the ferment of ideas that galvanized LATE, Rosen, Dixon's team, and Barnes' team were among the first teachers to enact the principle that the language that children bring to school constitutes the best means of their future development.

Chapter 7

Conclusion

The Three Schools: Contributions to Later Developments

In view of the subsequent prominence in English nationally of some of their teachers, it is clear that, as we explained in chapter one, two of our schools were indeed far from typical. Harold Rosen, John Dixon, and Leslie Stratta moved from Walworth and Douglas Barnes from Minchenden into institutions of teacher education; Simon Clements (Walworth) worked in BBC Schools Broadcasts and taught in a college of further education. Their contributions at the national level were made outside their teaching jobs, first through work on the committees of the Schools Council (Dixon and Barnes, along with James Britton), including writing key documents on English and influencing policy on the new Certificate of Secondary Education (CSE) examination; second, through their activities in NATE (while those still in London continued also to be active in LATE), part of their attention, again, being given to developing CSE; and third, through their publications and courses for teachers. Rosen and Barnes with Britton wrote *Language, the Learner and the School*,[1] one of the initiatives that radically transformed the climate of public discourse for English teachers (those, that is, who were receptive),and for which Martin Lightfoot of the new Penguin Education division was largely responsible. Rosen, Dixon, and Barnes also wrote independently: notable were Rosen's attack on Basil Bernstein's work on restricted and elaborated codes,[2] his collaboration with Connie Rosen on *The Language of Primary School Children*,[3] and his editorship of the Penguin English Project series of anthologies; Dixon wrote

Growth through English,[4] with Clements and Stratta edited the anthology/course book *Things Being Various*[5] and with Stratta produced a series of research papers on children's language and on writing in examinations. In the 1970s, Barnes produced the influential *From Communication to Curriculum*,[6]\ confirming his commitment to pupils' intellectual development beyond English and in the other subjects. Outside the United Kingdom, all ran courses that had an impact not only on other English-speaking countries, especially Australia and New Zealand, but also on parts of the United States and Canadian systems; Stratta's influence on English in Australia is remembered as giving an impetus to change.

Out of the three schools, Walworth was best placed to provide an example of possible ways forward for English, not least because it was one of the earliest schools of the comprehensive type toward which the whole system in England appeared to be moving, dating as it did from right after the war. Not only had new ways of doing English had time to develop there and begin to mature, but Walworth had also notably responded to the demands of the new postwar world and had taken seriously its responsibilities toward its pupils' needs.

Dartmouth and Two Versions of English

An early arena in which members of the same group (Barnes, Dixon, and Rosen) along with, again, James Britton, made prominent contributions was a ground-breaking transatlantic meeting at Dartmouth, New Hampshire:

> "What is English?" From August 20 to September 15 in 1966, more than fifty teachers from Britain, Canada, and the United States convened to answer this question and many more on the fundamentals of English at the Anglo-American Seminar on the Teaching of English, more commonly known as the Dartmouth Seminar. Sponsoring the seminar [were] the National Association for the Teaching of English (NATE) and [the US National Council of Teachers of English (NCTE)].[7]

Looking back in 1991, Joseph Harris, an American commentator, referring to all three countries, wrote about "the impact of the work on many teachers then and since—for whom Dartmouth has symbolized a kind of Copernican shift from a view of English as something one learns about to a sense of it as something one does."[8] We cannot say how far this was true of England nationally. As was mentioned in chapter two, the British contingent included both "participants [who] had studied at Cambridge with F. R. Leavis" and "James Britton and his colleagues at the University of London," a group with which Harris rightly associates Barnes and Dixon. It is interesting the degree to which he regards both the Leavisites and those around Britton as representing essentially the same approach to English:

> Both groups... took the work of students as seriously as that of poets or novelists... One of the most striking features of this British position was a renewed interest in personal and expressive forms of writing... [and in] lived experience, as shown either in literature or in the writings of students. Language was not so much to be studied as used. Growth in skill was expected to occur in an incidental fashion, not through direct training in stylistic or grammatical exercises... but as a natural outcome of meaningful practice in writing and reading... Students were encouraged to do in their own way what poets did—"bring a new, simplifying order to the complexity of life."[9]

Although the similarity was what struck this American, from the British perspective the two groups in the seminar occupied distinct positions that, centering as they did in part on the type of school and pupil each had in mind—grammar school and high academic ability on the one side, comprehensive school and the full range of children on the other—placed priority on either literature or the development of language; as Harris put it, on "lived experience, as shown *either* in literature *or* in the writings of students" (our emphases).

Medway has suggested that Leavisite values—above all, language as embodying life as lived with full awareness and a responsive sensibility—in order to be maintained with less academic groups, needed to be reinvested away from demanding literature into the children's writing.[10] This shift, often necessitated by the move of grammar school teachers into comprehensives, involved a transformation in a number of areas. Leavisites and *Scrutiny* had expressed little interest in children's writing processes—Holbrook's books were the first to articulate extensively how relevant to those teachers' concerns they were; and the need was entailed for a new respect for the language of young children and working-class language, both of which Harold and Connie Rosen, among others, brought to English. English teaching had never hitherto attempted to treat the qualities of vernacular language as a resource on which to build, a concern that was remote from *Scrutiny* preoccupations. Those who thought like Rosen and Britton sought to create new possibilities for pupils to put their native intelligence and linguistic capacity to productive use, in the interests of moving gradually into both more analytic and more literary forms of discourse, and of coming to grips with school knowledge. The pioneering works that analyzed children's writing and talking came from LATE and Penguin Education[11] rather than the *Use of English* people.

It has to be said that the distinction at Dartmouth between two separate groups did not emerge as clearly from the schools in our studies. While the Institute/LATE position was clearly in accord with the Walworth and later Minchenden work, English in Hackney Downs, although it was undoubtedly of a different kind and some of its most effective and influential English teachers had been taught by or were influenced by the writings of Leavis and the *Scrutiny* authors, was not different in coming across unmistakably as Leavisite in the way that teaching observed in some other schools did.[12] Rather, Hackney Downs English represented a range of good grammar school teaching, sometimes in highly unorthodox forms. We suspect that it was the case in many schools nationally that English teaching could be engaging, effective, and up-to-date without being definitely identifiable with either of the two versions articulated in the literature. It was not that Leavis' way of attending to literature did not influence the teaching in Hackney Downs and pre-1959 Minchenden; it presumably did affect teachers' choice and treatment of texts for study, as it also affected, without determining, the work of the other Leavis student in our study, Douglas Barnes. The Hackney Downs English staff seem like many intelligent grammar school teachers, well-read in Leavis but open to other influences as well. By the early sixties, for instance, David Ogilvie was in touch with Rosen about the role of language in learning, and Kemp grew interested in the work of Britton; Ted Hughes' teacher at Mexborough Grammar School in Yorkshire, John Fisher, seems to have been alert in this sort of way.[13]

We suspect that before the writings of Leavis and his associates began to affect English teachers, the study of literature in grammar schools may not have been taken as seriously or believed with such conviction to be central to children's development. In those schools where writing rather than literature had become the center, the Leavisites demonstration that writing in the best novels was more than merely a literary stylistic accomplishment helped to change writing in schools into a pursuit from which pupils would learn to discover and value important aspects of their own lives. To escape from the grammar school belles-lettrism described by Barnes, Barnes, and Clarke, as we reported in chapter two, and from elementary and secondary modern school barren functionalism and banality, an infusion of Lawrentian-Leavisite seriousness may have been needed. An English that put moral concerns at the centre at least wasn't trivial. It was a worthwhile pursuit for children to think about how one should live and relate to others. Although the belief at the center of this position, that literature was essentially an exploration of moral concerns, has not stood the test of time well and seems to leave too many valued literary texts unaccounted for, we suspect, as we said earlier, that in the background of teachers' consciousness in schools like Walworth and Minchenden, Leavis played a role alongside that of Gurrey and Britton, who were themselves also influenced.

The English That Emerged

The term "the New English" was used by Shayer and others in the 1970s but in so far as what it refers to is clear, and although Shayer seems to imply that it includes *Reflections*-type "social English," what those authors seem mainly to have in mind, as did many who referred vaguely to "1960s [or 1970s] English," was so-called creative and expressive approaches that involved writing in response to a "stimulus," such as objects brought into the classroom and photographs like those in the *Touchstones* poetry anthologies.[14] The sort of writing this seems to have been intended to elicit was of the Marjorie Hourd, *Education of the Poetic Spirit*[15] variety (see chapter six) and that favored in those primary schools, for instance, in the West Riding, where art work, writing, nature surveys, mathematics, science, and textiles work came together in stimulating classroom environments. The best results of this written work were impressive and John Dixon expertly points out its strength using West Riding examples in *Growth through English* and later productions. However, while Dixon found value in writing about experiences, like visiting a farm, for the sake of integrating the experience into the child's overall picture of the world, what often seemed particularly to be sought in the primary schools was the capturing in fresh and vivid language of the texture of immediate, usually visual impressions, what counted being authenticity of observation and response.

In contrast with the claims about "schools" of English teaching, it is often hard to distinguish the different strands that were present in practice once a body of teachers, especially in the new comprehensive schools, persuaded that a regime of language instruction and literary studies could not be effective with the range of pupils they were teaching, opted to make writing the focus. Their aim thereby was to engage pupils' intelligence, resources, creativity, interests, and concerns in a motivated activity through which their language would be extended. There were those who looked primarily toward arts-oriented expression and creativity and appreciated particularly the poetic qualities in pupils' language; others were concerned to help pupils articulate their experience, and perhaps in the process bring problematic personal topics under greater cognitive and emotional control and into an ordering that made sense. But in teachers' practice the two approaches often seemed entangled or blended.

In the English work that emerged from Walworth and Minchenden, the stated object of writing was not the creation and shaping of a beautiful verbal object but to enable reflection on life and social relations in the child's familiar world. In what were, of course, urban secondary schools for older children, not primary schools in rural or small town environments, the progression tended to go from stories and anecdotal memories in the first two years (11–13), which, while often comic, were intended to address themes important to the child like getting lost, taking on responsibility, or coping with fractious relatives; and to move on in the third and fourth years to matters of wider public import, addressed less in narrative genres than expository or argumentative modes. It was a principle in which this version of English differed from the "creative" one (though not from the Leavisite one), that, as Walworth's Simon Clements put it in conversation, every lesson should be about "something that mattered." This led to reading matter that was not only literary but also sociological or journalistic, writings in which factual accuracy, expository clarity, and argumentative power were the salient qualities. Hence the accusation that the work was leaving English behind and drifting toward social studies. (It was rarely borne in mind that in Walworth itself the work around the material that was eventually published as *Reflections* was only part of the fourth year English curriculum; literature was strongly represented in the rest.) This English work seemed also to be moving away from the governing principle of above all dealing with experience—unless experience included mediated experience, such as anything that was experienced by being read. The working principle was rather to start at 11 and 12 with experience, and then to move on. The question was, to what? The Walworth answer was to something that undoubtedly did take in subject matter that was the object of disciplines outside English, though not, as a rule, disciplines that were studied in school at the time. (What pupils would move on to write within the Hourd-Clegg approach as they reached more senior years is unclear.)

It seemed no single principle was capable of governing the choice of object of attention for English work from 11 or earlier to 15 or 16. Neither personal experience of day-to-day social life in family and community nor sensory experience of the surface of phenomena seemed to everyone capable of sustaining a curriculum after the earlier years.

There is an air of desperation about Britton's formulation in a paper delivered at Dartmouth that the business of English in relation to the curriculum was "the rest of the pastry after the other subject shapes [the cookies] have been cut out"[16]—hardly a resonant justification for the place of English at the center, particularly in schools where the traditional academic disciplines were what that curriculum was essentially about.

The *Reflections* response was not to settle for the disciplinary residue but to draw on matter that might otherwise be regarded as the specialist domains of sociology, criminology, urban planning and architecture, or international relations, thus moving English in the spirit of *Culture and Environment* along the lines being pioneered by Williams, Hoggart, and Hall (chapter two). It perhaps thereby lay itself open to an accusation from the other side, discussed in chapter four, of a disservice not to "real English" but to intellectual standards, in not taking seriously enough the need for a sound knowledge base when such issues were addressed; introducing them through extracts in an English book when they needed to be embedded in a disciplinary context was an inadequate approach; as it was, it could be claimed, pupils were allowed to articulate responses and opinions that were unchecked and *ill-informed*, a state of affairs against which an education that valued reason and knowledge should set its face. The obvious riposte was that these were important topics about which children *should* have the chance to think before leaving school at 15 or 16, and since no one else was tackling them in schools English was performing an important function, one for which, besides, it was well-equipped, if not in disciplinary expertise, then in its discussion-based classroom procedures, its ways of attending to texts, and its ways of supporting thinking through writing.

Misgivings about whether, in the absence of a large content of grammar and exercises, English had enough to go on apart from literature in the fourth and fifth years may have been why in the later 1960s and 1970s many schools, including Hackney Downs (when it became a comprehensive) and Walworth bought into schemes of "integrated humanities" or the like that combined English with some or all of history, geography, and social studies. It was as if English on its own had nowhere to go after the junior years (except to serious literary study, for an academically able minority) and had nothing that pupils "could get their teeth into" that provided both a degree of intellectual challenge and imaginative stimulation. The approach adopted by many teachers, however, was simply to act pragmatically on the criterion of what felt right and was broadly recognizable as English.

Perhaps the strangest feature of the new approaches to English that emerged in the 1950s and 1960s is an absence: none of them placed their main focus on *English itself*, as it were: developing effective uses of the language and advanced literate capabilities. In the Institute of Education/

James Britton version of English, language was to be developed not by making it the instructional focus but as the outcome that would be achieved in the course of directly pursuing other primary purposes, such as bringing order to experience, while in the "creativity" version the aim was poetic and imaginative production rather than a gain in overall language effectiveness. Undoubtedly, the understanding among teachers of those persuasions was that directly addressing language was generally ineffective, but it may be that setting out directly to teach accurate reading and "good writing," with a diet of grammar and exercises as its principal methods, had been irrecoverably discredited by its perceived failure with all but very able children, so that it was simply assumed that *all* such approaches could be dismissed. Other ways were, moreover, felt to be a superior alternative, so that perhaps no need was felt for yet another way of promoting the development of written and spoken language. Suggestions about the possibilities of exploiting modern linguistic understanding and approaches to the analysis of discourse in the interests of developing a modern and engaging approach to language work were made but not widely taken up, though both a strong case for that and the means to implement it were offered in the later *Language in Use* project that resulted from Michael Halliday's initiatives at University College, London.[17] The argument was, indeed, strongly made from that quarter even within or shortly after our period that such a development would do better justice to young people's language needs as they entered adult life than the other new approaches, which were seen as too exclusively literary in the types of written language they encouraged, particularly the widely espoused personal, expressive, and autobiographical modes.[18] Walworth English, however, did include an explicit language element in its notion of moving over several years from "primary" narrative modes of writing to more abstract and generalizing ones. This happened to chime with ideas put forward by the American James Moffett at Dartmouth that were taken up by Britton's Writing Research team.[19]

The Project's Claims

We set out to make a contribution to curriculum history and the history of English teaching and would claim that our work has indeed contributed something under both heads, less perhaps by substantial contributions to knowledge or new "findings" than through showing how complex and difficult to interpret the reality of education in the past is when set aside the confident summaries that we find in the literature. This may, of course, simply be a question of scale; an account that sets out to offer a general account of the state of affairs in a period will necessarily smooth over the differences, contradictions, and incompatibilities that close and detailed scrutiny render salient. However that is, we know of no other historical study from a period long enough ago to be relatively inaccessible, of individual English departments, or even subject departments, that has produced a detailed record, as far as traces, memories, and research resources allow, of what the ship was like before it foundered on the rocks of time.

And the more extensive the incomplete and fragmentary record is, the more intriguing we have found the questions. It was once we had started to know a little that they multiplied: How did this unorthodox practice arise in a school like that? Was it a one-off? When she wrote that in her teaching notes, was it a serious intention and did she carry it through? When he read that text with them, what did they make of it—surely it would have been far too difficult? (We were surprised, on re-reading the book, that Harold Rosen lent his own copy of *The Quiet American* to a boy who was dissatisfied with the books in the classroom; we can see that a 15 year old might have been pleased to be given an adult book to read, but surely he couldn't have got much out of it?) Was Dixon's bottom stream fourth year really so cooperative and engaged in the discussion on the occasion when he says the visiting scholar Barbara Hardy, was impressed? Was making a film really such a positive experience for Simon Clements' third year class, or were many simply bored with the unproductive hanging about? In other words, while the film is certainly impressive, what was the general educational benefit? School plays of the exceptional quality that Brearley produced at Hackney Downs likewise involved relatively small numbers of pupils and we might ask here, too, how pupils not involved benefited (although that activity did not occupy lesson time).

There are limitations in our study that we are well aware of, mainly to do with incompleteness and the impracticality of systematic coverage. We are satisfied that we learned what we could from the documentary sources we collected, given their deficiencies, such as our frequent ignorance about how a particular piece of writing had come to be kept. Our selection of people to interview was inevitably somewhat fortuitous; we would have liked to first draw up a list of possible informants and then make a rational selection by categories that our agenda indicated would be important. In practice people could not always be found who would represent a category we needed to include, and it often took an interview before we knew what category a person should be placed in. Moreover, potential interviewees who came forward after the research was well under way, too late for a prior sampling procedure, often proved the most valuable. We would have liked, too, as was our original plan, to interview everyone twice, in two separate rounds, our questions in the second round drawing on issues arising from the first and including the elicitation of comment on responses we had received earlier and on quotations from documents we had gathered. In the event it was impossible to separate the stages like that, not least because we never ended the "first" interview stage because of people who offered their help late in the day. One could contemplate setting up the design in the first place with an adequate gap between the two rounds, but against that is the consideration that some of our subjects were very old so that there was no guarantee they would still be available later.

Specific examples of the problems we faced include the case of Harold Rosen. Although we may have offered a quite rich account of his work, it is sobering to realize that almost all of this comes from his own writing and retrospective oral testimony. About what he did in the classroom at Walworth, or in his department meetings, we know almost nothing from independent sources and the testimony is sometimes contradictory (he was lively and inspiring, we learned, *and* he was miserable and gloomy). Again from Walworth, we learn a great deal about the impression Arthur Harvey made and the liveliness and originality of his teaching, but of the work his pupils did routinely in class and at home we have only a single pupil's collection—which is either very thin, considering we have one exercise book that covers years two to part of five, or incomplete, though she believes it is all there; and it does not confirm the impression we gain from ex-pupils' reports in interviews and email exchanges.

We may never have the answers to the questions implied earlier, but some broader questions would be amenable to further research projects. For example, while the philosophy behind the Walworth English of Dixon's team was never written down at the time, or not anywhere that we have found, though it can be glimpsed in passages from the *Reflections Teacher's Book*, it received extensive articulation in Dixon's writings shortly afterwards (*Growth through English*) and the NATE and Schools Council Papers which he wrote or had a hand in (see chapter six) where his general thrust parallels that of James Britton. The main themes were, on the one hand, helping older pupils to get a grip on some of the central social questions at issue in Britain and the contemporary world—a mission in line with notions of an adequate education for modern democratic citizens; and, on the other, about helping children to arrive at a position on their own experience and place in the world, particularly, in this case, their relationships, thereby attaining what came to be summed up in the expression "personal growth," a notion that contained a strong element of *moral* development. Both aspects were strongly present in Douglas Barnes' approach, though the writings we know that make this clear come from rather later.

Did that sort of "growth"—or moral development, or refinement and strengthening of the sensibility one brought to one's dealings with others—*really* result from these curricula in reading, talking and writing? We believe pupils' reports that they were often intensely engaged in the activities the teachers provided and it is hard to believe that learning, or, better, development, did not take place. But perhaps the effect that the teachers thought was moral growth and a psychologically beneficial ordering of experience was actually the development of *language*, in the broad sense that embraces "inner speech" or verbal *thought* and is involved in the ordering of ideas, impressions, and memories into more organized and usable form? And might not the educational effect be valuable and lasting enough on its own not to need any further rationale, of simply experiencing a great deal of varied writing and private reading and of considering books in common in class, together with constant discussion? The achievement would succeed in what English was conventionally *supposed* to do, to expand and refine pupils' abilities in English. This is not to mention the educational and social benefits of four or five years' experience of civilized interaction about nontrivial matters in English lessons, with all that sharing, arguing, and following of argument. (That sort of classroom seems, by the way, to have gone a long way toward achieving that development of democratic ways of thinking and relating that the London County Council (LCC) and Walworth's first head, Anne O'Reilly, wanted their postwar comprehensive schools to achieve.)

We would like to see researchers seeking out people who experienced such classrooms and asking them, "What did you get out of it? What did that education do for you, or to you?"

A related consideration is suggested by what we were told about Arthur Harvey at Walworth, that he used to write parts of pupils' essays and stories on the board so that he and the class could discuss how its expression could be improved—a concentration, that is, not on the subject matter but on the form and structure of the writing. We know almost nothing more specific about Harvey's procedure, but it is striking that we never hear of it again in the practice of later Walworth teachers. Did the later focus on the content addressed—experience and public issues—mean that pupils received less help in the "engineering" aspects of their writing process? It might be worth adding that we have sometimes been impressed by the well-expressed and well-structured written communications we have received in the course of the study from people who experienced English teaching at a time when *instruction* was still favored; we wonder if what they *didn't* get by missing out on that later English teaching was as great a loss as their apparently developed writing ability was a gain. This is a question that might be pursued with people who had experienced both instruction-based and experience-based forms of English. The problem with Harvey's practice in relation to writing, as his successors saw clearly, was that it tended to entail writing for the sake of producing a good piece of writing, whereas many children would do good work in writing only if the writing was for some purpose beyond writing itself, whether that be to communicate an experience to an interested listener or to entertain oneself and others with a humorous story. Then the effect if all went well would be that satisfaction was found in the process while something was perhaps learned about the content being written about, and/or about writing itself. It was regrettable if, after Rosen, English could appear to be about non-language-related subject matter *to the detriment* of attention to language. Walworth and Minchenden teachers themselves didn't see it like that; it is true that the balance between the two had shifted from Harvey's time, but in their view necessarily so.

Our own study did not yield a simple answer to the question, "What did your experience of English in school do for you?" A few individuals offered clear answers but they varied greatly in content. We would like to see it asked of many other former pupils from all types of school in the period before everything changed with the 1988 Education Reform Act. Curriculum studies as we see them should not get too far away from educational effects—what an education enabled or inhibited in its students and what the social effects were. It is an interest in the sort of people that were made by or emerged from English teaching that primarily motivated the two English teachers in our team to pursue this inquiry.

But there are other questions we would like to see pursued that are of more straightforwardly historical interest. Thus, we have objected to the attempt to force varieties of English teaching into a model of opposing "schools": how different in practice, we wonder, were the bulk of lessons in schools where the influence of Leavis was strong from those in others, when both groups are regarded as having been good, and were comparably situated grammar or comprehensive schools? In fact a study of Leavisite teachers would in itself be worthwhile because, for all the dogmatism they were said to display in some departments, they practiced an approach to literature that was strikingly incompatible with that which obtains widely in schools in England today; for all its earnestness, their approach was resolutely more than academic, refusing, as Leavis had refused, what they regarded as "mere study" as opposed to experiencing and responding to the text—an essentially Protestant process over which authority had no sway, and in which a course of literature could not be reduced to learning about genres, influences, techniques, historical correlates, and the like. For all the disciplined attention it required, Leavisite reading was closer to normal careful reading in the spirit of giving first-hand responses, discriminating and making judgments, which for Leavis was a moral activity. Being good at English was not a matter of knowledge that could be got from a textbook.

Another issue suggested by our study: it included two teachers, Rosen and Dixon, who had moved from grammar to comprehensive schools. (John Dixon had done this twice, from Holloway Grammar School to Holloway Comprehensive when it changed its status, and then to Walworth.) What in general happened to English teachers when they made this rather momentous move? Were they forced, by having to teach pupils with lower literacy levels, to adopt the solutions developed at Walworth, or were there other successful ways of teaching English successfully in their new situation?

Some further questions are, were grammar schools generally as hopeless in providing for their lower streams as has been reputed? What was English like before the war in grammar schools, elementary schools, and central schools? (Walworth was a respected central school before it went comprehensive in 1946, and English there was reported by inspectors to be good, including in its literature teaching and its use of a well-resourced library.) Again, we know there was good English teaching in secondary modern schools, but where, and what form did it take?

Studies would have to go well beyond 1965 in order to review the currents, tensions, and settlements in comprehensive school English. Questions might include, to what extent did the versions of English that became important in comprehensive schools derive from the initiatives of Walworth, Minchenden and LATE that we have described? And when elements from those sources were picked up and built into practice, how often did that take-up follow from an understanding of the underlying principles and how often as the piecemeal result of "eclectic pillaging"? Did the approaches to English that we have described prove adequate to the ablest students who were recruited into full comprehensives?

Broad questions of likely interest to curriculum studies remain, ones on which this study has, by its nature, not been able to throw much light. First, English is only one of the postwar subjects in which two traditions had to be combined or at least jointly drawn on in the comprehensive school, from their elementary school and grammar school prewar histories. One thinks, for instance, of mathematics and geography in which more and less abstract versions coexisted. Walworth English found a common rationale and method under which it was thought a real unity could be achieved and in which relative success was equally possible for children of varying academic abilities. How and to what extent did other subjects achieve this?

Secondly, the motor for change in English in the schools in the study was partly teachers' ideas and commitments about how *society* should be developing, worked out either in political engagement (CP and Labour Party activism, work for working-class advancement) or through attempting to create an education that produced citizens better fitted for a democratic society. Were the same motivations active in developments in other subjects?

Social Change

What insights might our research offer for those with an interest in how society developed in our period? Postwar developments in the teaching of English might understandably be viewed as of only professional interest; however, when seen as one instance of what happened in British society after the war, they acquire a wider relevance as manifestations of contemporary adjustments in social relations, policies, and culture. We can speculate, moreover, not implausibly, that they were significant also in *contributing* to social change by helping to produce a different kind of young adult, at least in conferring some legitimacy (as some teachers did) on ways of being a young person that were emerging anyway. An example would be the support received by Alex McLeod's two nonconforming self-styled existentialists in the mid-1950s, who were allowed an unusual degree of latitude in speech, writing, and other areas.

English teachers responsive to the currents of the times adapted their teaching, no doubt not always consciously; pupils emerging from their teaching had had a different education in English from those who had experienced a continuation of traditional approaches. English in its innovative forms, in comparison with its more academic versions and with other academic subjects, was exceptionally permeable to influences from the wider society since its topics tended to be drawn from pupils' experience and from social life and relations. Discussion occupied more time in class and ranged more widely, so that those topics were often gone over quite thoroughly. Thus changes in English may be presumed to have had social significance insofar as those educated in such curricula might be expected to have been more articulate, more skilled in narrative modes, less skilled in essays, more knowledgeable about a wider (and more international) range of literature, more assertive and less deferential, more openly unashamed of their own culture (e.g., if working-class), more habituated to initiating writing and critical inquiry for themselves, more attentive to the quality of their own experience, and more engaged with public issues and also perhaps cultural developments.

Those are the sort of outcomes we might have expected to result from Walworth and Minchenden English in the later part of our period, though we can only speculate on what the results actually were—and, further, about how differently a young person would have turned out if instead his English course had comprised working through *English through Experience* and writing to the "ad hoc" stimuli of bubble-blowing and like (see chapter two).

English: The Essential Findings

There is no doubt that the teaching of English in two schools was transformed in the second half of our period by Harold Rosen and then by the teams led by John Dixon and Douglas Barnes. We are assured in conversations with teachers from other parts of the country who were not in the study that the subject was transformed there too in some schools, in similar ways at around the same time. But what comes across finally from our case studies is not essentially related to English nor to the changes just referred to, and is probably something that has for a much longer period been a feature of some educational contexts. It is an educational point, rather than one that concerns English alone. Some teachers, and not just English teachers of the Walworth–Minchenden-LATE persuasion, and indeed not just English teachers, had a lasting effect on some young people that may be called *cultural enlargement* and that went beyond the confines of the subjects in the curriculum.

When it was English teachers who were responsible for this cultural enlargement—the cases which, of course, the focus of our study led us particularly to pick up—the quality and content of the worlds of which their pupils were helped to gain awareness appeared to have had little to do with the version of English they espoused. Harvey at Walworth and John Kemp at Hackney Downs, no less than those teachers who saw themselves as pioneering a new sort of English, would often simply chat with pupils out of class, a matter most obviously of having time for young people but more importantly of, as it were, placing in full view of their pupils their own minds, habits of thought and range of cultural reference while these were actively engaged on a variety of topics and issues. The result was that, as Pete Johnson said about a later generation at Walworth (chapter six), "we started to gravitate towards [teachers who thus made themselves available], a bit like thinking they were like the shining light of the school," part of the point being that in these interactions the pupils had *chosen* to associate with them rather than the teachers simply accepting the pupils as part of the package of their assigned duties.

The teachers were, of course, adults, and there comes an age when some adolescents want to be with adults—*some* adults, that is, as Johnson explained—and not just their peers. But these adults were also very different from their parents, relatives and neighbors, coming as they did not just from a different class but from three or more years in higher education. This was obviously true not only for working-class young people but also for many others; saying in the case of, say Minchenden, that the teachers and many of the pupils were "middle-class" occludes the fact that the middle class was far from homogeneous and included many, employed often in business and commerce, who had limited education and little interest in reading, culture or the arts, little, in fact, that could engage the lively intelligence of a bright adolescent. Several times we were told by pupils that they had never outside their secondary school encountered anyone like Teacher X. The initial impression might be of unfamiliar accents from other parts of the country and often other countries. As Mick Groombridge from Walworth explained, "So when you actually had an informal discussion, about cultural things, like music or politics...suddenly you realized, cor, yes, you can talk to these people, you know?"[20]

It was a type of exchange that impinged on both working-class and middle-class boys at Hackney Downs. Medcalf successfully passed on his specialist interest in medieval French and English texts to an exceptionally able working-class pupil, David Ogilvie, but pupils were also introduced to wider culture. Another working-class boy, Raoul Sobel, told us, "I was introduced to the theatre in that way. My parents had never gone with me to the theatre. It was just this new world," and Tim Dowley (middle-class) recalled that "The first opera I went to was [Brecht and Weill's] *The Rise and Fall of the City of Mahagonny*, which is not what you'd expect. He [John Kemp] got tickets, it was the fifth form, I think. Again, I don't know if my parents quite knew what I was going to." (Kemp's literature teaching had a lifelong influence on Dowley, a historian who became a successful publisher.) In the same spirit, Simon Clements took a group to see the Jackson Pollack show at the Whitechapel Gallery, because it seemed important although having nothing to do with English. Such teachers would take pupils along to an event that they themselves were going to anyway.

John Dixon reports (see chapter four) that he and his Walworth colleagues exclaimed after listening to recordings of young children talking, "Good God, what are we doing in school? We've got these amazing kids!" This referred—and the same attitude doubtlessly informed teachers in other schools—not to what were sometimes in those days called "sterling qualities" in the children, the same that officers were so gratified to find in working-class soldiers in both world wars, but to imagination, quick intelligence and linguistic facility, attributes that should always have been seen as vitally relevant to educability. The essential point was that these "linguistically and culturally deprived" children," in the 1960s phrase, in fact had a language that was capable of expressing and communicating their understanding of the world—the emphasis that distinguished the thinking of, say, Harold Rosen from that of George Sampson in the 1920s.

A relationship with a teacher might arise at first because the space arose for conversation, a scarce commodity in formal lessons, for instance, simply because the pupil was taking refuge in the library. Dowley again: "We didn't want to be marching with the cadets, so we'd tend to hang out in the library for an hour after school before we went home. And John (Kemp) was totally aware of what we were up to, I think—he encouraged it and would chat to us if he wanted to."[21] It was probably important with working-class children like those at Walworth that the starting point for these exchanges, that sometimes lasted for years, could be something brought to them by the pupils, such as enthusiasm for particular records. The occasion might simply be the 15-minute break between lessons, though a negotiated topic might have started to be aired in class, as is recalled in the following excerpts in which Mick Groombridge (Walworth) talks about his teacher Graham Reid (Cambridge and Leavis) and about how conversation with Reid led from the chance encounter with the recording of a contemporary literary work to a love of poetry that has taken him to places he could not have imagined at 11 or 12:

> I'd just got into Dylan, Bob Dylan, I was only eleven or twelve, and I had the first two albums *[sc. obtained from an adult acquaintance who had a less than respectable source]*...and I started talking to [Reid] rather a lot about it, and he liked a bit of Dylan, liked a bit of folk music, Joan Baez and that kind of thing...and he said bring some records in and we'll play them in class. And I remember I brought a couple in...he was a guy that really, with this cultural crossover, you learnt from. Because he was the first man I can ever recall talking to about a song lyric...I'd always chat to him...we talked about "Blowing in the Wind," which to me, before I discussed it with him, I never understood the references...But amongst all these records that nobody wanted was [Dylan Thomas's] *Under Milk Wood*, read by Richard Burton. And I put it on my dad's gramophone...and I thought wow, when I first heard the thing. Again, not really understanding any of the content..."spring, moonless [night]...bible-black"...that was my first brush with real poetry. He said...I'll play a bit, and I stayed in the break, and we played some of it, you know, Captain Cat, the blind seaman lying in his bunk...And yes, I just thought it was fantastic...I love it [poetry], you

know, and *[as an adult]* I made a sort of pilgrimage to South America, to a certain poet's three houses...Pablo Neruda.[22]

In the interview a conversation between Mick and his friend and former classmate Pete Johnson ensues:

> *Johnson*: Suddenly these people were kind of pushing the boundaries of what we regarded as normal teaching.
> *Groombridge*: Normal—didn't seem like schoolwork, it was what you wanted to do, it was culture.
> *Johnson*: They were doing things that interested you, at a time that suited you.

What was going on in such cases was more than the socialization and crossing of class boundaries envisaged by the LCC for their postwar democratic schools. Although it was in a sense democratic education, it went beyond that to education in a fuller and more permanent sense, that of the enlargement of minds through encounters with a wider world and other cultures. The vital role that teachers could fulfill in such informal conversations was to introduce the pupils to these other worlds and provide a live demonstration of what having access to them, in the ordinary course of living and thinking, could mean to an adult they respected.

Final Comments

We have looked at English teaching in three schools over the 20 years from the end of the Second World War, two grammar schools and a comprehensive. We can say finally something in summary about the picture that research has created, about stability and change in the schools, and about developments in English.

The scene that presents itself to us at the end of the study is on the one hand of an expanse of darkness sporadically illuminated by pools of light. Consider all the English lessons taught to all the classes in a school over 20 years; consider also all the teachers who taught English to at least one class for at least one year—by no means all of them members primarily of the English department, particularly in the larger comprehensive school. Of what went on in most of those lessons we know nothing, and of the few about which we know something our knowledge is mainly patchy—a reminiscence, a teacher's note, the textbook that was used, a piece of pupil work. Generalization, albeit sometimes speculative, does not nevertheless seem entirely impossible and we have felt able to suggest some general characterizations and broad patterns. The oral testimony we have received tends to present general pictures as well as bits of concrete detail. Each former pupil, after all, could talk from experience of four or more years in secondary school, normally under several teachers, and each former teacher who had stayed for some time had taught a large number of lessons, perhaps to some dozens of groups. Teachers also talked about their colleagues as well as themselves, and what they revealed went beyond memories of lessons to recollections of the climate among the staff and in the school, and the ideas and examples that influenced their thinking.

Both of the latter led us into taking account of university tutors, books, Institute of Education lectures, and speakers at LATE who and which had helped to shape teachers' sensibilities, all of them contributing to the education that was transacted in the teachers' lessons and their informal relations with pupils. Teachers brought those "ideational clusters" into the classroom with them in their heads, so that they were presences in the transactions in as real a way as the books on the pupils' desks. Thus the scene that has formed itself for us as we contemplated the diversity of the data is one in which ideas played an active part.

There was change in all three schools and major change in two, though in each case how widely the changes spread through all the teaching from first year to sixth form and across the practice of all who taught English remains unclear. One of our two grammar schools and our comprehensive experienced radical change. The case of the grammar schools is particularly interesting: English in one was disrupted—it might be said by new ideas as well as human agency—and in the other was not, although both experienced one or more changes of head of department. In Hackney Downs, the school that changed least radically, the heads of department were all internal appointments; they had been teaching there already. In the other schools, all the heads of department came from outside (except Witham, barely known to us, who transferred from Walworth Central School to its successor comprehensive in 1946) and appeared to bring change with them. Perhaps before the radical changes at Walworth and Minchenden a new head of department might not have affected other teachers very much, since the practice was to leave teachers more or less alone to do their own thing. There would have been little question of members of Arthur Harvey's department being regarded as either team players or not—there was currently no such thing, and perhaps there never was in the Hackney Downs department. It may have taken an outsider to introduce what seemed in London to be the new style of cooperative department. A result seems to have been the emergence of a new possibility of opposition to consensual department policy, as with Whittaker at Minchenden who argued with Barnes about grammar every morning. What Barnes and particularly the new teachers who joined the department saw as a positive movement—progress—in English teaching, Whittaker and perhaps others saw as retrogressive, as destruction and not as liberating creation. Behind the stances of both sides, of course, lay ideas or ideology, in sometimes more, sometimes less articulate form.

What happened to English teaching itself? Taking the two ends of the period, 1945 and 1965, and two ends of a spectrum of teaching with many gradations, in the later 1940s the teacher, at least in the grammar school, might have arrived in the classroom, explained some point of grammar or usage, often engagingly and with humor, and set an exercise to be done in the rest of the lesson with more for homework; or might have put a title on the board about which the pupils were expected, at home, to write a belles-lettristic essay. By the early 1960s, something interesting might be read in class *because* it was interesting and would stimulate a lively discussion, after which, with the juices flowing, the class would get started on a piece of writing to be finished at home, the intention of which would be both to give further experience of forming and giving written expression to thoughts and experiences of their own—not necessarily in full observance of the conventions of the essay form—and to make an intellectual or personal advance in some area of thought.

Beyond such crude snapshots, we have been able to an extent to distinguish movement, sudden changes of direction, and sometimes near immobility—all three on occasion in the same school at the same time; and sometimes but not always with tensions between them. Quite how the teachers of the younger groups and lower streams in the earlier Walworth were teaching, for example, we hardly know, but we imagine there was little common ground about the substance of English between, say, McLeod, the relaxed and experienced New Zealand graduate, and the Scottish-trained strict and formal Porchetta, and that that was so across the entire range of their teaching from handling of the books read in class to setting and responding to compositions, as well as the degree of their reliance on a textbook. In general we can see that those who would have regarded themselves as moving in a "progressive" direction tended to favor free-flowing classroom discourse and the elicitation of pupils' interpretations of literature in advance of giving authoritative versions; this description would have covered Brearley and Kemp at Hackney Downs as well as McLeod at Walworth. Beyond that there was a divide over arguments about the necessity of *telling* the pupils what a text meant and of exercises in grammar and usage beyond what O level demanded—the latter maintained also by those who would have seen themselves as preserving the strength of traditional practice; and over the sort of subject matter with which pupils should be engaging through the material they were given and the topics they were asked to write on. English for the innovators in the study involved prolific language use by pupils rather than instruction and study, their arriving at their own responses to literature, talking and writing about their experience and matters that deeply interested them, and encouragement of fluency in expressing or discovering meaning in preference to a constraining concern with orthographic accuracy and conventional acceptability of usage.

It was the innovators who tended to have the articulate justifications, drawing on ideas from the written and spoken discourse that had impressed them from the sources mentioned earlier. Their changes to previous practice applied to all aspects of English, arising as they did from consistent principles. Teachers outside this group, not necessarily offering opposition as long as their own teaching choices were not opposed, were either the conservatives alluded to above or individuals who devised or found in various places an arsenal of "good teaching ideas," such as Riddle at Minchenden. Since they were not pressing for change across the department or beyond, there was little need for these two groups to frame an articulate case, so that when it came to the arenas where clear exposition counted it was those who had successfully persuaded a team of teachers to innovate who tended to secure influential positions on the Schools Council, in NATE offices, at the Dartmouth Seminar, and in the expanding local advisory and inspection services. From there they were able to exert a disproportionate influence, in shaping the new CSE, on the projects they were invited to join, and in having a say in the appointment of teachers. In this way the version of English they promoted tended to become an orthodoxy—which is a different thing from being a generally understood and implemented practice; how far that was the case is beyond the scope of this study to judge.

Notes

Series Editors' Foreword

1. Durkheim, E. (1938/1977) *The Evolution of Educational Thought: Lectures on the Formation and Development of Secondary Education in France*. London: Routledge and Kegan Paul.
2. Ibid., 10.

1 Introduction

1. Maggie Fergusson, *George Mackay Brown* (London: John Murray, 2006), 52. Quotation is from Brown's *Northern Lights*, 4.
2. Board of Education, *The Teaching of English in England [Newbolt Report]* (London: HMSO, 1921).
3. Bernard Barker, "The History of Curriculum or Curriculum History? What is the Field and Who Gets to Play on it?," *Curriculum Studies* 4 (1996); Barry Franklin, "The State of Curriculum History," *History of Education* 28 (1999); Ivor Goodson, *Professional Knowledge, Professional Lives: Studies in Education and Change* (Maidenhead & Philadelphia: Open University Press, 2003); David Limond, "Risinghill Revisited," *History of Education* 31 (2002); Gary McCulloch, Gill Helsby, and Peter Knight, *The Politics of Professionalism: Teachers and the Curriculum* (London: Continuum, 2000).
4. Examples from this genre include Valerie E. Chancellor, *History for Their Masters. Opinion in English History* (New York: Augustus M. Kelley, 1970); David Layton, *Interpreters of Science. A History of the Association for Science Education* (Bath: John Murray/ASE, 1984); Michael H. Price, *Mathematics for the Multitude? A History of the Mathematical Association* (Leicester: Mathematical Association, 1994).
5. Harold Silver, "Knowing and Not Knowing in the History of Education," *History of Education* 21 (1) (1992).
6. Examples include: Ian Grosvenor, Martin Lawn, and Kate Rousmaniere, eds. *Silences and Images: The Social History of the Classroom* (New York: Peter Lang, 1999); Peter Cunningham and Phil Gardner, *Becoming Teachers: Texts and Testimonies 1907–1950* (London: Woburn Press, 2004).

7. For example, Thomas S. Popkewitz, "Curriculum Study, Curriculum History, and Curriculum Theory: The Reason of Reason," *Journal of Curriculum Studies* 41 (2009); Thomas S. Popkewitz, "Curriculum History, Schooling and the History of the Present," *History of Education* 40(1) (2011).
8. See Ivor Goodson and Stephen J. Ball, eds. *Defining the Curriculum. Histories and Ethnographies* (London: Falmer, 1984).
9. Philip Wesley Jackson, *Life in Classrooms* (New York and London: Holt, Rinehart & Winston, 1968).
10. They include Stephen Ball, Alex Kenny, and David Gardiner, "Literacy, Politics and the Teaching of English," in *Bringing English to Order: The History and Politics of a School Subject*, eds. Ivor Goodson and Peter Medway (London: Falmer, 1990); Tony Burgess and Nancy Martin, "The Teaching of English in England, 1945–1986: Politics and Practice," in *Teaching and Learning English Worldwide*, eds. James N. Britton, Robert Shafer, and Ken Watson (Clevedon and Philadelphia: Multilingual Matters, 1990); Anthony M. K. Burgess and John L. Hardcastle, "Englishes and English: Schooling and the Making of the School Subject," in *School Subjects in an Era of Change*, ed. Ashley Kent (London: Kogan Page, 2000); Margaret Mathieson, *The Preachers of Culture: A Study of English and Its Teachers* (London: Allen & Unwin, 1975); David Shayer, *The Teaching of English in Schools 1900–1970* (London: Routledge & Kegan Paul, 1972).
11. Ball, Kenny, and Gardiner, "Literacy, Politics and the Teaching of English," 47.
12. Harold Silver, "Case Study and Historical Research," in *Education as History: Interpreting Nineteenth- and Twentieth-century Education* (London and New York: Methuen, 1983).
13. Peter Medway, "Into the Sixties: English and English Society at a Time of Change," in *Bringing English to Order: The History and Politics of a School Subject*, eds. Ivor Goodson and Peter Medway (London: Falmer, 1990), 4.
14. Harold Rosen interview, May 4, 2005, British Library, C1469/63.
15. Grant number F/07 141/b.
16. The phrase that David Layton, Professor of Science Education at Leeds University, used when distinguishing technology from science, the former drawing on diverse sources from physics to tables of the gauges of wire in order to find practical solutions.
17. Our references to interviews in what follows have the BL catalogue number attached.
18. As exemplified by *Circular* 10/65.
19. Alan Allport, *Demobbed: Coming Home After the Second World War* (New Haven: Yale, 2009).
20. Peter Henry John Heather Gosden, *Education in the Second World War: A Study in Policy and Administration* (London: Methuen, 1976).
21. Gary McCulloch, *Documentary Research in Education, History and the Social Sciences* (London: RoutledgeFalmer, 2004), 129.

22. Bobbie Wells and Peter Cunningham, "'I Wanted to Nurse. Father Wanted Teachers'" in *The Uses of Autobiography*, ed. Julia Swindells (London: Taylor & Francis, 1995), 156.
23. See Silver, "Case Study and Historical Research," 297.
24. Also at the Institute of Education are the archives of James Britton, Nancy Martin, and the London Association for the Teaching of English.
25. The multivolume *Tales of a New Jerusalem* (London: Bloomsbury Publishing), still appearing.
26. One was in collaboration with Pat Jones, an independent researcher pursuing the story of the first head teacher.

2 THE PERIOD, THE EDUCATION SYSTEM, AND THE TEACHING OF ENGLISH

1. Barry Miles, *London Calling: A Countercultural History of London Since 1945* (London: Atlantic Books, 2010), 7.
2. Edward Shils, "An Age of Embarrassment," *Encounter* 54 (1978): 90.
3. James Hinton, *Nine Wartime Lives: Mass-Observation and the Making of the Modern Self* (Oxford: Oxford University Press, 2010), 11.
4. Ibid., 8.
5. Colin MacInnes, *England, Half English* (London: Chatto and Windus, 1986), 153.
6. Ibid., 45.
7. Harry Hopkins, *The New Look: A Social History of the Forties and Fifties in Britain* (London: 1963), 166–167.
8. Board of Education, *Secondary Education with Special Reference to Grammar Schools and Technical High Schools* (Spens Report) (London: HMSO, 1938).
9. And central schools, selective but non-fee-charging elementary schools with a wider range of subjects and a vocational bias.
10. TNA ED 147, 22 Tomlinson to FA Cobb, MP, March 24, 1949.
11. Ministry of Education, *The New Secondary Education* (London: HMSO, 1947).
12. Brian Cox, *The Great Betrayal* (London: Chapmans, 1992), 122.
13. Quoted by Francis Mulhern, *The Moment of "Scrutiny"* (London: NLB, 1979), 220.
14. Philip Vernon, *Secondary School Selection: A British Psychological Society Inquiry* (London: Methuen, 1957); Alfred Yates and Douglas A. Pidgeon, *Admission to Grammar Schools. Third Interim Report on the Allocation of Primary School Leavers to Courses of Secondary Education* (London: Newnes Educational Publishing, 1957).
15. Caroline Benn and Brian Simon, *Half Way There. Report on the British Comprehensive School Reform* (Harmondsworth: Penguin, 1972), 47.
16. Susan Crosland, *Tony Crosland* (Sevenoaks: Coronet, 1982), 148.

17. Hopkins, *New Look*, 151. Reference is to Jean Esther Floud, Albert Henry Halsey, and F. M. Martin, *Social Class and Educational Opportunity* (London: William Heinemann, 1956).
18. Brian Jackson and Dennis Marsden, *Education and the Working Class: Some General Themes Raised by a Study of 88 Working Class Children in a Northern Industrial City* (London: Routledge and Kegan Paul, 1962), 142.
19. Geoffrey Alderman, *The History of Hackney Downs School* (London: The Clove Club, 1972), 27.
20. Colin Lacey, *Hightown Grammar: The School as a Social System* (Manchester: Manchester University Press, 1970), 22, using figures based on Floud, Halsey, and Martin, *Social Class*.
21. Benn and Simon, *Half Way There*, 47.
22. Jackson and Marsden, *Education and the Working Class*.
23. Ibid., 137.
24. Ibid., 113.
25. Colin Lacey, "Schools and Academic Streaming," *British Journal of Sociology* 17 (1966).
26. Jackson and Marsden, *Education and the Working Class*, 110.
27. Ibid., 114.
28. Hopkins, *New Look*, 163.
29. Jackson and Marsden, *Education and the Working Class*, 114–115.
30. David Rubinstein and Brian Simon, *The Evolution of the Comprehensive School, 1926–1972* (London: Routledge and Kegan Paul, 1973), 45–46.
31. London County Council, *The London School Plan: A Development Plan for Primary and Secondary Education* (London: London County Council, 1947), 229.
32. Margaret Cole, *What Is a Comprehensive School? The London Plan in Practice* (London: London Labour Party Publications, 1955), 4.
33. Guy Boas, *A Teacher's Story* (London: Macmillan and St. Martin's Press, 1963), 86.
34. James Nimmo Britton, "How We Got Here," in *New Movements in the Study and Teaching of English*, ed. Nicholas Bagnall (London: Temple Smith, 1973), 13–29 and 19–20.
35. Margaret Mathieson, *The Preachers of Culture: A Study of English and Its Teachers* (London: Allen & Unwin, 1975); David Shayer, *The Teaching of English in Schools 1900–1970* (London: Routledge and Kegan Paul, 1972); Robin Peel, "'English' in England: Its History and Transformations," in *Questions of English: Ethics, Aesthetics, Rhetoric, and the Formation of the Subject in England, Australia, and the United States*, eds. Robin Peel, Annette Hinman Patterson, and Jeanne Marcum Gerlach (London; New York: Routledge, 2000), 39–115; Brian Doyle, *English and Englishness* (London: Routledge, 1989); Ian Reid, *Wordsworth and the Formation of English Studies* (Aldershot: Ashgate Publishing Ltd., 2004).
36. Simon James Gibbons, *The London Association for the Teaching of English 1947–1967: A History* (London: Trentham Books/University of London Institute of Education, 2013).

37. Douglas Barnes, Dorothy Barnes, and Stephen Clarke, *Versions of English* (London: Heinemann, 1984).
38. Douglas Barnes, *Becoming an English Teacher* (Sheffield: NATE, 2000).
39. Peter Medway, "Into the Sixties: English and English Society at a Time of Change," in *Bringing English to Order: The History and Politics of a School Subject*, eds. Ivor Goodson and Peter Medway (London: Falmer, 1990).
40. Wayne Sawyer did something similar for Australia (Wayne Sawyer, "Simply Growth? A Study of Selected Episodes in the History of Years 7–10 English in New South Wales from the 1970s to the 1990s." (Diss., University of Western Australia, 2002).)
41. A list of all the historical accounts Medway consulted is given there in note 3 on p. 34.
42. Stephen J. Ball, "Competition and Conflict in the Teaching of English: A Socio-Cultural Analysis," *Journal of Curriculum Studies* 14(1) (1982): 1–28; "A Subject of Privilege: English and the School Curriculum 1906–1935," in *Curriculum Practice*, eds. Martyn Hammersley and Andy Hargreaves (Lewes: Falmer, 1983), 61–88; "English for the English Since 1906," in *Social Histories of the Secondary Curriculum: Subjects for Study*, ed. Ivor Goodson (London: Falmer, 1985) 53–88.
43. Board of Education, *The Teaching of English in England [Newbolt Report]* (London: HMSO, 1921).
44. David Stevens and Nicholas McGuinn, *The Art of Teaching Secondary English: Innovative and Creative Approaches* (London: RoutledgeFalmer, 2004), 53.
45. Secondary Schools Examination Council (SSEC), *Report of the Committee of the Secondary Schools Examination Council on Curriculum and Examinations in Secondary Schools [the Norwood Report]* (London: HMSO, 1943), 97.
46. Ibid., 95.
47. See, for example, its magazine *English*.
48. Gibbons, *London Association*.
49. Charles Kay Ogden and Ivor Armstrong Richards, *The Meaning of Meaning: A Study of the Influence of Language Upon Thought and of the Science of Symbolism* (London: Kegan Paul, 1923).
50. Raymond Williams, *Writing in Society* (London: Verso, 1983), 184–185.
51. Frank Raymond Leavis, *The Great Tradition : George Eliot, Henry James, Joseph Conrad* (London: Chatto and Windus, 1948).
52. Frank Raymond Leavis, *New Bearings in English Poetry: A Study of the Contemporary Situation* (Harmondsworth: Penguin, 1963), 19. The last part is a quotation from Richards.
53. Andor Gomme, "Criticism and the Reading Public," in *The Modern Age. The Pelican Guide to English Literature*, ed. Boris Ford (Harmondsworth: Penguin Books, 1961), 350–376.
54. Frank Raymond Leavis and Denys Thompson, *Culture and Environment. The Training of Critical Awareness* (London: Chatto & Windus, 1933).
55. Work on advertising in English had begun between the wars. For example, *English on the Anvil* (1934) included a short section on "advertisements" with a set of composition exercises (James Nimmo Britton, *English on the Anvil.*

A Language and Composition Course for Secondary Schools (London: Foyles Educational, 1934).)
56. Denys Thompson, *Reading and Discrimination* (London: Chatto and Windus, 1934), vii.
57. Ibid., 5.
58. Denys Thompson, "Editorial: The Use of English and Conference Notes" *The Use of English* 1(1) (1953): 5.
59. Geoffrey Summerfield, "Great Expectations: Modern Trends in English 1," *New Education* 2 (1966): 8.
60. William Empson, *Seven Types of Ambiguity* (London: Chatto & Windus, 1930).
61. See Raymond Wilson Chambers, *The Teaching of English in the Universities* (Oxford: Oxford University Press, 1922); but also Hans Aarsleff, *The Study of Language in England, 1780–1860* (London: Athlone, 1983) (especially chapters V and VI) as well as Tony Crowley, *The Politics of Discourse: The Standard Language Question in British Cultural Debates* (Basingstoke and London: Macmillan, 1989).
62. Ian Pringle, "Jimmy Britton and Linguistics," in *The Word for Teaching Is Learning: Essays for James Britton*, eds. Martin Lightfoot and Nancy Martin (London and Portsmouth: Heinemann Educational Books, 1988), 264–265, 265.
63. Frank Raymond Leavis, *Mass Civilisation and Minority Culture* (Cambridge: Gordon Fraser, 1930), 3–5.
64. Thomas Stearns Eliot, *Notes Towards the Definition of Culture* (London: Faber, 1948), 48.
65. Mulhern, *The Moment of 'Scrutiny,'* 261.
66. Stefan Collini, *Absent Minds: Intellectuals in Britain* (Oxford: Oxford University Press, 2006), 438.
67. Hopkins, *New Look*, 247–248.
68. George Orwell, "Boys' Weeklies," in *The Collected Essays, Journalism and Letters of George Orwell*, eds. Sonia Orwell and Ian Angus, Volume 1 (Harmondsworth: Penguin Books in association with Secker & Warburg, 1970); and "The art of Donald McGill," in Orwell and Angus, *The Collected Essays*, Volume 2, 155–165.
69. George Orwell, *The Road to Wigan Pier* (London: Victor Gollancz, 1937).
70. Richard Hoggart, *The Uses of Literacy: Aspects of Working-class Life, with Special Reference to Publications and Entertainments* (London: Chatto & Windus, 1957).
71. Raymond Williams, *Culture and Society, 1780–1950* (London: Chatto & Windus, 1958).
72. Raymond Williams, "Culture is ordinary," in *Convictions*, ed. Norman Mackenzie (London: MacGibbon and Gee, 1958); reprinted in *Resources of Hope: Culture, Democracy, Socialism*, ed. Robin Gable (London: Verso. 1989), 1–18.
73. Peter Willmott and Michael Young, *Family and Class in a London Suburb* (London: Routledge and Kegan Paul, 1960).

74. For example, Floud, Halsey, and Martin, *Social Class*; and Olive Banks, *Parity and Prestige in Secondary Education: A Study in Educational Sociology* (London: Routledge and Kegan Paul, 1955).
75. Jackson and Marsden, *Education and the Working Class*.
76. Obituary, *The Times*, March 19, 1980.
77. Percival Gurrey, *The Teaching of Written English* (London: Longmans and Green, 1954), 3.
78. Percival Gurrey, *The Appreciation of Poetry* (London: Humphrey Milford for Oxford University Press, 1935).
79. Ibid., 9.
80. Ibid., 7.
81. Ibid.. Gurrey cites Percy Nunn, *Education: Its Data and First Principles* (London: Edward Arnold, 1920).
82. Gurrey, *Teaching Written English*, 5.
83. Ibid., 6.
84. James Nimmo Britton, "Literature," in *Studies in Education: The Arts in Education* (London: University of London Institute of Education, 1963), 35.
85. James Nimmo Britton, "How we got here," in *Prospect and Retrospect: Selected Essays of James Britton* (Montclair: Boynton Cook, 1982), 169–184, 170.
86. Douglas Barnes, James Nimmo Britton, and Harold Rosen, *Language, the Learner and the School* (Harmondsworth: Penguin, 1969); James Nimmo Britton, *Language and Learning* (London: Allen Lane The Penguin Press, 1970).
87. James Nimmo Britton, Tony Burgess, Nancy Coniston Martin, Alex McLeod, and Harold Rosen, *The Development of Writing Abilities (11–18)* (London: Macmillan, 1975).
88. John Dixon, *Growth through English: A Report Based on the Dartmouth Seminar 1966* (Reading: National Association for the Teaching of English, 1967).
89. David Holbrook, *English for Maturity: English in the Secondary School* (Cambridge: Cambridge University Press, 1961).
90. David Holbrook, *Visions of Life. Prose Passages for Reading and Comprehension Work.* (Cambridge: Cambridge University Press, 1964).
91. Frances Stevens, "The Uses of Literacy and the Use of English," *The Use of English* 9(4) (1958): 231–232.
92. David Holbrook, "Something They Call a Play…" *The Use of English* 10(1) (1958): 6.
93. DES (Department of Education and Science), *Language: Some Suggestions for Teachers of English and Others* (London: HMSO, 1954), 10–11.
94. Ibid., 6, quoting Ernst Cassirer, *An Essay on Man*.
95. Ronald Ridout, *English Today,* Books 1–5 (London: Ginn, 1947).
96. Cedric Austin, *Read to Write* (four volumes) (London: Ginn, 1954).
97. Nancy Coniston Martin, *Understanding and Enjoyment* (London: Oxford University Press, 1954).
98. Richard Palmer, *School Broadcasting in Britain* (London: BBC, 1948), 54.
99. Kenneth Vye Bailey, *The Listening Schools: Educational Broadcasting by Sound and Television* (London: British Broadcasting Corporation, 1957), 141.

100. John Dixon and Leslie Stratta, John Dixon email to Peter Medway, October 30, 2012.
101. Schools Council, *Working Paper No. 3: English: A Programme for Research and Development in English* (London: HMSO, 1965); John Dixon email to Peter Medway, January 9, 2012.
102. DES, *Language: Some Suggestions.*
103. Peter Medway's recollection.
104. TNA ED 176/2, Central Panel minutes and papers, 1948–1950.
105. TNA ED 158/31 Minutes 15–25, 1951–1955, Meeting 19 of 23 April 1953. LATE on O level is also discussed in Meeting 21 of 23 April 1954, Meeting 22 of 7–8 December 1954, and Meeting 34 of 15–16 April 1959.
106. TNA ED 158/30 Minutes 1–14, 1945–1950, Meeting 4 of 10–11 December 1946.
107. TNA ED 158/30 Minutes 1–14, 1945–1950, Meeting 13 of 18–19 April 1950.
108. TNA ED 158/32 Minutes 26–39, 1956–1960, Meeting 32 of 18–19 September 1958.
109. TNA ED 147/22 Wilson to Tomlinson, [n.d. November/December 1949].
110. Barnes, Barnes, and Clarke, *Versions*, 131–132.
111. TNA ED 158/31 Meeting 16 of 11–12 December 1951.
112. Medway, "Into the Sixties."
113. Ibid., 6–13.
114. James Britton, *The Oxford Books of Verse for Juniors* (London: Oxford University Press, 1957).
115. R. H. Charles, "English Teaching Today," *English. The Magazine of the English Association*, 8(43) (1950): 6–7.
116. J. S. Tudsbury, "The Teaching of English Literature," *Journal of Education* 79(1947): 117.
117. LATE, "Report on the Day Conference on the Work of the English Department," (1966): 2.
118. Ibid., 1.
119. Schools Council, *The First Ten Years, 1964–1974* (London: Schools Council, 1975), 1.
120. Schools Council, *Working Paper 3*; Schools Council, *The First Ten Years, 1964–1974*, 11.
121. Douglas Barnes, "The Significance of Teachers' Frames for Teaching," in *Teachers and Teaching: From Classroom to Reflection*, eds. Tom Russell and Hugh Mumby (London: Falmer, 1992), 11.
122. *Half Our Future. A Report of the Central Advisory Council for Education (England) [Newsom Report]* (London: HMSO, 1963).
123. Central Advisory Council for Education (England), *Children and Their Primary Schools: A Report of the Central Advisory Council for Education (England) (Plowden Report)* (London: Her Majesty's Stationery Office, 1967).
124. Alec B. Clegg, *The Excitement of Writing* (London: Chatto and Windus, 1964).

125. David Shayer, *The Teaching of English in Schools, 1900–70* (London: Routledge and Kegan Paul, 1972), 170.
126. Medway, "Into the Sixties," 13–21.
127. Albert Ward Rowe and Peter Emmens, *English through Experience* (five volumes) (London: Blond Educational, 1963). Over a million copies were sold (D. W. West, "The Moment of 1963: *Reflections* and the New English," *Changing English* 5 (1998): 41).
128. Summerfield, "Great Expectations: Modern Trends in English 1," 10.
129. Ian Serraillier, *The Silver Sword* (school edition, London: William Heinemann, 1957, original 1956). The Puffin edition was published in 1960 and a BBC children's television adaptation in eight parts was broadcast in 1957.
130. Wolf Mankowitz, *A Kid for Two Farthings* (London: William André Deutsch, 1953).
131. Britton, *The Oxford Books of Verse for Juniors*; David Holbrook, *Iron, Honey, Gold,* two volumes (Cambridge: Cambridge University Press, 1961); Michael Baldwin, *Billy the Kid, an Anthology of Tough Verse* (London: Hutchinson Educational, 1963); Ted Hughes, *Here Today* (London: Hutchinson Educational, 1963); Geoffrey Summerfield, *Voices* (three volumes) (Harmondsworth: Penguin Books, 1968).
132. Shayer, *Teaching of English*, 112.
133. George Allen, "English Past, Present and Future," in *New Movements in the Study and Teaching of English*, ed. Nicholas Bagnall (London: Temple Smith, 1973), 37–38.
134. Derek Sharples, "Literacy and Curriculum," *Higher Education Journal* 16 (1968).
135. V. Davis, "Prose Anthologies," *The Use of English* 20 (1968).
136. Allen, "English Past, Present and Future," 30, 33.
137. Frank Whitehead, *The Disappearing Dais* (London: Chatto and Windus, 1966), 238–239.
138. Harriet Chetwynd, *Comprehensive School: The Story of Woodberry Down* (London: Routledge and Kegan Paul, 1960), 63.
139. Summerfield, "Great Expectations," 8–9.
140. Excerpts shown in the BBC film, "At the Chalk Face," BBC4 on January 28 and 29, 2005. See "Were Secondary Moderns That Bad? asks BBC," TES January 21, 2005, http://www.tes.co.uk/article.aspx?storycode=2067297, consulted September 28, 2013.
141. Medway, "Into the Sixties," 23.
142. T. H. B. Hollins, "The Three-year Course and the Training of the Teacher of English," *English in Education* 2 (1968): 20.
143. The Swiss psychologist, Jean Piaget, discussed the claims of grammarians concerning the training of mind before the war (1935) in a piece that was subsequently included in *The Science of Education and the Psychology of the Child* (London: Longman, 1970).
144. Barnes, Barnes, and Clarke, *Versions*, 131–132.

145. Hollins, "The Three-year Course and the Training of the Teacher of English," 17.
146. Dixon, *Growth through English*.
147. Barnes, Barnes, and Clarke, *Versions*, 131–132.
148. Michael Baldwin, *Poems by Children, 1950–61* (London: Routledge and Kegan Paul, 1962).
149. Clegg, *Excitement of Writing*.
150. Summerfield, "Great Expectations," 9.
151. Medway, "Into the Sixties," 10.
152. Martin Lightfoot, "Teaching English as a Rehearsal of Politics," in *The Word for Teaching is Learning: Essays for James Britton*, eds. Martin Lightfoot and Nancy Coniston Martin (London and Portsmouth: Heinemann Educational Books, 1988), 246.
153. Michael Benton, "Review of English Teaching Since 1965: How Much Growth? By David Allen," *British Journal of Educational Studies* 29(2) (1981).
154. Stephen J. Ball, "A Subject of Privilege," 61–88; "Competition and Conflict in the Teaching of English," 1–28; Stephen Ball, Alex Kenny, and David Gardiner, "Literacy, Politics and the Teaching of English," In *Bringing English to Order: The History and Politics of a School Subject*, eds. Ivor Goodson and Peter Medway (London: Falmer, 1990), 47–86.
155. Lightfoot, "Teaching English as Rehearsal," 244.

3 Hackney Downs

1. Livery Companies are trade associations in the City of London.
2. Geoffrey Alderman, *Hackney Downs, 1876 – 1995: The Life and Death of a School* (London: The Clove Club, 2012), 5.
3. Barry Supple interview with John Hardcastle, 15 August, 2011, British Library, C1469/71.
4. HMI, *Report by HMI on London County Council Hackney Downs School, Hackney, London. Inspected on 29, 30, 31, May, 1951.* Issued September 28, 1951 (London: HMSO, 1951).
5. The phrase, "English for all" invokes the spirit of R. H. Tawney's seminal 1924 work, *Secondary Education for All: A Policy for Labour* (London: Hambledon, 1988). For a clear, engaged discussion of Tawney's ideas, see Raymond Williams, *Culture and Society, 1780–1950* (London: Chatto and Windus, 1958).
6. HMI, *Hackney Downs School*, 5.
7. Guy Pocock, *Grammar in a New Setting* (London: J. M. Dent, 1928), 57.
8. Surviving green and blue exercise books were donated by David Ogilvie's widow, following his death in 2010. David Ogilvie, *Green Exercise Book*. The exercise is from Guy Pocock, *Grammar*.

9. HMI, *Hackney Downs School*, 6.
10. Ibid.
11. Pocock, *Grammar*, vi.
12. Ibid..
13. See David Shayer, *The Teaching of English in Secondary Schools* (London: Routledge and Kegan Paul, 1972), 79–82.
14. Alderman, *Hackney Downs*, 64.
15. We have discovered no reliable way of distinguishing classwork from homework in surviving exercise books.
16. Supple interview.
17. An official position on the amount of grammar teaching is represented in a Department of Education and Science pamphlet of 1954, *Language: Some Suggestions for Teachers of English and Others*: one weekly lesson for about three years (in grammar schools) with more time in other secondary schools, and when this grammatical minimum has been mastered, the report recommends practice in continuous composition is more important than further elaboration. (Department of Education and Science, *Language: Some Suggestions for Teachers of English and Others in Primary and Secondary Schools and Further Education*, Education Pamphlet No 26, (London: HMSO, 1954), 45.
18. Terry Gasking interview with John Hardcastle, December 13, 2011, British Library, C1469/28.
19. Harvey Monte email to Hardcastle, August 22, 2010.
20. James Britton, "The Paper in English Language at Ordinary Level," *The Use of English* 4(3) (Spring 1955): 2.
21. Ogilvie, "Green Exercise Book."
22. Guy Pocock, *More English Exercises* (London: J. M. Dent, 1934).
23. HMI, *Hackney Downs School*, 6.
24. Ibid.
25. Supple interview.
26. Harvey Monte interview with John Hardcastle, October 20, 2009, British Library, C1469/48.
27. Barry Supple, *Doors Open* (Cambridge: Asher, 2008), 98.
28. See Shayer, *The Teaching of English*, 112–117.
29. The following extract is from a testimonial written by Medcalf's Commanding Officer in 1919, and it suggests something of his qualities as a soldier: "James E. Medcalf has served under my command in France and Belgium for 12 months or more, during which he has proved himself an excellent soldier, smart, energetic, intelligent, with a perfect knowledge of control. His advancement in education: Languages etc. was a great boon to me as Commander, also to the Army Education Staff, in the training of Officers after the Armistice. He had many times volunteered for action in the field but was withheld."
30. Raoul Sobel interview with John Hardcastle, March 15, 2010, British Library, C1469/66.
31. Spencer Moody, "Mr James Ellis Medcalf" in *The Review*, the Magazine of the Hackney Downs School (1956): 11.
32. Sobel interview.

33. This testimonial kindly made available to us by Gillian Medcalf, James Medcalf's granddaughter, from the Second Master, Cheltonia College, Streatham, suggests why Medcalf earned a reputation as an excellent teacher: "Mr. Medcalf has shown during that time exceptional ability as a teacher, and is particularly well qualified to handle a large number of boys. He has the knack of interesting his classes, without in any way allowing discipline to become slack, and has also exercised a very lasting and excellent influence upon boys out of school hours." HMI, *Hackney Downs School*, 6.
34. Moody, *The Review*, 11.
35. Supple, *Doors Open*, 98.
36. Harvey Monte email to John Hardcastle, August 22, 2010.
37. Supple, *Doors Open*, 98.
38. HMI, *Hackney Downs School*, 4.
39. Harvey Monte email to Hardcastle. The poetry anthology was almost certainly, W. A. C. Wilkinson and N. H. Wilkinson, *The Dragon Book of Verse*, with illustrations by Gillian Alington (Oxford: Oxford University Press, 1935).
40. Letter from Medcalf to Kemp, Thursday, December 31, 1953. The letter was deposited with us by John Kemp's daughter, Vicky Ward.
41. Brearley had recently been promoted to second master under the fifth headmaster, Vernon Barkway Pye.
42. Alderman, *Hackney Downs*, 90.
43. Ibid.
44. Steven Berkoff, "The Worst Days of My Life," *The Independent* newspaper on November 5, 1995.
45. Berkoff, "The Worst Days of My Life."
46. Monte email to Hardcastle.
47. Terry Gasking gave us a moving account of getting practical support from teachers, especially Les Mitchell, a physical education teacher at the school, and Joe Brearley. Gasking interview.
48. Gasking interview.
49. Ogilvie, "Green Exercise Book."
50. David Ogilvie's unpublished letters were made available to us by his widow, following his death in 2010. They are now available as a collection, David Ogilvie, *Thanks for the Boblet: The Wartime Letters of David Ogilvie*, ed. Glyndwer Watkins (Dinton: Twig Books, 2012).
51. Ogilvie, *Thanks for the Boblet*, 43.
52. Ogilvie, *Green Exercise Book*.
53. See Patrick Kingwell and Peter Medway, "A Curriculum in Its Place: English Teaching in One School, 1946–1963," *History in Education* 39 (6) (2010): 749–765.
54. Ogilvie, *Blue Exercise Book*.
55. F. R. Leavis complained about the frequent use of *Poems of Today* anthologies by teachers. See Frank Raymond Leavis, *New Bearings in English Poetry*, first published in 1932 (Harmondsworth: Pelican Books, 1972), 51.

56. David Ogilvie interview with John Hardcastle, April 23, 2010.
57. Joseph Brearley, *Fortune's Fool: A Life of Joe Brearley*, ed. G. L. Watkins (Dinton: Twigg Books, 2008), 146.
58. Ibid., 147.
59. Ibid.
60. Ibid., 150.
61. Barry Supple mentions "subversive moments"; Supple, *Doors Open*, 99.
62. Ogilvie left the school in 1949. GCE A levels were introduced in 1951. It seems likely therefore that he is referring to the Higher School Certificate examination that the A level replaced.
63. Ogilvie interview.
64. Sobel interview.
65. Supple interview.
66. Supple, *Doors Open*, 99.
67. Ibid., 101.
68. Henry Grinberg, "Pinter at School," in *The Pinter Review: Collected Essays, 1999 and 2000*, eds. Francis Gillen and Steven H. Gale (Tampa: University of Tampa Press, 2000), 3.
69. As Barry Supple remarks, "He [Brearley] is one of the few state secondary school teachers I know to have a website devoted to his role and life." Supple, *Doors Open*, 100. See also Billington's biography, Michael Billington, *Harold Pinter* (London: Faber and Faber, 1996), 443–446. Pinter frequently acknowledged his debt to Brearley as, for example, in his acceptance speech for the David Cohen British Literature prize in 1995.
70. Billington, *Harold Pinter*, 11.
71. Ibid. See also Pinter's "Introduction" to Brearley, *Fortune's Fool*, 7–9.
72. Billington, *Harold Pinter*, 1996, 11.
73. Grinberg, *Pinter*, 3.
74. Ibid.
75. *The Review* (1947): 11–12.
76. Harvey Monte email to John Hardcastle, August 22, 2010.
77. Derek Newton, "'Drama' in *Studies in Education: The Arts and Current Tendencies in Education*, ed. James Britton (London: Institute of Education, 1963), 102.
78. Sobel interview. The early twentieth century was the heyday of Yiddish theater in London, with plays performed in Yiddish. However, we have found no evidence to suggest that pupils were encouraged to visit, say, the Feinman Yiddish-People's Theatre that was nearby in Commercial Road in the heart of the traditional East End.
79. Brearley, *Fortune's Fool*, 163.
80. Monte interview.
81. Raoul Sobel told us, "I don't think any of the leads in the school plays, that I can remember, big leads, were recruited from the 'B' and 'C' streams, except perhaps once, and that was in, what do you call it, in *Midsummer Night's Dream*." Sobel interview.

82. Gasking interview.
83. Brearley wrote: "Forster's Indians are high-caste – at least those he is interested in. But what about the *Punka-wallah* and the Eurasian and the vast mass of Indians who are hardly hinted at in Forster's novel? You touch on an important point when you say that Forster is only interested in *individuals* – individuals, moreover, of a very limited group. Does Forster imply that the *punka-wallah* and his kind are fated to return to dung-hill? Is Forster too narrowly fatalistic?" Geoffrey Alderman kindly loaned surviving exercise books, several essays, and transcripts.
84. Supple, *Doors Open,* 101.
85. Monte interview.
86. Vicky Ward deposited with us a collection of Kemp's surviving undergraduate essays from 1948–1950.
87. Later, Kemp gained substantial preservice practical experience in Owen's Grammar School. Owen's was a similar kind of school to Hackney Downs, with links to the Worshipful Company of Brewers, a City Livery Company.
88. John Kemp's unpublished account of teaching at White Hart Lane Primary School.
89. Vicky Ward in conversation with John Hardcastle, December 12, 2010. Vicky remarked that John came from a Labour family and he was a lifelong Socialist.
90. John Kemp, "Some Diverse Views on the Position and Function of the Artist and His Work in Society as Seen in the Literature of the Years 1880–1920." (MA thesis, King's College, London University, 1953), 1.
91. Ibid., 1.
92. John Kemp interview with John Hardcastle, October 14, 1994.
93. Ibid.
94. Denys Thompson, "Editorial," *The Use of English*, 1(1) (Autumn 1949): 6.
95. Teaching about advertising did not start with *Culture and Environment.* Suggestions for work on adverts appear for example in James Britton, *English on the Anvil: A Language and Composition Course for Secondary Schools* (London: Foyles Educational Ltd, 1934).
96. Tim Dowley, "Blue Exercise Book."
97. Percival Gurrey, *The Teaching of Written English* (London: Longmans Green and Co, 1954), 224.
98. Ibid., Appendix B, 229.
99. Kemp's principle source is Gurrey. There are two reasons for suggesting this. First, *The Teaching of Written English* figures in an inventory of Kemp's private book collection; and second, a topic for descriptive writing recommended by Gurrey, "A Busy Railway Station," is among the writing tasks set for the same classes. See Gurrey, *Written English* 1954, 146–147.
100. This was confirmed by Kemp's daughter, Vicky Ward.
101. Thomas Sharp, *The Anatomy of the Village* (Harmondsworth: Penguin Books, 1946).
102. Tim Dowley interview with John Hardcastle, June 7, 2011, British Library, C1469/23.

103. Ibid.
104. Kemp's handwriting altered over the years. The MCC books are written in the same hand as Kemp's unpublished account of teaching at Whitehart Lane, 1949.
105. Dowley interview.
106. Roy Dunning, a former teacher, remarked: "He [Kemp] had a lot of difficulty in the early days with unruly classes, because he was not the most assertive of people." Jean and Roy Dunning, interview with John Hardcastle, July 16, 2009, British Library, C1469/25.
107. Kemp interview.
108. Ogilvie interview.
109. Cyril Poster, "Projects for the English Specialist," *The Use of English* 5(1) (Autumn 1953): 20–22.
110. "*The Brute*" was from a school anthology, Joseph Conrad, *Four Tales: A Selection from the Works of Joseph Conrad*, eds. Emile Victor Rieu and Peter Wait for Methuen's Modern Classics Series (London: Methuen, 1955). Tim Dowley recalled studying short stories including *The Brute* with Kemp for the O level examination: "We did *The Secret Sharer* and *The Machine Stops*, [and] *The Demolitionists.*" Dowley interview.
111. The narrator overhears someone say, "That fellow Wilmot fairly dashed her brains out, and a good job too!" The "person" spoken of is a ship.
112. Dowley interview.
113. Derek Traversi, *Shakespeare: The Roman Plays* (Stanford: Stanford University Press, 1963), and John Holloway, *The Story of the Night: Studies in Shakespeare's Major Tragedies* (London: Routledge, 1961).
114. Ralph Levinson interview with Georgina Brewis, June 13, 2011, British Library, C1469/44.
115. John Kemp, *The Last Thirty Years* (Whittlebury: The Clove Club, 1996), iii.
116. Joan and Roy Dunning interview with John Hardcastle August 7, 2009.
117. Kemp, *The Last Thirty Years,* iii.

4 Walworth

1. Seamus Perry, "The Shoreham Gang," *London Review of Books* 34(7) (2012): 30.
2. Replaced in 2007 by Walworth Academy.
3. There is further discussion of English at Walworth in Peter Medway and Patrick Kingwell, "A Curriculum in Its Place: English Teaching in One School 1946–1963," *History of Education* 39(6) (2010): 749–765, and Peter Medway, "Teachers Learning in a London School: Autonomy and Development in the 1950s," *L1 – Educational Studies in Languages and Literature* 12 (2012): 1–32.
4. This information is drawn from the National Archives.

5. LCC, "Organisation of Secondary Education and the Possibility of Early Experiment. Report from the Education Officer," LMA LCC/MIN/4037 (1946). Three more were added in 1947: LCC, *The London School Plan: A Development Plan for Primary and Secondary Education* (London: LCC, 1947), 152.
6. Accounts of interim London comprehensives are included in Brian Simon, ed., *New Trends in Education, A Symposium* (London: MacGibbon & Kee, 1957) including a chapter on Walworth (D. Levin, "Mathematics Teaching in Interim Comprehensive Schools," 175–182).
7. John Dixon, Simon Clements, and Leslie Stratta, *Reflections: An English Course for Students Aged 14–18* (London: Oxford University Press, 1963). It had sold its initial print run of 10,000 before the end of the year and went on to sell 200,000 by the early 1980s: D. W. West, "The Moment of 1963: *Reflections* and the New English," *Changing English* 5 (1998): 41.
8. Valerie Avery, *London Morning* (London: Kimber, 1964).
9. Now deposited in the Southwark Local History Library.
10. Patricia Jones, "Walworth School: Changing Aims and Organization (1946–76)." (MA thesis, Sussex University, 1976), 6–7. She has also helped us in person.
11. Most of these have since been destroyed in a fire.
12. The school reached six form entry (200 pupils) after the first few years and rose to eight f.e. in 1962.
13. Jones, "Walworth," 7.
14. Stuart Maclure, *A History of Education in London, 1870–1990* (London: Allen Lane, 1990), 172.
15. Jones, "Walworth."
16. Arthur George Hughes, T*he London School Plan. Some Reflections on Reading it in 1947. A Lecture to Heads of London Schools* (London: North-Western Polytechnic Printing Department, 1948).
17. LCC, *Walworth Secondary School: Report (14–9–51) of a Full Inspection* (London: LCC, 1951); Harold C. Shearman, "Some Claims Justified," in *Comprehensive Schools Today: An Interim Survey by Robin Pedley with New Critical Essays by Robin Pedley, H. C. Dent, Harold C. Shearman, Eric James, W. P. Alexander*, ed. Robin Pedley (London: Councils and Education Press, 1954): 44.
18. Jones, "Walworth," 27–28.
19. Walworth School Staff Bulletins 1954–55, 22.
20. Harry Hopkins, "Trying Out the Skyscraper School (Conclusion of a 4-Part Series, 'Going to School in 1951')" *John Bull*, (February 10, 1951), 23.
21. 1911 Census.
22. There is a record of a Mr Witham as senior master for English (LCC, Walworth Secondary Schools Interim Report (25.6.47). He left in December, 1948.
23. Jones, "Walworth," 48.
24. Boardman email, April 23, 2010. His evidence is more compelling than a reporter's claim that Harvey "had worked twenty years in Grammar Schools" (Hopkins, "Skyscraper School," 23).

25. His work appeared in John Lehmann's collection that featured five poets including David Gascoyne and Laurie Lee, *Poets of Tomorrow. Third Selection* (London: The Hogarth Press, 1942) and in John Lehmann, *Poems from New Writing, 1936–1946* (London: J. Lehmann, 1946).
26. Arthur Harvey, "Experience and Experiment at Walworth," *New Era* (July 7, 1954): 128–133; "English in a Modern Secondary School," *The Use of English* 5(4) (1954): 149–153.
27. LCC 1951.
28. Avery, *London Morning*; Valerie Avery, *London Spring* (London: William Kimber, 1982) and *London Shadows* (Leeds [Oxford]: Arnold-Wheaton [Pergamon], 1985).
29. Kathleen Harris [now Boxall], English Exercise Book, 1950–52.
30. Boardman email, 2009.
31. Brian Morton interview with Patrick Kingwell and Peter Medway, July 27, 2009, British Library, C1469/50; Boardman emails, July 8–10, 2010.
32. Morton interview.
33. Arthur Harvey, English Syllabus, undated.
34. Boardman email, 2009.
35. Harold Rosen, "What Shall I Set?" *The Use of English* 10(2) (1958): 91.
36. Sheila Love née Hopwood email to Kingwell, April 8, 2008.
37. Boardman email, July 28, 2010.
38. Valerie Noakes interview with Kingwell and Medway, February 23, 2009, British Library, C1469/51.
39. Boardman email, 2009.
40. Ibid.
41. See chapter two.
42. Kathleen Boxall née Harris interview with Kingwell and Medway, July 16, 2012, British Library, C1469/51.
43. Boardman email, July 28, 2010.
44. Ibid.
45. Boardman email, July 5, 2010.
46. John Sparrow letter to Medway, May 23, 2010.
47. Roy Boardman and Valerie Avery.
48. Ronald Ridout, *English Today, Books 1–5* (London: Ginn, 1947).
49. 273 Old Kent Road, according to a photograph in Southwark Local Studies Library and Kelly's Post Office Directory, 1952.
50. Jones, "Walworth," 35–36.
51. Boxall interview.
52. Jones, "Walworth."
53. John Sparrow interview with Kingwell and Medway, April 22, 2010, British Library, C1469/67.
54. Sparrow interview.
55. Sparrow letter to Medway, May 6, 2010.
56. Levin, "Mathematics."
57. Harvey, "Experience," 129.
58. Sparrow interview. In Harvey's period there were 15–22 passes a year in O level English Language and from 3 to 15 in Literature.

59. Roy Boardman interview, February 24, 2012, British Library, C1469/67.
60. Sparrow letter, May 6, 2010.
61. Harvey is reminiscent, at least in his literary connections if not his teaching, of another Oxford educated teacher, John Garrod, as recorded in Paul Vaughan's memoir, *Something in Linoleum: A Thirties Education* (London: Sinclair-Stevenson, 1994).
62. Noakes interview; Betty Rosen interview with Medway, May 26, 2011, C1469/58.
63. Derrick Catchpole, "School Memories and Impressions from September 1946 to 1948." (document sent to Kingwell, March 13, 2008).
64. LCC 1951.
65. "The Strange Case of Midas Moneybags." Typescript donated by John Sparrow.
66. Borough councils.
67. For example, Boardman email, 2009. The Old Vic was a short bus ride away from the school.
68. Harold Rosen interview with Hardcastle and Medway, November 30, 2004, British Library, C1469/61.
69. See, for instance, Valerie Avery's fictional treatment of both teachers in her trilogy of novels (*London Morning, London Spring, London Shadows*)—though her initial uncritical stance has noticeably changed in the later ones—and our interview with Brian Morton.
70. Harold Rosen, *Troublesome Boy* (London: English & Media Centre, 1993).
71. Harold Rosen interview 2004.
72. Alex McLeod conversation with Medway (recalled without date).
73. For a discussion of the syllabus, see Simon Clements and John Dixon, "Harold and Walworth," *Changing English* 16(1) (2009): 15–23.
74. Harold Rosen interview 2004.
75. Harold Rosen, Walworth School English Syllabus [Provisional, 1958], 1. The position taken by Rosen in his syllabus is strikingly consistent with that of a 1956 LATE pamphlet for India in the writing of which, in view of his prominence in LATE, we suspect he may have worked closely with Britton.
76. Harold Rosen interview 2004.
77. Ibid.
78. Rosen Syllabus, 1.
79. Harold Rosen interview with Hardcastle and Medway, May 4, 2005, British Library, C1469/62.
80. Harold Rosen interview 2004.
81. Philip J. Hartog, *Words in Action. The Teaching of the Mother Tongue for the Training of Citizens in a Democracy* (London: University of London Press, 1947), 16.
82. Rosen Syllabus, 1.
83. Ibid., 1–2.
84. Ibid., 1.
85. Rosen, "What Shall I Set?" 92.
86. Harold Rosen interview 2004.

87. "Now I wouldn't have dreamt of doing *Anthony and Cleopatra* in any grammar school I'd been to. But in that sense they were sophisticated. It is a very mature person's play, and they made a wonderful fist of it." Harold Rosen interview 2004.
88. In the mid-1960s the school still had a class set of Gorki's *My Childhood*, published in Moscow, that had been bought by Rosen. *Schweik* (by Jaroslav Hašek) he must have read aloud or passed round for individual reading.
89. Harold Rosen interview 2004.
90. Rosen Syllabus, 4.
91. Ridout, *English Today*.
92. Harold Rosen interview 2004.
93. Rosen Syllabus, Appendix I, "Composition Scheme."
94. Ibid., 4–5.
95. Ibid., 5–6.
96. Betty Rosen interview. (It was long after the experience she describes that she met Harold again and became his second wife.) She described the incident in *And None of it Was Nonsense: The Power of Storytelling in School* (London: Heinemann, 1988), 10, where "Mr Rees" is Rosen.
97. Panamanian but brought up in Jamaica.
98. John Dixon email to Medway, November 24, 2012.
99. John Dixon, "A Golden Age? v1." (unpublished paper, project archive). The work at Holloway is described in S. C. Brown, John L. Dixon, and H. Wrigley, "The Common English Syllabus in the Comprehensive School," in Simon, *New Trends*, 159–166.
100. Dixon email, November 24, 2012.
101. For example, Simon Clements interview with Hardcastle and Medway, March 20, 2006, British Library, C1469/15; Dixon email, November 24, 2012.
102. Leslie Stratta and Simon Clements came in September 1958, a term ahead of Dixon.
103. John Dixon interview with Hardcastle and Medway, June 4, 2004, British Library, C1469/21.
104. "Two Bob's Worth of Trouble," 1962. Now deposited, for possible digitization, with the British Film Institute.
105. Simon Clements phone conversation with Medway, September 6, 2012. We are aware of doing less than justice to Stratta, though he is recalled as a brilliant teacher. He was too ill to be interviewed and died in 2011.
106. Simon Clements, "Postcript to the Meeting at ULIE Wednesday 25th May 2011." (unpublished document, June 1, 2011).
107. John Dixon interview with Simon Gibbons, July 11, 2007. Quoted with Dr Gibbons' kind permission.
108. John Dixon email to Medway, October 22, 2012.
109. E. L. Black, *Précis and Comprehension Practice* (London: University of London Press, 1953); Geoffrey Frederick Lamb, *Précis and Comprehension for School Certificate* (London: George G. Harrap & Co., 1947).
110. Raymond Morgan O'Malley and Denys Thompson, *English One [etc.], Illustrated by J. S. Goodall* (London: Heinemann, 1955).

111. Cedric Austin, *Read to Write* (four volumes) (London: Ginn, 1954); Nancy Coniston Martin, *Understanding and Enjoyment* Books 1 & 2 (Oxford: Oxford University Press, 1954–1955).
112. Algernon Methuen, *An Anthology of Modern Verse*, with an Introduction by Robert Lynd (London: Methuen, 1921).
113. Frederick Edward Simpson Finn, ed., *The Albemarle Book of Modern Verse*, Volume 1 (London: John Murray, 1962). Brian Catling interview with Kingwell and Medway, January 24, 2012, British Library, C1469/13.
114. Dixon, Gibbons interview.
115. Clements interview.
116. Jennifer Johnson (née Fraser) interview with Kingwell and Medway, September 21, 2009, British Library, C1469/37.
117. Dixon interview.
118. Ibid.
119. Irene Bassey, *Walworth Pilgrim* [magazine], Spring 1963.
120. Robert and Mary Lou Thornbury interview with Hardcastle and Medway, December 10, 2007, British Library, C1469/76. Nancy Martin had argued in a talk that the pressure of excitement in writing led children into sophisticated conceptual compression.
121. "The fourth year teachers included Pip Porchetta, Val Avery, Leslie and me," (Dixon interview).
122. John Dixon, "Letter to James R. Squire, 16 May 1966," Archives of National Council of Teachers of English, http://archives.library.illinois.edu/ncte/about/about_images/dartmouth/correspondence01.jpg/, consulted November 5, 2012.
123. Dixon interview.
124. Dixon, Clements, and Stratta, *Reflections*.
125. David Shayer, *The Teaching of English in Schools 1900–1970* (London: Routledge and Kegan Paul, 1972).
126. Ibid., 154.
127. Thornbury interview.
128. Dixon, Clements, and Leslie Stratta, *Reflections*.
129. The final pages had essay suggestions and exercises relating to each section.
130. Geoffrey Summerfield, "Great Expectations: Modern Trends in English 1," *New Education* 2(3) (1966), 10.
131. Dixon email, November 24, 2012.
132. Michael Louis, "As Man has," *3H Magazine*, July 1965.
133. Michael Gallagher, 4H, *Walworth Magazine*, 1963.
134. Michael Baldwin, *Poems by Children, 1950–61* (London: Routledge and Kegan Paul, 1962).
135. *3H Magazine*, July 1965.
136. *3H Magazine*.
137. Leslie Withers, "Omniology!," *5H Magazine 1967*.
138. Dixon interview.
139. Dixon emails, January 9 and April 28, 2012.
140. Brown, Dixon, and Wrigley, "Common Syllabus," 164.

141. John Dixon email to Medway, July 18, 2010.
142. Dixon interview.
143. Dixon interview.
144. Email to Kingwell, May 3, 2008.
145. For example, Marjorie Hourd, *The Education of the Poetic Spirit. A Study in Children's Expression in the English Lesson* (London: Heinemann, 1949); Margaret Langdon, *Let the Children Write: An Explanation of Intensive Writing* (London: Longmans, 1961).
146. "Our Schools," 1962, sponsored by the National Union of Teachers, http://www.screenonline.org.uk/film/id/1078626/index.html.
147. Janet Midwinter email to Medway, March 4, 2012.
148. Schools Council, *An Approach through English, Humanities for the Young School Leaver* (London: HMSO, 1968), 2.
149. Dixon interview. The reference is to Bretton Hall College where he worked after Walworth.
150. Brian Catling interview with Kingwell and Medway, January 24, 2012, British Library, C1469/13.
151. John Dixon experimented with new modes of written questions that were shortly to be adopted in the new national Certificate of Secondary Education (CSE) (Dixon interview).
152. Barry Miles, *London Calling: A Countercultural History of London Since 1945* (London: Atlantic Books, 2010), 61.
153. Peter Jones and Tony McLean interview with Kingwell and Medway, November 3, 2009, British Library, C1469/38.
154. John Sparrow (a colleague) in a letter to Medway, February 3, 2011.
155. Gillian Stevens née Palmer, third year English "rough book," 1965–1966.
156. Previously Valerie Avery who while still a pupil at the school has written *London Morning* (see note 28 above).
157. Patrick Kingwell interview with Hardcastle and Medway, February 13, 2007, British Library, C1469/43.
158. That would be mainly the women.
159. "A good education," blog post October 11, 2012, http://beetleypete.wordpress.com/2012/10/11/a-good-education.
160. Thornbury interview.
161. Ibid.
162. Maclure, *History*, 162.

5 Minchenden

1. The borough became part of the London Borough of Enfield in 1965.
2. Alan Dumayne, *Southgate: A Glimpse into the Past* (London: Macdermott and Chant Ltd, 1987), 9.
3. *Southgate Official Guide, 1959/60* (London: Pyramid Press, 1960), 75.
4. "Foreword" in *Southgate Official Guide, 1954/5*, 13.
5. *Southgate Official Guide, 1956/7*, 35–40.
6. *The Magazine of the Minchenden School* 8 (1934): 3.

7. James Kirkup, *I, of All People: An Autobiography of Youth* (London: Weidenfeld and Nicolson, 1988), 120.
8. Peter Blakebrough interview with Mary Irwin, March 25, 2010, British Library, C1469/04.
9. Ibid.
10. *Southgate Official Guide, 1956/7*, 30–33.
11. *Youth in Southgate, 1963–64* (London: Southgate Youth Service, 1963), 10–17.
12. *Southgate Official Guide, 1959/60*, 54.
13. *Southgate Official Guide, 1956/7*, 56.
14. Joseph Frayman, "The History of the Cockfosters and North Southgate Synagogue," *Heritage: An Historical Series in the Jewish Inhabitants of North London* 1 (1982), Jewish Research Group of the Edmonton Hundred Historical Society.
15. *Magazine* 7 (1933): 3.
16. Both former residents of the house. Ibid., 7.
17. *Magazine* 11 (1937): 34.
18. K. E. Nolan, "Fifty Years in Retrospect," *Minchenden School Golden Anniversary 1919–69*, 1969: 35–37.
19. *Magazine* 19 (1945): 1.
20. *Southgate Official Guide, 1964/5*, 51.
21. *Magazine* 19 (1945): 3.
22. Ibid., 2.
23. Peter Borrows interview with Mary Irwin, October 8, 2009, British Library, C1469/07.
24. Valerie Whittle interview with Mary Irwin, November 24, 2009, British Library, C1469/73.
25. Marion Kane, *Dish: Memories, Recipes and Delicious Bites* (Toronto: Whitecap Books, 2005), 36.
26. "Conference with Governing Body 28 March 1958" in Ministry of Education, *Report by HM Inspectorate Reports on Minchenden County Secondary School, Southgate, Middlesex, 1958*. National Archives.
27. Richard Morss interview with Mary Irwin, March 26, 2010, British Library, C1469/49.
28. Blakebrough interview.
29. "Conference with Governing Body," 1.
30. Whittle interview.
31. James Watts-Phillips interview with Mary Irwin, December 15, 2009, British Library, C1469/72.
32. HM Inspectorate Reports on Secondary Institutions: Minchenden School 1948.
33. *Magazine* (1966).
34. *Magazine* 15 (1941): 3.
35. *Magazine* 7 (1933): 6.
36. George Whitfield, ed., *Poetry in the Sixth Form* (London: Macdonald, 1950), vii–viii.

37. *Report of the Consultative Committee on Secondary Education: With Special Reference to Grammar Schools and Technical High Schools* [Spens Report] (London: HMSO, 1938), 221.
38. "Shorter notices," *English* 3(14) (1940): 97.
39. LATE, "Report of the LATE Study Group on Textbooks," January 1949. LAE 5/8, Institute of Education Archives.
40. Jerome Hanratty, "Courses," *The Use of English* 12(4) (Summer, 1961): 262–266.
41. *Magazine* 19 (1945): 2.
42. *Magazine* 21 (1947): 4.
43. HMI Report, 1948.
44. Kirkup, *I, of All People*, 190.
45. Mike Riddle interview with Mary Irwin, October 20, 2009, British Library, C1469/55.
46. HMI Report, 1958, 8.
47. Terry Hearing interview with Mary Irwin, October 27, 2009, British Library, C1469/32.
48. C. G., "Shakespeare," *The Use of English* 12(1) (Autumn 1960): 270–274.
49. W. M. McIlry, "Shakespeare," *The Use of English* 14(4) (Summer 1963): 270–274.
50. *Magazine* 33 (1959): 4.
51. Yvonne Bradbury email to Douglas Barnes responding to questions asked by Social Change and English project team, March 16, 2011.
52. Hearing interview.
53. HMI Report, 1958, 8.
54. Nolan, "Fifty Years in Retrospect," 41.
55. *Magazine* 33 (1958): 24.
56. *Magazine* 32 (1958): 25.
57. HMI Report, 1948.
58. Riddle interview.
59. HMI Report, 1948.
60. Whittle interview.
61. We are grateful to Daphne Dean (née Chitty), Roger Dean, and Monica Wafford (née Medows) for loaning us their English exercise books.
62. Francis Isaac Venables and Donald Cameron Whimster, *English for Schools: A Planned Course in Comprehension and Expression* (London: G. Bell and Sons, 1939).
63. HMI Report, 1948.
64. Robert Hardman interview with Mary Irwin, October 21, 2009, British Library, C1469/31.
65. Whittle interview.
66. Madeline Salter, interview with Mary Irwin, October 12, 2009, British Library, C1469/65.
67. HMI Report, 1948.
68. Riddle interview.
69. Letter from Steve Butters to Georgina Brewis, November 23, 2011.

70. Steve Butters interview with Georgina Brewis, November 10, 2011, British Library, C1469/10.
71. Borrows interview.
72. Norman Ellis interview with Georgina Brewis, October 4, 2011, British Library, C1469/26.
73. Peter Boot interview with Mary Irwin, September 22, 2009, British Library, C1469/06.
74. *Magazine* 24 (1950): 29.
75. HMI Report, 1958, 8–9.
76. Ibid., 9.
77. Douglas Barnes, *Becoming an English Teacher* (London: NATE, 2002), 48.
78. Douglas Barnes interview with John Hardcastle and Peter Medway, October 15, 2007, British Library, C1469/01.
79. Barnes interview 2007.
80. Letter from Steve Butters to Georgina Brewis, November 23, 2011.
81. Bradbury email to Barnes.
82. Barnes interview 2007.
83. Ibid.
84. Ibid.
85. Elizabeth Hardman, hand written memoir, 2009.
86. Douglas Barnes, ed., *Twentieth Century Short Stories* (London: Harrap and Co, 1958); Douglas Barnes, ed., *Short Stories of Our Time* (London: LATE, 1963).
87. Dennis Roberts interview with Mary Irwin, October 9, 2009, British Library, C1469/57.
88. Sandra Newton interview with Georgina Brewis, September 20, 2011, British Library, C1469/52.
89. Irving Finkel interview with Mary Irwin, February 25, 2010, British Library, C1469/27.
90. Ellis interview.
91. Barnes interview 2007.
92. Letter from Steve Butters to Georgina Brewis, November 23, 2011.
93. Margaret Roberts interview with Georgina Brewis, September 20, 2011, British Library, C1469/56.
94. Robert Hardman, hand written memoir, 2009, 5.
95. Douglas Barnes interview with John Hardcastle and Peter Medway, March 3, 2011, British Library, C1469/02.
96. *Magazine* 34 (1960): 20; Nolan, "Fifty Years in Retrospect," 46.
97. *Magazine* 34 (1960): 20.
98. Margaret Roberts interview with Georgina Brewis, September 20, 2011, British Library, C1469/56.
99. Margaret Roberts interview.
100. Barnes, *English Teacher*, 36.
101. Dennis Roberts interview.
102. Barnes, *English Teacher*, 36.

103. Whittle interview.
104. Douglas Barnes, "To Help You Write Well," *English in Education* [Previously NATE Bulletin] A2(1) (March 1965): 10–14.
105. Ibid., 10.
106. Barnes, *English Teacher*, 36.
107. Department of Education and Science, *The Examining of English Language: Eight Report of the Secondary School Examinations Council* (London: HMSO, 1964), 22.
108. Morss interview.
109. Blakebrough interview.
110. Barnes, *English Teacher*, 101.
111. Elizabeth Hardman interview with Mary Irwin, October 21, 2009, British Library, C1469/30.
112. Barnes, *English Teacher*, 101.
113. Barbara Brooks interview with Mary Irwin, November 20, 2009, British Library, C1469/08.
114. Robert Hardman interview.
115. Yvonne Bradbury, "A Representative Lesson," *English in Education* 1(1) (March 1967): 62–63.
116. Robert Hardman interview.
117. Barnes, *English Teacher*, 67.
118. Douglas Barnes, "Talking and Writing in the Secondary School English," in *Talking, Making and Writing* (Enfield Association for the Advancement of State Education, 1966), 21.
119. Barnes interview 2011.
120. Robert Hardman memoir, 3.
121. Barnes, "To Help You Write Well," 11.
122. Maggie Butt English exercise book; Maggie Butt interview with Mary Irwin, February 4, 2010, British Library, C1469/09.
123. Blakebrough interview.
124. Barnes, "Talking and Writing."
125. Barnes, *English Teacher*, 37.
126. Robert Hardman interview.
127. Elizabeth Hardman interview.
128. Elizabeth Hardman memoir.
129. Ibid.
130. Barnes, *English Teacher*, 49.
131. Elizabeth Hardman memoir.
132. Barnes interview 2011.
133. Elizabeth Hardman interview.
134. Finkel interview.
135. Barnes interview 2011.
136. Butt interview.
137. Barnes, *English Teacher*, 122.
138. Robert Hardman interview.

139. HMI Report, 1958, 9.
140. Barnes, *English Teacher*, 122.
141. Barnes interview 2007.
142. Butters interview.
143. Barnes interview 2011.
144. Ibid.
145. Ibid.
146. Ibid.
147. Jan Wilson interview with Georgina Brewis, June 12, 2012, British Library, C1469/75.
148. Dennis Roberts interview.
149. Ibid.
150. Elizabeth Hardman interview.
151. Barnes, *English Teacher*, 44; Barnes interview 2011.
152. Scrap of paper written on the back of "House Records Broomfield (Girls) 1971/2," Enfield Local History Library, LR13/19.
153. *Magazine* (1966).
154. Barnes, *English Teacher*, 121.
155. Ibid., 116.
156. Robert Hardman memoir, 6.
157. Dennis Roberts interview.
158. Barnes interview 2007.

6   The Three Schools—What We Have Learned

1. This point was made by Harry A. Davies, *The Boys' Grammar School* (London: Methuen, 1945), 32.
2. Tim Dowley interview with John Hardcastle, June 7, 2011.
3. Harold Rosen, "What Shall I Set?" *The Use of English* 10 (1958): 92.
4. Algernon Methuen, *An Anthology of Modern Verse*, with an Introduction by Robert Lynd (London: Methuen, 1921).
5. The expression often used by James Britton that derived from wartime bombing raids, such as those of the "Dambusters," in which a bombing run, on being aborted, might be classified as practice only and labeled a "dummy run."
6. Denys Thompson, "Editorial," *The Use of English* 1(3) (1953): 116.
7. John Mullan, "As If Life Depended on It," *London Review of Books* 35 (2013): 12.
8. LATE, "Report on the Day Conference on the Work of the English Department," 1966.
9. Margaret Hewitt, "The English Department from the Point of View of the New Teacher," in LATE, "Report on the Day Conference on the Work of the English Department," 1966, 2.

10. LATE, "Report on the Day Conference," 2.
11. Albert Ward Rowe and Peter Emmens, *English through Experience* (five volumes) (London: Blond Educational, 1963). See chapter two.
12. David Shayer, *The Teaching of English in Schools 1900–1970* (London: Routledge & Kegan Paul, 1972).
13. Ibid., 139.
14. James Britton is listed in the index only in one connection; Nancy Martin and Harold Rosen not at all.
15. Not in the index.
16. However, John Kemp associated Holbrook with a certain kind of religious intensity: "in Holbrook it [literature] was almost like a religious thing, almost like the idea of receiving the light, almost like the idea of acquiring a virtue from revelation, and the literature is revelation." John Kemp interview with John Hardcastle, October 14, 1994.
17. Marjorie Lovegrove Hourd, *The Education of the Poetic Spirit. A Study in Children's Expression in the English Lesson* (London: Heinemann, 1949).
18. Shayer, *Teaching of English*, 138.
19. Ibid., 142.
20. Harry Hopkins, "Trying Out the Skyscraper School" (conclusion of a 4-part Series, "Going to School in 1951"), *John Bull* (February 10, 1951), 22–24: 23.
21. Shayer, *Teaching of English*,185.
22. George Allen, "English Past, Present and Future," in *New Movements in the Study and Teaching of English*, ed. Nicholas Bagnall (London: Temple Smith, 1973), 30.
23. Margaret Mathieson, *The Preachers of Culture: a Study of English and Its Teachers* (London: Allen & Unwin, 1975), 122–141.
24. Kemp interview.
25. Peter Medway, "Into the Sixties: English and English Society at a Time of Change," in *Bringing English to Order: the History and Politics of a School Subject*, eds. Ivor Goodson and Peter Medway (London: Falmer, 1990).
26. Positional and personal authority are sociological terms ultimately from Max Weber via Talcott Parsons.
27. Pete Johnson and Mick Groombridge interview with Hardcastle and Medway, August 17, 2011, British Library, C1469/38.
28. Percival Gurrey, *The Teaching of Written English* (London: Longmans, Green, 1954), 2.

7 Conclusion

1. Douglas Barnes, James Nimmo Britton, and Harold Rosen, *Language, the Learner and the School* (Harmondsworth: Penguin, 1969).
2. Harold Rosen, *Language and Class: A Critical Look at the Theories of Basil Bernstein* (Bristol: Falling Wall Press, 1972).

3. Connie Rosen and Harold Rosen, *The Language of Primary School Children* (Harmondsworth: Penguin, 1973).
4. John Dixon, *Growth through English: A Report Based on the Dartmouth Seminar 1966* (Reading: National Association for the Teaching of English, 1967).
5. Simon Clements, John Dixon, and Leslie Stratta, *Things Being Various. Teachers' Book* (London: Oxford University Press, 1967).
6. Douglas Barnes, *From Communication to Curriculum* (Harmondsworth: Penguin, 1976).
7. "Global Goals for English: NCTE and the Dartmouth Seminar," NCTE Archives, http://archives.library.illinois.edu/ncte/about/july.php#_jmp0_, accessed October 20, 2013.
8. Joseph Harris, "After Dartmouth: Growth and Conflict in English," *College English* 53 (1991), 631.
9. Harris, "After Dartmouth: Growth and Conflict in English," 637–638. The quotation is from Dixon, *Growth through English*.
10. Peter Medway, "Into the Sixties: English and English Society at a Time of Change," in *Bringing English to Order: The History and Politics of a School Subject*, eds. Ivor Goodson and Peter Medway (London: Falmer, 1990), 26.
11. Carol Burgess et al., *Understanding Children Writing* (Harmondsworth: Penguin, 1973). Nancy Coniston Martin et al., *Understanding Children Talking* (Harmondsworth: Penguin, 1976).
12. Caroline St John-Brooks, "The Transmission of Values in English Teaching." (Unpublished PhD Thesis, University of Bristol, 1981); James R. Squire and Roger K. Applebee, *Teaching English in the United Kingdom* (Champaign: National Council of Teachers of English, 1969).
13. See David Smart, "John Fisher at Mexborough Grammar School: a memoir," http://joseflocke.co.uk/heritage/MGS02.htm, accessed October 21, 2013. Also see Fisher in the index to Ted Hughes, *Letters of Ted Hughes /Selected and Edited By Christopher Reid* (London: Faber, 2007).
14. Michael Benton and Peter Benton, *Touchstones: A Teaching Anthology in 5 Vols.* (London: English Universities Press, 1968).
15. Marjorie Lovegrove Hourd, *The Education of the Poetic Spirit. A Study in Children's Expression in the English Lesson* (London: Heinemann, 1949).
16. Britton, "Response to Kitzhaber"; David Allen, *English Teaching Since 1965: How Much Growth?* (London: Heinemann, 1980), 54.
17. On the initiative that arose from Halliday's work, see Richard Hudson and John Walmsley, "The English Patient : English Grammar and Teaching in the Twentieth Century," undated, http://www.phon.ucl.ac.uk/home/dick/texts/engpat.pdf, accessed October 25, 2013.
18. The author who most forcefully articulated that view was an LATE member, Peter Doughty, director of the Nuffield Programme in Linguistics and English Teaching at University College, London. See papers by him published in 1968 by Longmans for University College, London.

19. James N. Britton et al., *The Development of Writing Abilities (11–18)* (London: Macmillan, 1975).
20. Pete Johnson and Mick Groombridge interview with Hardcastle and Medway, August 17, 2011, British Library, C 1459/38.
21. Sobel and Dowley interviews.
22. Johnson and Groombridge interview.

Index

11 plus test, 19, 20, 22, 24, 25, 32, 81, 82, 84, 87, 95, 98, 117, 144, 145, 166. *See also* psychometric testing
  dissatisfaction with, argument for comprehensives, 20
1945–65, 2, 17, 188
  children's experience, 11
  stagnation and change, 17, 18
1950s, mood
  difficulties, economic, military, national pride, 18
  optimism in some quarters, reasons for, 19

A level examination (GCE Advanced level), taken at, 18, 36, 64, 108, 117, 120, 121, 123, 137, 203. *See also* examinations
Aarsleff, Hans, 196
Absolute Beginner, 1959, novel about new teenagers, 108. *See also* MacInnes, Colin
academic disciplines influencing English
  anthropology, 30
  linguistics, 28, 30, 31, 33, 34, 54, 176
  list, 28
  literary studies, 28, 30, 32, 51, 159
  philosophy, 28, 30, 32, 33, 36, 87, 157
  psychology, 33
  sociology, 28, 32
  sociology of class, 32
  sociology of education, 32
accents, 65
"ad hoc excitements," 43, 154
Adlam, Roger 1924– (HDS teacher 1956–1989), 55

Alderman, Geoffrey 1944– (HDS pupil 1955–62), 58, 59, 66, 194, 200, 201, 202, 204
Allen, David, 200, 218
Allen, George, 37, 42, 199, 217. *See also* HMI
Allport, Alan 1970–, 192
Amis, Kingsley, *Lucky Jim* (1954), 18, 147
Anglo-Saxon, 63
anti-intellectualism in English teachers, 155, 158
Applebee, Roger K., 218
architecture and planning, 18, 71, 72, 73, 95, 175
archives, 10, 209
Arnold, Matthew 1822–1888, 32, 158
art, 95, 116, 129, 131, 173, 196
  children's, 156
  contemporary—Jackson Pollack show, visits to, 48, 184
associations of former pupils, 81
Austin, Cedric 1912–, 37, 98, 197, 210
Australia, English teaching in, British influence, 35, 111, 170, 194, 195
Avery, Valerie (later Noakes), Walworth pupil 1953–?, teacher 196?–4, and novelist, 84, 96, 206, 207, 208, 210, 211

backward children, old term for children with special educational needs, 68
Bailey, Kenneth Vye, 197
Baldwin, Michael 1930–2014, 42, 44, 103, 199, 200, 210
Balk, Thomas Oscar 1889–1970 (HDS headteacher, 1935–1952), 56

Index

Ball, Stephen J., 5, 26, 45, 192, 195, 200, 220
Barker, Bernard, 3, 191
Barkway Pye, Vernon 1900–1989 (HDS headteacher, 1952–1960), 58, 59, 202
Barnes, Dorothy, 26, 38, 195, 198, 199, 200
Barnes, Douglas R., 26, 38, 40, 41, 44, 118, 120, 124, 125, 127–42, 151, 156, 157, 159, 161, 166, 167, 169, 170, 171, 172, 178, 183, 187, 195, 197, 198, 199, 200, 213, 214, 215, 216, 217, 218
   background, 169
   edited LATE story collections, 129
   learning across the curriculum, 158
   Leavis, student of, moved away from, 151
Barnes, Douglas R. et al, *Versions of English*, 26, 38, 198, 199, 200
BBC (British Broadcasting Corporation), 17, 32, 37, 42, 44, 94, 169, 199. See also BBC schools broadcasts
BBC schools broadcasts, 17, 32, 37, 42, 44, 94, 169, 199
   Listening and Writing, 44
   Senior English, Poets and Poetry, 37
BBC Third Programme, 32
belles lettres, belles-lettrism, 38, 44, 172, 188
Benn, Caroline, 193, 194
Benton, Michael 1939–, 200, 218
Benton, Peter 1934–, 218
Berkoff, Steven 1937– (HDS pupil, 1950–55), playwright, 59, 202
Bernstein, Basil 1924–2000, sociologist of education, known among teachers for his theory of linguistic codes, 169
Beveridge Report (1942), 18
Billington, Michael 1939–, biographer of Harold Pinter, 65, 203
Birkbeck College, University of London, 119, 128
Blakebrough, Peter 1951– (Minchenden pupil 1962–1969), 114, 136, 212, 215

Boardman, Roy (Walworth pupil 1948–52), 206, 207, 208
Boas, Guy, 194
Boot, Peter 1942– (Minchenden pupil 1953–1960), 125, 214
Borrows, Peter 1942– (Minchenden pupil 1953–1960), 125, 212, 214
Boxall née Harris, Kathleen 1937– (Walworth pupil 1948–54), 207
Bradbury, Yvonne (Minchenden teacher c1954–196?), 127, 213, 214, 215
Brearley, Joseph 1909–1977 (HDS teacher, 1939–1972), 55, 58, 59, 63–7, 68, 70, 71, 77, 151, 152, 153, 158, 164, 177, 188, 202, 203, 204
   favours literary criticism over scholarship, 151
   Fortune's Fool (2008), 63
   influenced by Richards, 63
   taught by Leavis, 63, 151
   teacher education and training— none, 153
Britton, James Nimmo 1908–94, 6, 9, 25, 27, 28, 31, 33, 34, 35, 37, 39, 41, 42, 44, 45, 53, 71, 72, 89, 105, 107, 129, 132, 148, 150, 151, 152, 153, 155, 156, 157, 169, 170, 171, 172, 173, 174, 176, 178, 192, 193, 194, 195, 196, 197, 198, 199, 200, 201, 203, 204, 208, 216, 217, 218, 219, 220
   career and importance, 34
   ideas
      on children's speech, 34
      democratic, not elitist, starts from common resources, 34
      ordering experience, 157
      effects on teachers' practice, 155
      shared with his tutor, Gurrey, and taken further, 33, 34
   works
      Britton et al, *The Development of Writing Abilities, 11–18*, 34
      English on the Anvil (1934), 71, 72, 148, 195, 204
Bronte, Emily 1818–48, 70, 85, 125
Brooks, Barbara 1946– (Minchenden teacher 1969–1974), 133, 215

Brown, George Mackay 1921–96, 1, 191, 220
Burgess, Anthony M. K., 192. *See also* Burgess, Tony
Burgess, Carol, 218
Burgess, Tony, 192, 197, 220
Butt, Maggie 1955– (Minchenden pupil 1966–1972), 215
Butters, Steve 1942– (Minchenden pupil 1954–1961), 139, 213, 214, 216

Cambridge University, 2, 27, 28, 30, 31, 32, 34, 35, 45, 55, 63, 116, 127, 128, 150, 151, 153, 171, 185
Canada, English teaching, 111, 170. *See also* Dartmouth
Cary, Joyce 1888–1957, 85, 86
Catchpole, Derrick (Walworth pupil 1946–8), 208
Catling, Brian (Walworth pupil 1959–67), 108, 210, 211
central schools, 80, 81, 181, 193
Chambers, Raymond Wilson 1874–1942 (HDS pupil) philologist, Quain Professor of English at University College, London, 196
Chancellor, Valerie E., 191, 220
Charles, R. H., 198
Chetwynd, Harriet, 199
cities, urban experience, 161
  acknowledged in English, 39, 101 (*see* English, aims, priorities, values, assumptions: world referenced)
Clarke, Stephen, 26, 38, 195, 198, 199, 200
classics (Greek and Latin), 27
classrooms, design of, 51
clause analysis (grammatical exercise), 53, 60, 75, 84, 86, 122, 132, 133
Clegg, Alexander (Alec) Bradshaw, Sir, 1909–86, Chief Education Office, West Riding of Yorkshire (1909–74), author of *The Excitement of Writing*, 41, 44, 156, 174, 198, 200
Clements, Simon (Walworth teacher, 1958–64), 96, 99, 106, 110, 151, 153, 169, 174, 177, 184, 206, 208, 209, 210, 218

background, 169
CND, Campaign for Nuclear Disarmament, 114, 120, 140
Cockney, 54, 144
cognitive, 43, 59, 157, 174
Cold War, 18
Cole, Margaret 1893–1980, 194
Coleridge, Samuel Taylor 1772–1834, 28, 33, 157
Collini, Stefan 1947–, 196
communication, 90, 150
Communist Party, communism, 67, 89
composition, 73, 150, 196, 204. *See* writing
comprehension, type of exercise, 37, 38, 43, 51, 60, 72, 86, 98, 102, 122, 134, 136, 140, 146, 148
comprehensive schools, 4, 6, 9, 10, 18, 20, 23, 24, 25, 40, 42, 70, 80, 82, 84, 89, 161, 173, 179, 181, 186
  1960s increase, 21
  appeal of for graduates, 23
  conversions from grammar schools, 40, 48, 77, 95, 145, 160
  graduates teaching full range of children, 24
  interim or experimental comprehensives, 21, 79, 81, 110, 145, 159
  experimental in curriculum as well as structure (Walworth), 110
  Labour policy on, 20
  mission set out in London School Plan, 25
  motives and rationales, 20, 95
  slow to be established, numbers, 20
  teachers moving from grammar schools—experience and effects, 46, 181
Conservative Party, in government 1951–1964, 17, 114
counterculture, 1960s, 163
Cox, Brian 1928–2008, 193
creative writing, 84, 106, 156, 157
creative, creativity, 3, 41, 46, 59, 136, 144, 150, 157, 173, 174
Crosland, Anthony 1918–77, Labour Secretary of State for Education, 1964, 21, 193
Crosland, Susan, 193

cross-curricular collaboration across subjects, 131
Crossley, Miss, Minchenden head of English 1941 to 1959, 115, 119, 120, 123, 127, 152
Crowley, Tony, 196
cultural studies, 28, 32, 33, 70, 110, 175
cultural visits—theater, art, opera, ballet, 131. *See also* individual entries
culture
　challenge from working-class and popular culture, 32 (*see also* Orwell, Hoggart, Williams)
　contemporary, 164 (*see also* architecture, art, film, opera, theater)
　degradation of, 29 (*see also* industrial society)
　high, elite, literary, 31, 34, 83, 121
　　declining dominance of, 31
　　necessity of maintaining—Leavis and Eliot, 31
　　theorists of, 32
　popular, 17
　working-class—Orwell, Hoggart, Williams, 32
Culture and Environment (1933) by Frank Raymond Leavis and Denys Thompson, 29, 70, 71, 195, 204
Cunningham, Peter 1948–, 191, 193, 220
curriculum history
　and English, 1, 2, 3, 4, 176
　works drawn on, 3
curriculum, school
　common, 87, 88, 95
　no government control, 20
　range of subjects, 115

Dartmouth, Anglo-American Seminar on the Teaching of English, 1966, 34, 129, 170, 172, 174, 176, 189, 218
　contribution by teachers in this study, 170
　Leavisites, 171
Davies, Harry A., 216
Davis, V., 199
Day, Stanley 1901–1957 (HDS teacher 1936–45), 55

democratic, democracy, 13, 14, 25, 31, 34, 67, 73, 82, 83, 109, 113, 155, 178, 182, 186
DES (Department of Education and Science), 197
development
　centrality of language and symbolic thinking, 30, 33
　focus of education and English rather than instruction, 166
　personal and moral aims for education and English, 146
discussion, 123, 124
Dixon, John, 34, 37, 41, 44, 83, 95–105, 106, 107, 111, 151, 153, 156, 157, 159, 163, 166, 167, 169, 170, 171, 173, 177, 178, 181, 183, 184, 197, 198, 200, 206, 208, 209, 210, 211, 218
　background, 169
　biography, 95
　Growth through English, 35, 111, 152, 197, 200, 218
Doughty, Peter 1934–2013, director of the Nuffield Programme in Linguistics and English Teaching, critic of much practice in English, 218
Dowley, Tim 1946– (HDS pupil, 1957–1964), 71, 73, 76, 184, 204, 205, 216
Doyle, Brian 1943–, 26, 194
drama, 46, 52, 57, 59, 68, 74, 76, 88, 96, 99, 107, 121, 122, 129, 131, 133, 134, 139, 144, 164
　alternative to experience as source of content, 107
　improvised, 68, 74, 88, 98, 99, 107, 139
　play reading groups, 121
　plays read, studied, performed or seen, 57, 65, 121, 123, 131 (*see also* Shakespeare)
　　Brecht, Bertolt 1898–1956, *The Life of Galileo*, (1955), 66
　　Eliot, T. S. 1888–1965, *Murder in the Cathedral* (1935), 66, 121
　　Ibsen, H. 1828–1906, *An Enemy of the People* (1882), 65

Index

Miller, Arthur 1915–2005, *Death of a Salesman* (1949), 66
Shaw, George Bernard 1856–1950, 31, 46, 65, 88, 121, 123
Sheridan, Richard Brinsley 1751–1816, *School for Scandal* (1777), 66
Sophocles *Oedipus Rex*, 66
Webster, John 1580–1634, *The The White Devil*,(1612), 65
Wilder, Thornton 1897–1975, *Our Town*, (1938), 66
Dunning, Jean (Minchenden teacher), 128, 135, 137, 205
Dunning, Roy 1927– (HDS teacher, 1952–), 77, 205
Dylan, Bob 1941–, 185

economy, austerity to affluence, 2, 17, 19
educability, 89, 109, 157, 185. *See also* O'Reilly
 relevant qualities observed in pupils, 185
education, 31
 attitudes to, rising demand, 21, 47
 as cultural enlargement, 183
 democratic, 186 (see also *main entry* democratic)
 as enlargement of minds, 186
 transformative power for working class, socialist and communist belief in, 68, 89
Education Acts, 19
 1918, 19
 1944, 9, 19, 20, 21, 22, 55, 116
 attitudes to reforms, 20
Education and the Working Class (1962) by Brian Jackson and Dennis Marsden, 32, 194, 197
education system and policy, 21, 181. *See also* school types
 1940s, social before academic priorities, 25
 1960s, child-centered learning, comprehensive schools, 18
 spending increase, 18
 terminology, pre- and post-1944, 19, 68
elementary schools, 20, 23, 24, 80, 151
Eliot, Thomas Stearnes 1888–1965, 20, 31, 66, 98, 121, 125

Ellis, Norman 1943 (Minchenden pupil 1955–1962), 214
Emergency Training, Trent Park Emergency Training College, 56
Emmens, Peter, secondary modern teacher, 41, 43, 106, 150, 154, 155, 156, 157, 199, 217. *See also* Rowe and Emmens
 in TV film, 41, 43, 106, 150, 154, 155, 156, 157, 199, 217
employment, 18, 65, 79, 113, 117, 165
Empson, William 1906–84, 30, 33, 196
endowed schools, created under Endowed Schools Act, 1869, 47
English (school subject), 3. *See* English
English (university subject), 2, 27. *See also* Birkbeck, Cambridge, King's College, London, London, Oxford, UCL
English Association, 27. *See also* English, teachers' associations
 ineffectual, 27
English departments, 15, 16, 28, 32, 40, 55, 57, 83, 85, 87, 88, 89, 95, 96, 101, 107, 109, 118, 119, 120, 126, 127, 128, 129, 130, 132, 135, 145, 148, 153, 159, 178, 187
 emergence, 40
 heads of department
 internal or external appointment, 187
 roles, 40, 57, 58, 87, 89, 119, 143, 145, 146, 152, 153
 interactions—tolerant, collaborative, conflictual, 95, 96, 101, 120, 126, 127, 135, 137, 141, 145, 152, 153, 188
 meetings, 57, 86, 87, 96, 120, 128, 137, 152
English method texts
 Poster, Cyril, "Projects for the English Specialist" (1953), 74, 205
English teachers
 ability to articulate justifications characteristic of innovators, 189
 generations and traditions coexisting, 4
English teaching, the study of, 1, 2, 4, 24, 90, 183

English, aims, priorities, values, assumptions
  democratic, not elitist, based on universal capacities, 34, 35, 50, 78, 145, 164, 166, 200
    not only elite could write, 35
    see also Rosen, Holbrook
  divide over center of subject, literature or language and experience, 171, 172
  elevate above environment, 70, 83, 87
  "English itself," rhetoric, capability in language—not found as central focus, 175
    but happened nevertheless?, 179
  growth—personal, sometimes intellectual, 157, 178
    see also Dixon, John, *Growth through English*
  honesty and sincerity, 61, 91, 135, 156
  intellectual development, 3, 70, 91, 97, 109, 155, 158, 170
  intellectual values, disdain for anti-intellectual, 43, 46, 143, 144, 146
  language development the center, 146
    focus use over instruction, 158, 166
    through focus on experience, 89, 91, 130, 134, 151
    supported by LATE and Institute, 150
    in two versions, 175
  literature the center, 43, 44, 45, 144
  moral concerns, 43, 102, 104, 172
  public rationality, 45, 91, 157
  pupils' productions in speech and writing
    content valued over manner, 150
    honesty, sincerity of expression, authentic voice, 35, 75, 156, 173
    own language accepted, 149
  realism, attention to ordinary life and pupils' experience, 35, 44, 45, 101, 135, 141, 148, 149, 150
  worlds referenced: actual/ideal, familiar/remote, rural/urban
    city, 44
English, books
  old books in use although newer and better available, 42
    postwar shortage, few new or modern, 36, 57, 98, 146
English, character of, 52, 55
  in 1950s, Medway survey, 38
  between the wars, 27, 181
  in different school types, 181 (*see* English, in elementary schools *etc.*)
  overall 1945–65, 188–9
  recent and current, 14
English, continuity, change, innovation, 13, 32, 42, 159, 163, 181
  change and its causes
    accelerated from 1960, 42
    concern for fairness, effectiveness, ideas and principles, 146, 160, 161, 181
    motivating considerations, 166, 187, 188
    response to difficulty of pupils, 45, 163
  inherited practice, 42, 53, 158, 159, 162
  innovation, 7, 13, 96, 110, 158, 189
  nature of, 158, 159
English, critiques, dissatisfaction
  artificial and meaningless, 42, 61
  egalitarian and expressivist sell-out, 158
  HMI dissatisfaction, 38
  writing types too literary, 176 (*see also* Doughty, Peter)
English, curriculum and pedagogy
  "ad hoc excitements," 43, 154
  contact with writers and poets, 87, 88
  curriculum elements and their organization, 38, 43, 51, 73, 133
    see reading, literature, drama, poetry, fiction
  Britton's theme-based model, Island project, 72, 135
  coherence/incoherence of curricular experience, 51, 53, 71, 74, 98, 133, 134, 148
  lessons separate and unconnected, 38, 39, 121, 134
  organized by instructional topic or exercise type, 122
  organized by themes, 44, 67, 71, 72, 74, 98, 100, 148 (*see* English, themes, content, topics)

INDEX 227

the street, 148
topics/activities extended over more
  than one lesson, 98, 148
village project, 71, 72
exercises and tasks, 50, 52, 53, 56, 61,
  75, 77, 122, 123, 126, 136, 141,
  200, 204, 213, 215
  examples, 50, 53, 60
  see also writing
group work, 124, 137, 138
happenings, 154
instruction and exercises, place of relative
  to language *use*, 34, 39, 50, 102,
  104, 106, 107, 108, 133, 150, 156,
  158, 160, 166, 173, 176, 179, 189
Copernican shift, 170
out-of-school activities, 86
planning lessons and programs, 53, 73,
  75, 120, 152, 155
procedural principles—pupil choice, 135
progression, nature of, 53, 72, 91, 100,
  101, 145, 174–5
  personal to social, concrete to general
    and abstract, 91, 100, 145, 172,
    174, 176
pupils' culture affects lessons, 52, 144
relationships, teacher-pupil, 65, 67, 87,
  107, 109, 142, 144, 187
rolling curriculum, collaborative
  development at Minchenden, 134,
  135, 152
Rosen syllabus at Walworth, 89, 91, 92,
  93, 100, 104, 157, 160, 166, 208
syllabuses, 5, 42, 50, 57, 59, 64, 72, 84,
  85, 88, 89, 91, 92, 93, 95, 96, 100,
  122, 129, 134, 144, 153, 160
English, historiography, 3, 4, 5, 7, 16, 26.
  See also Ball, Doyle, Mathieson,
  Peel et al, Shayer
English, history of the subject
  established recently, 2
  insecure, 2, 27, 61
  seen as means of national renewal, 27
English, in comprehensive schools, 108,
  109, 181, 183
  outside the study—sources, 183
English, in elementary schools, functional
  literacy, 27, 38, 60, 172

English, in grammar schools, 27, 36, 38,
  39, 45, 103, 109, 118, 144, 145,
  150, 159, 187
  critiques, 39
  exciting, 145
  outside the study schools, 45
  schools outside the study,
    experiences, 161
  university influence, 36, 45, 53, 145,
    151, 153, 159, 187
English, in secondary modern schools, 27,
  30, 38, 109, 151, 172, 181
English, official control and guidance,
  35, 37
  Language, Some Suggestions (DES, 1954),
    35, 38
English, other countries
  influenced by UK, 170
  US, Canada, 34 (*see also* Dartmouth)
English, other subjects, relation to,
  130, 175
English, resources, teacher-produced
  materials, 41
English, social change, relationship to, 182
English, teachers' associations
  no national assoc. until 1964, 27
  School Libraries Association, 56
  see also English Association, LATE,
    NATE, 10, 118, 131, 162
English, themes, content, topics, 39, 41,
  44, 45, 64, 123, 126, 131, 135, 138,
  140, 141, 145, 174, 175, 182, 189
  social and political issues, 67, 100, 101,
    102, 109, 139, 141, 164
  taken from history and geography
    curriculum, 107
  worlds referenced by English, 39, 125
  rural bias, 149
English, theory and ideas
  role of language in organizing
    experience, 35, 173, 174
  sources, 28, 32
    Cambridge, 32
    ideas from educational thought or
      literary studies, 33
    see also academic disciplines
      influencing English, Institute of
      Education

English, versions, approaches, models, 26
    "Cambridge" or Leavisite, 35 (*see also* Leavisite)
        rejected academicism, 180
    creative and expressive approaches, 3, 173, 176
        in writing and drama, 46, 144
    effects on pupils, 182, 183
    engagement with lives, experience, interests, concerns, 92, 146, 148, 158, 189
    for less academic pupils, 145, 171
        lessons could be boring *or* lively, 144
    more recent—genre etc, 180
    pragmatic, eclectic, 8, 174, 181, 189
    "social studies approach," characterization of *Reflections*-style English, 102, 134, 154, 174, 175
    strands of practice, coexisting/ competing
        1960s, two main strands, perceptions of, 34, 35, 171
            Leavisite and Institute of Education (University of London)/LATE/ NATE, seen as opposed, 35, 172
            reality more blurred than the perception, 45
        traditional teaching, inherited traditions, 150
            elementary and secondary, 38
            successful integration of two traditions, 181
estates, 48, 117. *See also* housing: council housing
examinations (public), 27, 36, 40, 42, 53, 57, 93, 102, 141, 144, 146
    Certificate of Secondary Education (CSE), 40, 42, 169, 189, 211
    offered by university examination boards at 16 and 18
        General Certificate of Education (GCE), 36, 49, 58, 203
        GCE Advanced (A) Level, dissatisfaction with, 36 (*see also* A Level)
        GCE Ordinary (O) Level, 36 (*see also* O Level)
        GCE Ordinary (O) Level alternative versions, 40, 133
        GCE Ordinary (O) Level Language, 53, 58, 104, 146, 207
        GCE Ordinary (O) Level Language and Literature examined separately, 36, 49
        GCE Ordinary (O) Level Literature, 85
        GCE Ordinary (O) Level set texts, 85
        GCE Ordinary (O) Level: dissatisfaction shared by HMI, 20, 28, 36, 38, 42
    School Certificate and Higher School Certificate, 36, 49, 55, 120, 123, 146, 203, 209
    School Certificate and Higher School Certificate, dissatisfaction, 28
    vocational
        offered by City and Guilds, 102, 104
        offered by Royal Society of Arts, 102, 104
examinations (school internal), innovations in, 107, 132
experience, pupils', as content for speech and writing, 8, 11, 28, 34, 35, 39, 44, 84, 85, 86, 89, 91, 92, 93, 99–102, 107, 110, 118, 134, 137, 145, 148, 150, 152, 155, 157, 158, 161, 167, 171, 173, 174, 176, 178, 180, 182, 189
    eliciting in discussion, 97, 99
    HMI seek honest expression of, 38
    urban, 161 (*see also* English, aims, priorities, values, assumptions: worlds referenced)

fiction authors and works, 57, 73, 75, 77, 85, 92, 122, 137
Achebe, Chinua 1930–2013, *Things Fall Apart*, 138
Aesop, *The Lion Going to War*, 60
Amis, Kingsley William 1922–95, *Lucky Jim* (1954), 18, 147
Austen, Jane 1775–1815, 76, 85, 123
    Emma (1815), 76
authors and titles, 105
Beowulf, 99, 107

INDEX

Blackmore, Richard Dodderidge 1825–1900, *Lorna Doone* (1869), 41, 57, 61
Clearly, Beverly *Fifteen* (1956), 138
Conrad, Joseph 1857–1924, 75, 76, 85, 205
  The Brute (1906), 75
  The Secret Agent (1907), 76
  The Secret Sharer (1910), 73, 205
Day-Lewis, Cecil 1904–1972, *The Otterbury Incident* (1948), 37, 77, 105, 147
Dickens, Charles 1812–70, 76, 85, 92, 123
  Great Expectations 1860–61, 66
Eliot, George 1819–80 *Silas Marner* (1861), 39, 41
Forster, Edward Morgan, 1879–1972, 67, 85, 204
  A Passage to India (1924), 67
  The Machine Stops, (1928), 73, 205
Golding, William 1911–93, *The Lord of the Flies* (1954), 37, 76, 137
Gorki, Maxim 1868–1936, 92
Greene, Graham 1904–1991, 39
  The Quiet American, 92, 147, 177
Hašek, Jaroslav 1883–1923, *The Good Soldier Schweik* (1923), 92, 209
Heinemann's New Windmill, 36, 174
Hemingway, Ernest 1899–1961, 37, 39
Hugo, Victor 1802–85, *The Hunchback of Notre Dame* (1831), 107
Huxley, Aldous *Brave New World* (1932), 76
Joyce, James 1882–1941 *Portrait of the Artist as a Young Man* (1916), 76
Lawrence, David Herbert 1885–1930 "Odor of Chrysanthemums" (1909), 73
Lessing, Doris 1919–2013, 137
London, Jack 1876–1916 *Call of the Wild, The* (1903), 37
Mankowitz, Wolf 1924–98, *A Kid for Two Farthings*, 41
Orwell, George 1903–50, *Animal Farm* (1945), 32, 37, 125, 196
Priestley, John Boynton 1994–1984 *Good Companions* (1929), 57

recent, adult, American, European and other
  Simenon (Maigret), Micky Spillane and Hank Jansen, 85
Salinger, Jerome David 1919–2010, *The Catcher in the Rye* (1951), 147
Serraillier, Ian 1919–1994, *The Silver Sword* (1956), 41, 77, 137, 147, 199
Sewell, Anna 1820–1878, *Black Beauty* (1877), 57, 122
Sillitoe, Alan 1928–2010, *The Loneliness of the Long Distance Runner* (1959), 137, 147
Steinbeck, John 1902–1968, 37, 85
Stevenson, Robert Louis 1850–94, *Treasure Island*, (1883), 57
Tolkien, John Ronald Reuel 1892–1973, *The Hobbit* (1937), 107, 137, 138
Van Der Loeff, Ann Rutgers 1910–90, *Children on the Oregon Trail*, 1963, 107
Wain, John 1925–1984, *Hurry On Down* (1953), 147
Wells, Herbert George 1866–1946, 31, 37, 85, 115, 125, 131
Wells, Herbert George 1866–1946, *War of the Worlds, The (*1898), 37
Woolf, Adeline Virginia 1882–1941, *To the Lighthouse* (1927), 76
fiction, categories
juvenile and adolescent, 42, 85, 105, 147
recent, adult, American, European and other, 76, 85, 92, 105, 125, 136, 147
film, contemporary British
working class, 95, 149
Finkel, Irving 1951– (Minchenden pupil 1962–1970), 129, 138, 214, 215
Firth, John Rupert 1890–1960, new linguistics, 30, 31, 34
Foyles bookshop, Charing Cross Road, 70, 85
Franklin, Barry, 3, 191, 220
Friends Reunited website, 11, 81

Gandhi, Mahatma, (1869–1948), assassination, 1948, 67
Gardiner, David, 192, 200, 220

Gardner, Phil, 191, 220
Gasking, Terry 1939– (HDS pupil 1951–7), 53, 59, 66, 201, 202, 204
Georgian, movement in poetry from around reign of George V, influence on Medcalf, 70
Gibbons, Simon James, 26, 27, 194, 195, 209, 210
Gomme, Andor, 195
Goodson, Ivor, 3, 191, 192, 195, 200, 217, 218, 220
Gosden, Peter Henry John Heather, 192
Government committees and reports
   Bullock Report, *A Language for Life*, 1975, 34
   Newbolt Report, 1921, *The Teaching of English in England*, 2, 27, 34, 166, 191, 195, 220
   Newsom Report, *Half Our Future*, 1963, 41, 198
   Norwood Report, 1941 (with chapter on English), 27
   Plowden Report, *Children and their Primary Schools*, 1967, 41, 198
   Spens Report, 1938, 19, 81, 118, 166, 193, 213
   tripartism, 19, 20
governments 1945–65, 17
grammar schools, 4, 7, 10, 19–26, 27, 29, 33, 34, 35, 38, 40, 42, 53, 55, 68, 80, 81, 82, 89, 98, 116, 118, 144, 145, 151, 160–1, 162, 165, 172, 181, 186, 201
   abolition of fees and its effects, 19, 22
      Eliot deplores, 31
      no access by wealth alone, 31
   character of, academic and social, 21, 23, 50, 161
   closure of, opposition to, 25, 82
   curriculum, 21
   defenders of, 20
   government resistance to closure, 26
   opposition to, 21
   progressive alternative to public schools, 25
   teacher attitudes to pupils and pedagogy, 23
   teacher unease about selection, 77

grammar teaching, 27, 33, 39, 43, 50, 51, 53, 75, 84, 86, 93, 118, 121, 122, 127, 132, 133, 136, 146, 148, 201
   based on Latin, 31, 39, 54
   formal grammar, 51, 148
   HMI find provision 'over-generous,' 50, 51
   HMI seek reduction, 38
   linguistics, 133
   reduced to spelling and punctuation, 104, 148
   Standard English, 54
Great Tradition, The, 29. See also Leavis
Grinberg, Henry (HDS pupil), 64, 65, 164, 203
Grocers' Company School, later Hackney Downs School, 47. See also endowed schools
Groombridge, Michael (Walworth 1962–7), 184, 185, 186, 217, 219
Grosvenor, Ian, 191, 220
Growth through English, 35, 111, 152, 170, 173, 178, 197, 200, 218. See also Dixon, John
Gurrey, Percival 1890–1980, 27, 28, 33, 34, 35, 72, 118, 151, 152, 153, 155, 157, 166, 173, 197, 204, 217
   career, 33
   ideas on English
      experience, giving expression to, 33
      influence of other disciplines, 33
      intellectual development the aim, rather than linguistic accomplishment and literature, 33
      response to literature a creative activity, 33
   works
      The Appreciation of Poetry (1935), 33, 197
      The Teaching of Written English (1953), 72, 153, 155, 197, 204, 217

Hackney Downs Grammar School, 10, 11, 15, 22, 26, 47–78, 101, 119, 121, 143, 147, 148, 152, 153, 154, 156, 158, 159, 160, 161, 164, 166, 172, 175, 177, 183, 184, 187, 188, 200, 201, 202

curriculum, 144
  English, 143, 159, 160, 172
    Mankowitz not used, 150
  fire, 1963, 41, 48, 77
  no women teachers, 15
  taken over by LCC 1907, free scholarships taken up by working-class pupils, 22
Hall, Stuart 1932–2014, London teacher, leader of the New Left and cultural studies, 10, 110, 175
Halliday, Michael 1925–, 31, 176, 218
Halsey, Albert Henry 1923–, 194
happenings, 154
Hardcastle, John Lawson 1948–, 1, 6, 9, 10, 14, 45, 220
Hardman, Elizabeth 1942– (Minchenden teacher 1964–1968), 129, 133, 137, 140, 214, 215, 216
Hardman, Robert 1937– (Minchenden teacher 1962–1967), 121, 123, 127, 131, 134, 137, 141, 213, 214, 215, 216
Hardy, Barbara 1930–2012 lecturer at Birkbeck College, 122, 123, 128, 177
Harris, Joseph, 170, 171, 218
Harrow Weald Grammar School, Middlesex, where Britton and Nancy Martin were senior English teachers and Harold Rosen taught before his military service, 72
Hartog, Philip Joseph 1864–1947, 208
Harvey, Arthur 1905–1981 (Walworth senior English master, 1949–55), 63, 83–8, 89, 91, 93, 94, 96, 98, 106, 145, 151, 152, 153, 155, 159, 178, 179, 183, 187, 206, 207, 208
Harvey, Brenda (Walworth teacher 1963–89), 94, 96, 101, 108
Hearing, Terry 1930– (Minchenden pupil 1941–1948), 120, 213
Heinemann New Windmill series, modern novels in school editions, 36, 137
Helsby, Gill, 191
higher grade schools, 79
Hinton, James, 193

HMI (His/Her Majesty's Inspectors of Schools), 37, 38, 42, 49, 50, 51, 54, 56, 57, 86, 116, 119, 120, 121, 122, 123, 124, 125, 138, 158, 200, 201, 202, 213, 214, 216
  Allen, George, 37, 42
  English Panel, progressive views of, 37
  guidance from, 35
  influence of, on schools, 37
  influence of, through official bodies, 37
  inspections, 49
  Wilson, Percy, 38 (*see* entry)
Hoggart, Richard 1918–2014, 10, 32, 110, 175, 196
Holbrook, David 1923–2011, Leavisite school English teacher, author of *English for Maturity*, 35, 42, 157, 171, 197, 199, 217
  anthologies for schools, 35, 156, 157
  critique by Kemp, 159
Hollins, T. H. B., 43, 44, 154, 199, 200
Holloway Boys Grammar School (Comprehensive School from 1955), 95, 98, 99, 104, 157, 181, 205, 209
homework, 23, 52, 75, 84, 116, 122, 125, 136, 138, 140, 147, 188
honesty as value in pupils' productions, 75, 135, 136, 141, 164
Hopkins, Harry, 23, 125, 193, 194, 196, 206, 217
Hourd, Marjorie Lovegrove, *The Education of the Poetic Spirit*, 1949, 156, 157, 173, 174, 211, 217, 218
housing, 48, 60, 79, 113, 117
  council housing, estates, 117
Hughes, Ted 1930–98, 42, 106, 172
Hungary crisis, 1956, 95

ILEA (Inner London Education Authority), 24
imagination, imaginative, 28, 43, 65, 107, 108, 133, 157, 185
  alternative to realism as governing value in fiction, writing, 107
immigration
  from central and eastern Europe, 48, 114
  Cypriot, Turkish and Greek, 79

industrial society, critique—degradation of culture, 29, 70
  duty of English to counteract (Leavisites), 35
inspection, inspectors, national and local, 13, 37, 50, 51, 56, 84, 116, 125, 126, 138, 189. *See also* HMI, LCC
Institute of Education (University of London), English department, 6, 9, 10, 27, 28, 32, 33, 34, 38, 45, 72, 81, 89, 95, 97, 110, 116, 119, 127, 129, 151, 156, 166, 172, 175, 187, 209
  ideas on teaching of English, 32–4
  main source of fresh thinking, 28
integrated humanities, combining English with social studies/history and geography, 175
intellectuals, changing character of, 31
intensity, poetic or expressive, 156. *See* Hourd
"Into the Sixties," Medway, 5, 41
island project, 71, 148
Israel, 67

Jackson, Brian 1932–2009, 22, 194, 197
Jackson, Brian & Dennis Marsden, *Education and the Working* Class 1962, 194, 197
  findings, 22
Jackson, Philip Wesley, 192, 220
Jewish, 11, 48, 52, 54, 57, 65, 89, 114, 141, 142, 144, 150, 164, 212
Johnson (née Fraser), Jennifer (Walworth pupil 1961–6), 210
Johnson, Peter (Walworth pupil 1962–1968), 109, 165, 183, 186, 217, 219
Jones, Patricia, researcher, 81, 193, 206, 207
Jones, Pete (Walworth pupil 1955–?57), 107, 207

Kemp, John 1929–2009 (HDS teacher, 1954–1989), 55, 57, 58, 67–78, 119, 147, 148, 151, 152, 153, 155, 156, 158, 160, 164, 172, 183, 184, 185, 188, 202, 204, 205, 217
  critique of Holbrook, 159

teacher education and training PGCE at King's, 153
Kenny, Alex, 192, 200, 220
Kidbrooke School, 1954, purpose-built comprehensive, 26
King's College, University of London, 6, 55, 58, 60, 63, 68, 70, 74, 151, 153
Kingwell, Patrick, co-researcher (Walworth pupil 1961–69), 6, 12, 108, 149, 202, 205
Kirkup, James 1918–2009, poet and Minchenden teacher, 114, 119, 212, 213
Knight, Peter, 191
Knockshinnock pit disaster, 1950, 68
Korean War, 18, 39
Kynaston, David 1951–, 15

Labour Party and Labour governments, 9, 13, 20, 95, 182, 204
  1945 government, 2, 17, 18, 65
  policy on school types, rejection of tripartism, 25, 81, 166
  1964 government, 2, 17, 21
Lacey, Colin 1936–, 22, 194
language
  of children, 31
  freshness of valued, 86, 173
    admired by Harvey in Joyce Cary, 86
  of ordinary people, vernacular, 54, 171
  of working-class children, 89, 91, 99
  of young children, 171
language and learning across the curriculum (also 1970s movement), 3, 34, 158
Language in Use project, 176
LATE (London Association for the Teaching of English), 26, 27, 28, 34, 38, 40, 41, 42, 43, 45, 81, 89, 90, 95, 97, 99, 110, 118, 119, 120, 127, 129, 131, 132, 133, 134, 137, 139, 140, 143, 147, 150, 152, 153, 156, 159, 163, 166, 167, 169, 172, 181, 187, 198, 208, 213, 214, 216, 217, 218
  activities, 28
  conferences, 40
  founded 1947, 10, 27, 81, 193

interest in primary education, 41
short story collections, 147
significance for teachers, 89, 153
Law, Bernard HDS Teacher, 55
Lawn, Martin, 191, 220
Lawrence, David Herbert 1885–1930, novelist and poet, 35, 43, 45, 107, 140
Layton, David (1925–2010), 191, 192, 220
LCC (London County Council, as LEA), 10, 24, 25, 26, 47, 73, 77, 79, 80, 82, 84, 88, 95, 179, 186, 206
  educational aims, social over academic stressed, 82
  replaced by ILEA 1965, 24
  Savage, Graham (Sir Edward Graham) 1886–1981, LCC Education Officer 1940–51, 25
  takes over grammar schools after 1903, 22
LEAs (local education authorities)
  little involvement in curriculum, 24
  take over existing grammar schools and establish new ones, 22
leaving school, age of, 85, 98, 123, 175
Leavis, Frank Raymond 1895–1978, 29, 31, 33, 35, 43, 55, 63, 70, 71, 127, 150, 151, 158, 159, 160, 165, 171, 172, 180, 185, 195, 196, 202
  ideas, 29
  influence of
    on Barnes (moved away), 151
    on Kemp, 151
    made study of literature serious, 172
    pervasive on teachers, 151, 172
  and Leavisites, 30, 32, 34, 150, 158, 171, 172, 174, 180
    views on literature and culture, nostalgia for pre-industrial society, 35
  Leavisites, followers of FRL, 30, 32, 43, 45, 171
  see also literary studies
  taught Brearley, Barnes, Reid, 151
  works
    New Bearings in English Poetry (1932), 70, 195, 202
    The Common Pursuit (1952), 70
    The Great Tradition (1948), 70, 195
Leavis, Frank Raymond and Denys Thompson *Culture and Environment* (1933)
  for teachers, 29, 70, 165
Leavisite teachers, replaced literature with writing in comprehensives, 171
Levinson, Ralph 1950– (HDS pupil, 1961–1969), 76, 205
libraries, school, 52, 56, 57, 73, 123, 147, 181
Lightfoot, Martin, 45, 169, 196, 200
Limond, David, 3, 191
linguistic diversity, 54
literary criticism, 29, 33, 34, 45, 70, 75, 144, 151
  inflated claims for, 29, 43
  replacing literary appreciation and scholarship, 64, 144, 151, 152, 159
  Brearley, 151
  Thompson finds impracticable for less academic pupils, 151
literary studies, 29, 43. *See also* Leavis, Richards, Williams, Eliot
literature, 2, 27, 28, 29, 30, 31, 33, 34, 38, 39, 42, 43, 44, 45, 49, 56, 57, 60, 68, 70, 73, 75, 76, 78, 84, 85, 87, 90, 98, 100, 107, 118, 121, 122, 123, 124, 125, 126, 130, 133, 134, 136, 137, 138, 140, 143, 144, 145, 151, 152, 158, 159, 160, 161, 165, 166, 171, 172, 173, 174, 175, 180, 181, 184, 188, 217
  experienced as unrelated to ordinary reading, 39, 42
  mode of teaching, 43, 75, 76, 85, 105, 121, 124
  more accessible selections, 165
  preparing texts, 73, 75, 120
  pupils' response to, 30, 44, 75, 105, 188
  pupils' work, examples, 75, 123
  range of, 124, 146, 160, 182
  study of, Leavis made more serious, 172
  substitute for religion, 158
  to understand it is to create it oneself, 33
Lodge, David John 1935– *Out of the Shelter* (1970), 18

London, 113
  areas and districts
    Bow, 48
    East End, traditionally comprising Whitechapel, Hoxton, Shoreditch, Mile End, Stepney and Bow, 41, 48, 54, 66, 73, 79, 89, 108, 149, 203
    Hackney, 47, 48, 50, 59, 60, 63, 64, 68, 74, 114, 160, 164, 194, 200, 204
    Hoxton, 48
    Mile End, 48
    outer London, 10, 24, 113
    Shoreditch, 48, 114
    Southgate, 113, 114, 115, 116, 117, 135, 141, 212
    Stepney, 48
    Walworth, 79
    Whitechapel, 48, 184
  attracted young teachers, 109
  education, 24
  effects of war, 17, 24, 60
  local culture, 114
  meaning of in the study, 24
  Metropolitan Boroughs, London local government until 1965
    Bermondsey, 79
    Camberwell, 79
    Southwark, 79, 206
  population movement, 48, 113, 114, 164
London School Plan, 1947, 25
  comprehensive schools mission, academic not the priority, 25
London School, the, in Ball's model, 45, 119, 194, 206
Louis, Michael (properly Loizou), 1950– (Walworth pupil 1962–?9), 210
Love née Hopwood, Sheila (Walworth pupil), 207
Luria, Alexander 1902–77, Soviet psychologist, 134

MacInnes, Colin 1914–1976, 193. See also *Absolute Beginner*
Maclure, Stuart 1926–, 206, 211
MacNeice, Louis 1907–63, poet, friend of Arthur Harvey, visited Harvey's club at Walworth, 83, 87

Malinowski, Bronislaw 1884–1942, 30
Mankowitz, Wolf 1924–1998, *A Kid For Two Farthings* (1953), 108, 149, 199
mark books, teachers' records, 5, 7, 13, 71, 81, 155
marking and correcting, 56, 61
Marsden, Dennis 1924–1998, 22
Martin, F. M., 194, 197
Martin, Nancy Coniston 1927–2003, 6, 9, 27, 28, 37, 45, 89, 98, 129, 132, 150, 153, 169, 191, 192, 193, 196, 197, 200, 210, 217, 218, 220
mass media, teaching with newspapers, advertising, film, 38, 71, 159, 165
  extension of literary criticism, 29
  HMI deplore excessive use of, 38
Mass-Observation, 19, 193
Mathieson, Margaret, 26, 157, 158, 192, 194, 217, 220
McCulloch, Gary, 3, 11, 191, 192, 220
McGuinn, Nicholas, 195
McLean, Tony (Walworth pupil 1953–58), 107, 207
McLeod, Alexander O. (Walworth teacher 1952–58, head of English 1963–6), 6, 83, 88, 94, 95, 96, 98, 99, 106, 107, 110, 182, 188, 197, 208
Medcalf, James Ellis 1891–1962 (HDS teacher, 1920–1956), 50, 55, 56–63, 64, 66, 70, 152, 184, 201, 202
Medway, Peter George 1941–, 1, 6, 9, 11, 14, 45, 81, 106, 192, 193, 198, 199, 200, 202, 205, 217, 218, 220
  "Into the Sixties," 26, 38, 44, 149, 163, 171
metropolitan boroughs, 24. *See* London: Metropolitan Boroughs
Mexborough Grammar School, Yorkshire attended by Ted Hughes, 172, 218
Middle English, 63
Middlesex County Council (as LEA), 10, 24, 72, 73, 89, 113, 116, 212
  comprehensives proposal rejected by government, 24
Midwinter, Janet 1951– (Walworth pupil 1962–), 211
Miles, Barry, 193, 211

Mina Road, 79. *See also* Walworth School
Minchenden Grammar School, 6, 10, 11, 16, 24, 42, 68, 70, 73, 113–42, 143, 146, 147, 148, 149, 150, 151, 152, 153, 154, 156, 159, 160, 169, 173, 181, 184, 187, 189, 211
   Minchenden English, 127–32, 156, 159, 161
   female head of English, 16
   LATE connection, 146
Ministry of Education, 193, 212
Moffett, James, American participant at Dartmouth, 176
Monte, Harvey 1934– (HDS pupil, 1945–52), 54, 57, 59, 66, 67, 202, 203, 204
Moody, Spencer 1898– (HDS teacher, 1930–1947), 56, 201, 202
Morss, Richard 1951– (Minchenden pupil 1962–1970), 212, 215
Morton, Brian 1939– (Walworth pupil), 207, 208
Mossbourne Academy, 48
Mulhern, Francis, 31, 193, 196

narrative, 75, 91, 93, 118, 145, 154, 174, 176, 182
Nasser, Gamal Abdel 1918–70, President of Egypt 1956–70, 67
NATE (National Association for the Teaching of English, founded 1964), 28, 34, 37, 40, 41, 42, 43, 45, 132, 169, 170, 178, 189, 195, 214, 215
National Archives, 13, 205, 212
National Service (postwar two-year military conscription), 63, 95, 119, 128
nature, as theme in literature and writing, 61, 126, 136, 173, 174, 181. *See also* rural bias
Nelson School, secondary modern amalgamated with Walworth 1962, 94, 96, 104, 108
Neruda, Pablo 1904–73, Chilean poet, 186
New Education Fellowship, 82
New English, the, 3, 155, 173, 206
New Jerusalem, 13

New Left, 10, 114, 120, 164
New Zealand, 88, 96, 107, 110, 111, 120, 170, 188
Newbolt Committee, 2, 27, 34, 166, 191, 195, 220. *See also* Government committees and reports
Newton, Derek, 203
Newton, Sandra 1951– (Minchenden pupil 1962–1969), 129, 214
Noakes, Valerie, née Avery, 84, 88, 96, 108, 207, 208. *See* Avery
non-fiction authors, works, material, 46, 85, 125, 134, 137
   Durrell, Gerald *My Family and Other Animals*, 137
   extracts in *Reflections*, 102
   Heyerdahl, Thor 1914–2002, *Kon-Tiki Expedition*, 105, 137
Nunn, Sir Thomas Percy 1870–1944, Principal of London Day Training College (later Institute of Education), 33, 197

O level (GCE Ordinary level), 35, 36, 38, 40, 49, 53, 58, 59, 85, 88, 104, 106, 125, 133, 137, 140, 141, 146, 149, 150, 188, 198, 205, 207. *See* examinations (public)
observation, value placed on, 65, 86, 101, 106, 173
Ogden, Charles Kay 1889–1957, 28, 30, 195
Ogden, Charles Kay and Ivor Armstrong Richards *The Meaning of Meaning*, 1923, 28, 30
Ogilvie, David 1930–2012 (attended HDS 1942–1949, taught at HDS 1957–1965), 55, 60, 61, 63, 64, 68, 74, 77, 172, 184, 200, 201, 202, 203, 205
opera, 129, 131, 184
   Brecht, Bertolt 1898–1956 and Kurt Weill 1900–50, *Rise and Fall of the City of Mahagonny* (1930), 184
O'Reilly, Anne Winifrede 1891–1963, head of Walworth, 1947–55, 81, 82, 83, 88, 109, 157, 179
   democratic aims met by English, 179
   on educability, 157

Orwell, George 1903–1950, 32, 37, 125, 196
Oxford University, 2, 27, 31, 39, 42, 60, 63, 83, 95, 108, 128, 151, 159
  tradition of literary appreciation and philology, 2, 27

Palmer, Richard, 197
Parker, Charles 1919–1980, BBC radio producer, creator of the *Radio Ballads*, 139
pastry left over, Britton's image of the subject matter of English, 175
Peel, Robin, 26, 194
Penguin Books, publisher, imprints included Pelican and Penguin Education, 32, 42, 169, 172
PGCE (Postgraduate Certificate of Education), 24, 28, 38, 68, 74, 89, 106, 127, 153
  value and effects, 153
Piaget, Jean 1896–1980, developmental psychologist, 30, 199
Pidgeon, Douglas A., 193
Pinter, Harold 1930–2008 (HDS pupil, 1944–1948), playwright, 55, 64, 65, 66, 145, 203
  and Joe Brearley, 65
planning lessons and programs, 42, 53, 72, 73, 95, 102, 120, 148, 152, 153
poetry reading, 29, 39, 52, 61, 122, 123, 125
  learning by heart, 52
  pupils' experience of, 59
poetry texts, 125, 140
  anthologies
    Baldwin, Michael 1930–2014, *Billy the Kid. An anthology of tough verse* (1963), 42, 199
    Britton, James Nimmo, *Oxford Books of Verse for Juniors* (1957), 39, 42
    Daffodil Poetry, Books, I and II (1920), 52, 61
    English Association, *Poems of Today* (three series, 1915–38), 61, 202
    Finn, Frederick Edward Simpson *Albemarle Book of Modern Verse* (1962), 99

Holbrook, David 1923–2011, *Iron, Honey, Gold* (1961), 42, 199
Hughes, Ted, *Here Today* (1963), 42, 199
Methuen, Algernon, *Anthology of Modern Verse* (1921, and many other editions), 123
Summerfield, Geoffrey, *Voices* (1968), 42, 199
Wilkinson, W. A. C. and N. H. *The Dragon Book of Verse* (1935), 202
Chaucer, Geoffrey, *The Franklin's Tale, The Pardoner's Tale* and *The Nun's Priest's Tale*, 76, 123
Goldsmith, Oliver 1728–74, 76
Longfellow, Henry Wadsworth 1807–82, *The Slave's Dream* (1842), 59
Milton, John 1606–74, 76
Pope, Alexander 1688–1744, 76
Tennyson, Alfred 1809–92, 64, 122
Wordsworth, William and Coleridge, Samuel Taylor, *Lyrical Ballads* (1798), 64, 70
poetry writing, 29, 102, 103, 110, 126, 144
  competitions, 121
Pollack, (Paul) Jackson 1912–1956, 184
Porchetta, Prosimia Isabella (Pip) (Walworth teacher, 1953–76), 88, 94, 96, 107, 188, 210
practical criticism, 29, 30, 38, 64, 158. *See also* Richards I. A.
précis, 33, 38, 51, 60, 72, 86, 122, 126, 133, 134, 146
Price, Michael H., 191, 220
primary schools, primary education, 41, 117, 162, 173, 174
  influence on English, 68, 99, 163
  LATE interest in, 41
  primary experience neglected in secondary, 162
Pringle, Ian, 196
professions, expansion of, enhanced role for planners, 18
progressive, 27, 41, 43, 61, 74, 82, 83, 93, 118, 138, 156, 188
projects, 74, 131, 135

Index

psychometric testing, 19, 20. *See also* 11 plus
  questioned, 20, 22
pupils
  with cultural and linguistic background different from middle-class norm, 144
    London working-class accents (and Cockney) deplored by HMI but tolerated by staff, 54
    pupils' own language and culture, 45, 53
  culture of, affects character of lessons, 52, 144
  dispositions and aspirations in relation to school and English, 52, 74, 129, 141, 142
  from immigrant backgrounds, 145, 164
  interests and concerns, engagement of, 45, 145
  language and culture, 53, 78, 144, 161
    overlooked, 53, 78, 144
  with languages other than English, 54, 149
    German, 54, 115
    Polish, 54
    Russian, 54, 131, 134
    Yiddish, 54, 203
  novels by, 81, 84
  social background and class, 117
  the term, 8

Quirk, Charles Randolf, 1920–, linguistics scholar, 31

Raine's Foundation School, 59
reading
  in class, 52, 85
    books, 41, 105, 147
    short sets, 137, 147
  a creative activity, 157 (*see also* Richards)
  includes non-literary texts, 174
  private, 39, 52, 65, 105, 147, 179
    experienced as unrelated to school literature, 39, 42
    reading lists, 57, 77, 105, 137, 147
reconstruction, post-war, 2, 18, 19, 61, 73

Reflections by Clements, Dixon and Stratta, 81, 96, 98, 101–5, 107, 108, 111, 140, 148, 153, 154, 157, 160, 174, 175, 178, 206, 210
  academic/intellectual values, 102
  influence of, 102, 108
Reid, Graham (Walworth teacher 1964–5), 151, 185, 218
  taught by Leavis, 151
Reid, Ian, 26, 194
relations, teacher-pupil
  enabling spaces, common topics, 73, 185
  music, 108, 185
  music, Bob Dylan, 185
research project, "Social Change and English—A Study of Three English Departments 1945–1965," 81
  achievements, 176
  adequacy of data, 155
  case studies, 3, 5, 7
  design
    archive of data, 91
    interviewees, selection of, 12, 177
    interviews, 5, 7, 11, 12, 15, 81, 94, 162, 192, 219
    London, meaning of, 10
    mixed methodology, 3, 11
    period, selection of, 10
    schools, selection of, 7, 11, 141, 143
    Walworth, reasons for selecting, 81
  documentary sources, 1, 7, 9, 12, 13, 14, 81, 155, 178
  evidence of social change, 182
  hypotheses & questions, 13
  interpreting data, 8, 13, 94, 98, 154, 178
    teachers' statements, 155
  limitations, 177, 186
  need for, previous lack, 5
  origins & intentions, 1, 6, 44, 176, 177
  process and experience, 14
    adventitious findings, 14
    interviews, 12, 15
    participants' eagerness, 15
    participants' inquiries, 15
    project events, 15
    range of sources, 5, 15
    use of websites—Friends Reunited and project, 11, 81

research project—*Continued*
  sources of evidence
    documentary—pupils' work, 50, 51, 53, 71, 81, 84, 95, 123, 125
    documentary—school administrative documents, 81
    documentary—teachers records, 50, 71, 81
    informants' memories, 1, 12, 15, 93, 116, 129, 130, 139, 149
    use of school, pupil and teacher data, 3
  team's previous experience, 9, 14
  unanswered questions, future research, 177, 178, 179
    growth or just language development?, 179
    Leavisite teaching?, 180
    long-term effects of English approaches, 180
  what is new, 3
Richards, Ivor Armstrong 1893–1979, 28, 29, 33, 34, 64, 88, 157, 159, 195
  reading a creative activity, 157
  on reading, practical criticism, 28
  Science and Poetry, (1926), 64
Riddle, Mike c.1927–2011 (Minchenden teacher 1955–1963), 119, 120, 122, 124, 127, 131, 213
Roberts, Dennis c.1936–2011 (Minchenden teacher 1962–1972), 120, 128, 129, 130, 131, 132, 134, 137, 140, 141, 214, 216
Roberts, Margaret 1940– (Minchenden teacher 1962–1968), 131, 132, 138, 214
Rodgers W. R. 1909–69, poet, visited Harvey's club at Walworth, 83, 87
Rogers, Guy 1919–2012 (Walworth deputy head 1952, head 1955–1956), 82, 88, 96, 105, 147
Rosen, Betty, second wife of Harold, 208, 209
Rosen, Connie, 41, 132, 163, 169, 171, 218
Rosen, Harold 1919–2008, 1, 5, 6, 9, 13, 40, 41, 58, 83, 84, 85, 88–94, 95, 96, 98, 99, 105, 106, 109, 110, 129, 132, 145, 147, 149, 150, 151, 153, 156, 159, 160, 163, 165, 166, 167, 169, 170, 171, 172, 177, 178, 180, 181, 183, 192, 197, 207, 208, 209, 216, 217, 218, 220
  approaches, views, positions—English for all, not just elite, 145
  background, 169
  Walworth syllabus, 89, 148
Rousmaniere, Kate, 191
Rowe, A. W. and Peter Emmens, *English Through Experience* (1963), 41, 154
  influence of, 154
  Summerfield's critique, 41
Rubinstein, David, 194
rural bias, 149. *See also* English, themes, content, topics: worlds referenced

Salkey, Andrew 1928–1995, Caribbean writer and poet, Walworth teacher (c1957–59), 94
Salter, Madeline 1932– (Minchenden pupil 1943–1950), 121, 123, 213
Sampson, George 1873–1950, member of the Newbolt committee, author of *English for the English* (1922), 34
Savage, Graham 1886–1981, LCC Education Officer 1940–51
  comprehensives schools idea from North America, 25
Sawyer, Wayne, 195
scholarship boys and girls, 95
scholarships to grammar school, LCC, 22, 49, 89, 95
  Junior Scholarships awarded to working-class Jewish boys, 47
school aims and ideologies, 83, 109
School Board for London, education authority before the LCC took over in 1903, 24
school buildings and spaces, 24, 25, 47, 48, 51, 73, 77, 115, 116, 117, 161
  classrooms, 51
  Hackney Downs, 65
school mock elections, 67
school types, 21, 181
  pre-war, 181
school-leaving age, statutory raised to 15, 1947, 19

Schools Council for Curriculum and
    Examinations, 34, 37, 40, 41, 44,
    107, 111, 162, 169, 178, 189,
    198, 211
  English Committee, role of HMI, 37,
    111 (*see also* Allen, G. and
    Wilson, P.)
  Working Paper 3, authors Allen and
    ?Britton, 37
schools of English teaching, Ball's model,
    45, 158, 161, 173
Scrutiny, journal founded by Leavis, 29,
    30, 31, 33, 70, 151, 159, 171, 172,
    193, 196
Second World War, 9, 11, 17, 18, 20, 24,
    49, 50, 52, 55, 63, 67, 80, 116, 119,
    121, 182
  evacuation, 24, 63, 65, 66, 115
  in memory, 18
secondary modern schools, 4, 10, 19, 20,
    24, 30, 35, 38, 40, 42, 43, 78, 83,
    94, 95, 98, 104, 106, 108, 109, 116,
    128, 145, 151
  problem of English for, 30, 35 (*see also*
    Holbrook)
secondary, 20. *See* education system:
    terminology
Shakespeare, William 1564–1616, 36, 57,
    65, 74, 76, 85, 86, 88, 92, 96, 118,
    120, 121, 122, 123, 125, 138, 140,
    205, 213
  Antony and Cleopatra, 66, 76, 92
  pupils' aversion to, 39
  Julius Caesar, 65, 92, 105
  King Lear, 76, 85
  Macbeth, 57, 61, 65, 74, 129
  Merchant of Venice, 57, 122
  Midsummer Night's Dream, 57, 65,
    122, 203
  Richard II, 76
  Twelfth Night, 96, 120
Sharples, Derek, 199
Shayer, David, 26, 41, 42, 101, 155, 156,
    157, 158, 173, 192, 194, 199, 201,
    210, 217, 220
Shearman, Harold Charles 1896–1984,
    Chairman of LCC 1961–62,
    82, 206

Shils, Edward 1910–1995, 193
Silver, Harold 1928–, 3, 5, 41, 191, 192,
    193, 220
Simon, Brian 1915–2002, 193, 194, 206
sixth form, 46, 49, 64, 67, 87, 102, 117,
    128, 142, 144, 151
  teaching prized by grammar school
    teachers, 46
Smart, David, 218
Sobel, Raoul 1932– (HDS pupil 1945–52),
    56, 64, 66, 184, 201, 203, 219
social attitudes, 95, 133, 164
  decline in deference, 17, 19, 67, 164
  democratic optimism vs retrenchment,
    13, 18, 95
  time-honored, challenges to, 17, 52, 165
  youth—new social assurance, 19
social change, 2, 11, 13, 18, 19, 23, 163,
    164, 165
  and change in English
    consumer economy, 163
  change in public discourse, 164
  English as contributing, 182
  generations of pupils and teachers, 11,
    18, 165
  see also teachers: generations
  new groups successful in media,
    including working class, 164
  reduced racial and class prejudice, 164
  relations between adults and children,
    styles of authority, 165
  social relations more egalitarian, 19
social class, 12, 19, 22, 32, 65, 77, 113,
    117, 128, 161, 184, 186. *See also*
    working class
social English. *See* mass media
  teaching with newspapers, advertising,
    film, 38, 173
social history, use of, 4
social studies, curriculum subject
    combining history and geography,
    82, 88, 102, 134, 139, 154,
    174, 175
  when taught by English teachers, 107
societies, clubs, groups, 85, 121, 131
  reading groups, 142
Sparrow, John (Walworth teacher
    1952–56), 84, 88, 94, 207, 208, 211

speech, spoken language, speaking and
    talking, 16, 27, 38, 40, 43, 44, 45,
    52, 54, 57, 64, 67, 74, 76, 82, 84,
    90, 91, 97, 98, 99, 100, 101, 107,
    120, 123, 124, 133, 134, 138, 140,
    141, 144, 147, 149, 152, 157, 160,
    164, 176, 179, 182, 188
  children's speech, opinions about
      Britton contrasted with Newbolt
      Report and Sampson, 34
  debates, 67, 73, 121, 124, 164
  increasingly important, 165
  speech, pupils'
    correction of, 160
      Jewish, teachers' prejudice, 54, 164
    tape recorders, use of, 138
spelling, 43, 75, 93, 104, 133, 148
St John-Brooks, Caroline 1947–?2003, 218
Standard English, 53, 91, 160
Stevens née Palmer, Gillian (Walworth
    pupil 1963–), 211
Stevens, David, 195
Stevens, Frances, two positions on English,
    35, 197
Stevenson, Robert Louis 1850–94, 71
Stratta, Leslie 1926–2010 (Walworth
    teacher 1958–64), 96, 106, 169,
    198, 206, 209, 210, 218
  background, 169
streams, streaming, grouping by ability, 58,
    59, 60, 66, 68, 71, 82, 84, 88, 94,
    100, 104, 108, 115, 144
  allocation of teachers, 59, 160
  effect on pupils in lower streams, 23, 58,
    59, 88, 95, 121, 144, 181
suburbs, suburban life, 7, 11, 44, 48, 68,
    113, 114, 126, 140, 141, 161
Suez crisis 1956, 18, 67, 95
Summerfield, Geoffrey, 41, 42, 43, 44,
    102, 107, 154, 196, 199, 200, 210
Supple, Barry 1930– (HDS pupil, 1942–
    1949), 54, 56, 64, 67, 200, 201,
    202, 203, 204
syllabuses, 5, 42, 50, 57, 59, 64, 72, 84,
    85, 88, 89, 91, 92, 93, 95, 96, 100,
    122, 129, 134, 144, 153, 160. *See
    also under* English, curriculum and
    pedagogy

symbols, symbolizing, identified as core of
    human thinking and development,
    33, 34, 35, 36

tape recorders, use of, 42, 64, 138, 139
Tawney, Richard Henry 1880–1962, 200
teachers
  ability to articulate justifications
      route to national influence, 189
  appeal of comprehensives for graduates,
      24 (*see also* comprehensive schools)
  communist, 89
  education and training, 24, 28, 38, 68,
      74, 89, 106, 127, 153, 154
    Brearley, 153
    Clements, 153
    emergency training, 56
    Kemp, 153
    see PGCE
  engagement with culture and
      politics, 164
  female
    few in the study, 15, 119
    leaving teaching on marriage, 16
  generations, 6, 9, 49, 109, 116, 129, 164,
      165, 183
    young teachers, 109, 116, 129,
      165, 166
  graduates, 23, 119, 151, 188
  grammar school, 31
  influences on, 53, 71, 187
  innovatory, Walworth and Minchenden,
      subsequent contributions, 169
  involvement in organizations outside
      English, 120, 132, 182
  literary and linguistic enthusiasms,
      63, 86
  military service, 20, 55, 63, 89, 116
  motivated by social ideas, 181
  political engagement—Labour Teachers,
      New Left, 95, 164
  postwar attitudes—recovering the old or
      building the new, 20
  shortages of, 55
  social class of, 68
    middle-class stereotype, 184
  specialists and non-specialists, 38, 55,
      119, 186

who touched pupils' lives, 162, 183–6
teaching profession, 3, 23
  divided, university graduates vs. college-trained, gender, appeal of comprehensives, 23
technical schools, 19, 20, 116
teenagers, emergence of, money, life styles, 19, 101, 165. *See also* youth
textbooks and course books, 3, 26, 29, 36, 39, 41, 50, 51, 53, 54, 57, 59, 60, 64, 71, 81, 92, 98, 102, 115, 118, 122, 123, 134, 140, 146, 147, 148, 149, 158, 170
  Austin, Cedric, *Read to Write* (1954), 37, 98
  Clay, Norman L., *School Certificate English Practice* (1933), 55
  Dent, J. C. *Thought in English Prose* (1930), 50, 55, 59
  dissatisfaction with, 146
  Marriot, J. W., *A Year's Work in English* (1921), 50, 59
  O'Malley, Raymond Morgan and Denys Thompson, *English One etc.,* (1955), 98
  Pocock, G. *Grammar in a New Setting* (1929), 50, 51, 53, 55, 72, 200, 201
  Pocock, G., *More English Exercises* (1934), 53, 55, 201
  pre-war, 55
  Reflections by Clements, Dixon and Stratta, 81, 96, 98, 101, 102, 103, 104, 105, 107, 108, 111, 140, 148, 153, 154, 157, 160, 174, 175, 178, 206, 210
  reliance on, 41, 50, 51, 53, 60, 64, 115, 122, 123, 146
  Ridout, Ronald 1916–1994, *English Today*, 37, 86, 92, 98, 132, 146, 197, 207, 209
  Walsh, J. H. *Complete English* (1949), 51
The Use of English, journal, 30, 32, 45, 70, 71, 73, 74, 148, 160, 172
theater, 18, 95, 129, 130, 131, 203
theater visits, 66, 88, 118, 121, 184
themes, 41, 92, 102
  Britton, island theme, 72
  Hackney Downs, village theme, 148

Walworth, street theme, 148
Thomas, Dylan 1914–53, poet, 83, 185
Thompson, Denys 1907–88, 20, 29, 30, 32, 35, 70, 71, 98, 151, 195, 196, 204, 209, 216
Reading and Discrimination, 29, 196
Thornbury, Robert (Walworth teacher 1962–66), 100, 102, 110, 210, 211
Touchstones, 173, 218
Tower, the, Brearley's domain, 65
tripartite system, tripartism, 19, 25, 81, 166
Tudsbury, J. S., 198

U.S. observers, 43, 155
United States, English teaching in, 170. *See also* Dartmouth
Universities and Left Review, 10, 95
University College, London (UCL), 30, 151
Use of English Groups, 30

Venables, Francis Isaac, Minchenden senior English master to 1941, joint author of *English for Schools* (1939), 118, 119, 121, 122, 213
Versions of English (Barnes, Barnes and Clarke), 172, 195
village project at Hackney Downs, 72, 101
vocabulary, 43, 75, 106, 150
  collecting on the board, 106, 150
Vygotsky, Lev Semyonovich 1896–1934, 134

Waddell, Helen, scholar of medieval vernacular Latin, 63
wall displays, 52, 68, 85, 107
Walters, J. H., head of Minchenden, 119, 120, 123, 125
Walworth English, 91, 96, 97, 99, 105, 107, 108, 109, 110, 143, 146, 147, 148, 152, 160, 170, 172, 174, 176, 178, 180, 181, 183
  film, *Two Bobs' Worth of Trouble*, 15, 96, 209
  heads of English all male, 83
  model for comprehensive school English, 146
  reflects nature and ideology of the school, 109

Walworth School, 6, 10, 11, 13, 16, 24, 37, 79–111, 149, 150, 151, 152, 153, 157, 159, 170, 173, 175, 181, 183, 187
  aims and ideology, 109, 145
  democratic spirit, 14
  project events, 15
  see also O'Reilly
Watts-Phillips, James 1928– (Minchenden pupil 1945–1952), 212
We are the Lambeth Boys, film, dir. Karel Reitz (1959), 95
welfare state, 18
Wells, Bobbie, 193
West, D. W., 199, 206
White Hart Lane Primary School, Tottenham, 68, 204
Whitehead, Frank, 43, 199
Whittle, Valerie 1932– (Minchenden pupil 1943–1948), 116, 123, 212, 213, 215
Wilkinson, N. H., 202
Williams, Raymond Henry 1921–88, 10, 29, 32, 70, 72, 73, 110, 175, 195, 196, 200
  "Stocktaking I, English and the Background" (1950), 70, 72
Willmott, Peter 1923–2000, 196
Wilson, Jan 1949– (Minchenden pupil 1960–1967), 216
Wilson, Percy, HMI, 35, 37. *See also* HMI
  on futility of essay writing, 38
  role in Schools Council, 37
Witham, Lewin Arthur (Walworth senior English master 1946–48), 187, 206
Wordsworth, William 1770–1850, 64, 70
working class, 11, 21, 47, 49, 54, 68, 77, 78, 79, 89, 95, 144, 149, 164
working-class pupils, 22, 23, 27, 44, 47, 54, 68, 90, 96, 109, 117, 150, 160, 161, 164, 166, 171
  language and speech, 23, 44, 148
  school experienced as alien world, 23, 91, 160
  seen as deficient in culture and language, 27, 58, 144, 185
  "working-class bohemians," 107

writing, 33, 34, 38, 39, 41, 43, 44, 46, 50, 57, 61, 65, 75, 78, 84, 85, 86, 91, 92, 97, 98, 100, 101, 103, 104, 106, 110, 125, 131, 132, 133, 134, 135, 136, 140, 144, 145, 148, 149, 150, 152, 155, 156, 157, 160, 162, 164, 170, 171, 172, 173, 174, 175, 176, 177, 179, 182, 189, 204, 210
  dummy runs, 150
  extended, free, 160
  following discussion, 149
  a general capability, not confined to the academically ablest, 157
  HMI seek honest expression of experience, 38
  improved when speech valued, 44
  intensity as a value, 156 (*see also* Hourd)
  modes and genres
    Charlie stories (in 1st year at Walworth), 98, 100
    children's poetry hard to interpret, 103
    novel (in 3rd year at Walworth), 101
    poetry, 103, 156 (*see also* poetry writing)
    reflective, argumentative, dealing with ideas, 104
    serial stories (in 2nd year at Walworth), 101
    the essay, dominant grammar school genre, 27, 33, 38, 150, 160, 182, 188; Percy Wilson HMI on its futility, 38
  with no purpose beyond mere production, 180
  "rhetorical engineering"—its abandonment a loss?, 106
  selection of topics, 39
  as self-discovery and formation, 172
  teaching of, 44, 85, 106, 133, 150, 188
    about shaping a verbal object, 174, 176
    assignments, subjects, topics, 85, 91, 100, 125, 135, 141
    assignments with quotation as title, 61, 86
    assignments with title only given, 85

Index

audiences for writing, display, circulation, publication
dissemination with magazines, 13, 39, 93, 102, 104, 134, 135
dissemination by wall displays, 85
writing a means of reflecting on social life, 174
modeling, attention to construction, "rhetorical engineering," 106
abandonment of modelling a loss?, 179
models and influences, 126
motivation and interest, away from formalism, 106
responding to, dealing with, 56, 61, 62, 104, 136
pupil comment on work, 104
sense of audience, 38
use of stimuli, 135, 173, 183
views of Percy Wilson, HMI, 38
Writing Research, the, *The Development of Writing Abilities 11–18*, Britton et al., 40, 44

Yates, Alfred, 193
Yorkshire, West Riding of, 41, 163, 173
Young, Michael 1915–2002, 196
youth, 18, 114, 117
   youth culture, 18, 117

GPSR Compliance
The European Union's (EU) General Product Safety Regulation (GPSR) is a set
of rules that requires consumer products to be safe and our obligations to
ensure this.

If you have any concerns about our products, you can contact us on

ProductSafety@springernature.com

In case Publisher is established outside the EU, the EU authorized
representative is:

Springer Nature Customer Service Center GmbH
Europaplatz 3
69115 Heidelberg, Germany

www.ingramcontent.com/pod-product-compliance
Lightning Source LLC
LaVergne TN
LVHW011812060526
838200LV00053B/3744